Striking Women

Struggles and Strategies of South Asian Women
Workers from Grunwick to Gate Gourmet

Striking Women

Struggles and Strategies of South Asian Women
Workers from Grunwick to Gate Gourmet

Sundari Anitha & Ruth Pearson

Lawrence & Wishart
London 2018

Lawrence and Wishart Limited
Central Books Building
Freshwater Road
Chadwell Heath
RM8 1RX

Typesetting: e-type
Cover design: Kirsty Capes
Cover images: TUC Library Collections, part of Special Collections at
London Metropolitan University

First published 2018
© Sundari Anitha and Ruth Pearson 2018

British Library Cataloguing in Publication Data.
A catalogue record for this book is available from the British Library

ISBN 9781912064861

For Paul Johnson, Megan Jenkins, and Tom and Mat Frere-Jenkins – who have supported and inspired us.

Contents

Acknowledgements viii

1. Striking Women from Grunwick to Gate Gourmet 1

2. Beyond the stereotypes: South Asian women workers
   in Grunwick and Gate Gourmet 18

3. South Asian women in the UK: Histories of migration
   and settlement 38

4. Women in a gendered and racialised labour market:
   Everyday accounts of resilience, struggle and resistance 64

5. 'We are the lions, Mr Manager': The Grunwick dispute 101

6. 'You have to fight for your rights [...] No one gives them
   to you on a plate': The Gate Gourmet dispute 141

7. Minority women and unionisation in a changing
   economy – where are we now? 185

Bibliography 204

Index 227

ACKNOWLEDGEMENTS

The authors would like to thank both the Grunwick strikers and the women who were involved in the Gate Gourmet dispute for their time, courtesy and courage in speaking to us about their experiences. With the exception of Jayaben Desai, who generously allowed us to name her, we have respected their request for anonymity, whilst frequently quoting verbatim from their interviews.

We would also like to acknowledge the encouragement and cooperation from a range of key actors both within and outside the trade union movement, including Linda McDowell (our co-researcher on the DMI project), Graham Taylor, Chris Coates, and Jeff Howarth (TUC Library Collections), Ben Rogaly, Jane Holgate, Dan Jones, Sujata Aurora, Chris Thomas and Suryakant Desai, the (now deceased) widower of Jayaben Desai. We would also like to thank the Arts and Humanities Research Council which provided funding for the research, both as part of the Diasporas, Migration and Identities programme, and for the follow-on grant which enabled us to produce materials for schools, community groups and trade unions, which can be found on www. striking-women.org.

CHAPTER 1

Striking Women from Grunwick
to Gate Gourmet

This book is based on research carried out between 2006 and 2016 – the years that marked the thirtieth and fortieth anniversary of the Grunwick strike which began in 1976. The story of the Grunwick strike is well established. In August 1976, a group of workers walked out of the film processing plant in Willesden, North London, in protest against the arbitrary and repressive actions of the management of this establishment. Grunwick was a mail order business, which processed films sent in by post from customers all over the UK. This was a time of expansion for the domestic photographic market which was flourishing in the wake of cheap package holidays abroad and the associated enthusiasm for family photos. Business was so good that George Ward, the Anglo Indian owner of the Grunwick plant, had already expanded his capacity with the opening of this second establishment in Willesden in 1974, which doubled the capacity of the initial factory which had been established in 1965. By 1975, the company leased additional premises from Brent Council in Chapter Road, adjacent to the Dollis Hill tube station, the location that became the backdrop to the confrontations between strikers, pickets and police in 1976 and 1977.

Keeping labour costs down was central to the success of the Grunwick operation. With the tight labour market of the 1970s, Grunwick had come to rely more and more on cheap labour supplied by South Asian women migrants, mostly recruited from Indian-origin families who had settled in North West London following their forced re-location from nationalist post-independence regimes in Uganda, Kenya and Tanzania. As in other labour intensive industrial production processes, increasing productivity depended on the intensification of the labour process to maximise the output per unit of labour – and the Grunwick management style reflected the company's ambitions to make the workers do more for minimum rewards.

Our research, based on verbatim accounts from some of those involved in the initial action, indicates that the tipping point for this particular group of South Asian workers, led by the indomitable Jayaben Desai, was their fury at being treated – as they saw it – like animals rather than human beings and their refusal to put up with it any more. Desai's response represented the first step in a struggle to reclaim the dignity of workers who were being systematically mistreated by their employer and his representatives. The Grunwick strikers initially walked out because they had had enough. They subsequently fought to get the company to recognise the union they then joined – Association of Professional, Executive, Clerical and Computing Staff (APEX) – in order to pursue collective bargaining to achieve their demands for improved working conditions and pay. Their cause was then taken up – for a time – by the wider trade union movement in the UK. A range of progressive forces including the women's movement and anti-racism activists joined trade unions members from all over the UK in an escalating campaign which included mass pickets and frequent clashes with the police – until politics and circumstances dictated the withdrawal of union support.

This widely disseminated history is not disputed. Nor is the fact that the strike ended after four South Asian strikers staged a hunger strike outside the Trades Union Congress (TUC, the umbrella organisation for trade unions in Britain) headquarters in London. The hunger strikers were protesting because, in spite of oft repeated declarations of solidarity by the TUC and other unions, the Grunwick Strike Committee had been told to scale down the mass protests. In 1976, the then TUC general secretary Len Murray declared, 'We're not just behind you, we're up there with you all the way' (Socialist Worker 2016). But his words were ultimately not turned into action as the union leadership, particularly that of APEX and the Union of Postal Workers (UPW) failed to maintain the momentum against George Ward, the intransigent and ideologically-driven owner of Grunwick. The withdrawal of support for the strikers, and even the withdrawal of strike pay from those on hunger strike, represented for many the way that 'defeat was snatched from the jaws of victory' (Novara Media 2016).

This tragic end to the Grunwick strike has not prevented it being heralded as the moment in which the UK labour movement took the cause of black and women workers to its heart. Nor has time dented the fervent belief – evidenced in a lot of the Grunwick40 commemorations and celebrations in 2016 – that the strike, although initially prompted by the Grunwick workers' refusal to accept oppressive and insulting management practices, was primarily a struggle for union recognition.[1]

For the Grunwick strikers, union recognition was a means to an end – and that end was justice for migrant women workers. The Grunwick strikers wanted their management and co-workers to respect them – as workers, as women and as migrants – and recognise that they brought to the workplace not just their labour, but also their dignity and experience as fully fledged working women who had settled in London in the expectation that Britain offered them the promise of equal opportunities to build their futures.

The trade union movement in the UK has indeed taken the Grunwick strike into their collective consciousness. 2006 saw the celebration of the thirtieth anniversary of the Grunwick dispute with a lively event at the Tricycle Theatre in North West London. At this event, which one of the authors attended, trade unionists who had been involved in the dispute in the 1970s including Jack Dromey (from the Transport and General Workers Union, TGWU), Arthur Scargill (ex-president of the National Union of Miners, NUM), and Derek Walsh (UPW) recalled their roles in the strike and supporting action, and talked about the significance of Grunwick for workers' solidarity and unionisation. The Grunwick strike leader, Jayaben Desai, then a frail woman in her seventies, also spoke briefly. One of the most fiercely contested parts of the day involved writer and activist Amrit Wilson who, with two workers who were part of the ongoing dispute at the Gate Gourmet airline food processing facility at Heathrow, decried the lack of union support for the struggles of migrant women workers currently engaged in industrial disputes. This was hotly contested by Dromey who talked about union support for Eastern European workers in the catering and hospitality sectors. However, he failed to mention the recently concluded compensation package, which committed two former TGWU shop stewards – who had led solidarity action at Heathrow Airport – to silence over recent events (Hencke 2006). The gap between the authorised account and the reality of Grunwick's legacy, in terms of unconditional support for migrant women workers, was beginning to show.

By 2016, ten years later, when the celebrations of the Grunwick40 anniversary took place, the earlier widely held consensus about the causes and significance of the Grunwick strike had become some-what modified. In some respects, the traditional voices dominated the commemorative events. The GMB sponsored a second edition of the 1978 Dromey and Taylor book, which included a new introduc-tion by the principal author Graham Taylor, as well as short prefaces from Tim Roache, the current general secretary of the GMB, and Jack Dromey, now Labour MP for Birmingham Erdington and former Deputy Secretary General of the TGWU. The new prefaces and introduction stress the significance of a group of unorganised women, predominantly of South Asian descent, defying all assump-tions about their docility and their willingness to accept low wages, poor working conditions and aggressive management. They resisted these expectations by challenging their employers and taking on the massed ranks of the state, the police and the right-wing political forces of the day. As Dromey notes, the strike was 'for the basic human right to respect and union recognition' and saw 'the biggest mobilisation in labour movement history around a local dispute' (Dromey and Taylor 2016, 6). His co-author, the historian Graham Taylor, who was himself a member of the Strike Committee, stresses in his introduction that the Grunwick strike was the first in UK history involving South Asian women workers to receive the proper backing from trade union officials, which proved that white trade unionists were prepared to support black and Asian strikers. Taylor acknowledges the extraordinary leadership of Jayaben Desai throughout the seventeen months of the strike and predicts that 'the light of the Grunwick candle will shine brightly into the future' (Dromey and Taylor 2016, 16).

However, for all that, this account, as so many others, remains very much 'the union's story', rather than 'the workers' story'. A recent account that reiterates this trade union perspective (Butler

2016) claims that 'Times have changed, and although the leadership of almost all the trade unions are still white men, these men are enlightened and are the leaders at the forefront of the struggle against inequality and discrimination'. The trade union account remains the one that has dominated mainstream media representation of the Grunwick dispute, though alternate narratives do proliferate on some radical left, anti-racist and feminist websites (see Wilson 2016 and Aurora 2016).

In contrast to the commemorative events organised by the trade union leadership, those that were organised by Grunwick40 – which comprised of local trade unionists, community members, local historians and feminist/anti-racism activists, including the authors of this book – articulated a more complex perspective on the legacy of the Grunwick dispute in relation to trade unions' representation of minority and women workers. These celebrations focused on the legacy of solidarity, the importance of ongoing anti-racism struggles and the alliances that the Grunwick strike evoked among a range of progressive organisations and individuals.

The dispute at Gate Gourmet took place some thirty years later in the summer of 2005. A different group of South Asian workers were employed by the airline catering company Gate Gourmet to prepare in-flight meal trays. In 2002, the US venture capital Texas Pacific bought the Heathrow facility from British Airways (BA) who were seeking to outsource unprofitable parts of their operation. Faced with declining profits and determined to reduce labour costs, Gate Gourmet imposed a series of changes in workers' conditions and pay. In spite of threatening large scale redundancies, the management introduced 'seasonal' agency staff – mostly Eastern European migrants – onto the production line in August 2005. The regular workforce withdrew to the canteen with their shop stewards, ready to negotiate with the company. Instead, they were given verbal warnings, then sacked by megaphone. About 800 workers were dismissed in total. After a two-day walkout by baggage handlers employed by BA who were also TGWU members, the union negotiated a Compromise Agreement which offered voluntary redundancy and led to the reinstatement of the majority of those who had been locked out. However Gate Gourmet refused to reinstate some 200 workers labelled as 'trouble makers'. Of these, fifty-six workers –

mainly women in their fifties – rejected the redundancy offer and continued to protest and picket for about four years afterwards, seeking support from a range of anti-racism campaigners and labour organisations. Unfortunately ongoing support from their trade union was not forthcoming.

The union narrative which dominated the fortieth anniversary celebrations of the Grunwick dispute hails it as the tipping point, after which the UK labour movement embraced the priorities of women and migrant workers. This overshadows any discussion of the complex history and struggles of minority workers, the whittling away of trade union rights and power, and the feminisation of the labour force, which has been reflected in the deterioration of conditions, security and rights at work for both women and men. The Grunwick celebrations, in the main, seem to inhabit a curious insulated place where the focus is on the heroic acts of a small group of South Asian women and a larger group of white male organised workers mobilised to support the striking workers' demands for improvements in pay and working conditions, for union recognition and for reinstatement. As many have pointed out, the fact that none of these were ultimately achieved does not diminish the importance of these events for a whole generation of trade union activists and other parts of the progressive movements in the UK.

The Grunwick dispute did indeed put the presence of South Asian women in the UK's labour force firmly on the map, and it is right that it should be remembered and celebrated. But a number of things need to be taken into account that temper the celebratory manner in which the dispute has been integrated into the political memory of those events: firstly, both immigration policies and trade union legislation have progressively worsened since that event, making it even harder for women and migrant workers to claim their rights and protect their jobs. Secondly, the photographs of the small but powerful figure of Jayaben Desai speaking through a megaphone across serried ranks of policemen are icons rather than signifiers of change. Subsequent strikes and disputes in which South Asian women workers played a dominant role, including the Gate Gourmet dispute, have not enjoyed the universal trade union support that was temporarily offered to the Grunwick strikers. And thirdly, the bold vision of South Asian women as industrial militants and independent agents has been overshadowed in recent decades by the public discourse that asserts the dominance of religious over other minority identities, depicting South Asian women as docile victims of patriarchal Islamic cultures – a far cry from the celebration of the brave and plucky striking women at Grunwick (Ahmed 2003).

The authorised version of both the events and the legacy of the Grunwick strike continues to be the dominant discourse some forty years after the event. A close examination of the documentation and history of the dispute gives some insight into how the definitive account of Grunwick has been represented and reproduced. There were a number of accounts published during or immediately after the strike, particularly by Joe Rogaly (1976) and Dromey and Taylor (1977 and the new edition 2016). There have also been a series of documentary films on DVD, radio and TV, which have told and re-told the Grunwick story, mainly focusing on the trajectory of the dispute, the mass picketing in 1977 and the highs and lows of union support and solidarity action in support of the women workers.[2]

One of the noticeable features of the Grunwick40 celebrations, as well as the thirty year anniversary in 2006, is the dominance of white male voices – journalists and writers, trade union officials and members, documentary producers and film makers. This is not to say that no women have been heard. Retrospectives documentaries and rallies have featured a range of media personalities and journalists in an attempt to make the discussion more inclusive, such as the presence of two elderly former strikers at a number of events in 2016. The dominance of white male voices has not disturbed the symbolism of the strike leader Jayaben Desai as the emblematic South Asian woman who took on all comers in the fight to expand unionisation in the UK workforce. But very often it seems that much of this celebration focuses on a single woman, rather than the integration of all South Asian and black women into the narrative about industrial resistance and militancy in the intervening decades.

But it is not only the insistence of the male lens that makes the ongoing analysis of the Grunwick dispute so problematic. It is also the fact that the celebration of the strike increasingly resembles a kind of political nostalgia, a longing backward glance to the muscular activism of mass picketing, confrontation with the police and a centrifugal drawing together of all the progressive elements in the labour movement and the wider left. While the events of 1976-7 did indeed include all these elements, it is perhaps an overstatement to assume that activism and the long struggle to achieve union recognition and reinstatement of the Grunwick workers effectively represented the internalisation of the interests of migrant women workers within UK trade unions. When we set out to understand the dynamics of the strike – what led up to it, what precipitated it, what the priorities were for the workers involved and how the events of those years fitted into their work and life history – we uncovered a much more complex reality which is often absent from the essentialist debates that have surrounded Grunwick ever since. Our concerns are: that the events of those years have been isolated from what came before, and what followed for the women concerned; what the priorities and experiences were that led them to take the action they took; and what the consequences for them – and other minority workers – were of the two year long dispute in which they were involved. Certainly joining a trade union made it possible for many workers to sustain their participation in the strike, although it is interesting to note that in spite of the strike pay, many of the black women of African Caribbean descent involved in the dispute were forced to return to work either at Grunwick or elsewhere because they did not have recourse to other community or family support. Some of them even benefitted from the fact that the Grunwick management did increase basic wages in 1977 in an attempt to tempt back waverers amongst the strikers.

The failure of the trade union movement to maintain its celebrated solidarity with women workers from migrant communities since the 1970s is at its most evident in the case of the South Asian women who refused to accept voluntary redundancy at Gate Gourmet in 2005. In stark contrast to the concerted support for the Grunwick workers, trade union solidarity for these women was conspicuous by its absence. The trajectory of the dispute – which is explored extensively in Chapter Six – illuminates the ways in which increasingly restrictive trade union legislation was combined with general deterioration of workers' rights and protection in the UK labour market to leave the Gate Gourmet workforce supremely vulnerable to arbitrary decisions by their employers. It is to the credit of the baggage handlers at BA that they took action in solidarity with fellow union members – although it is also understandable that the union leadership felt obliged to end this action which was deemed illegal under legislation enacted in 1980.

However, what followed does cast doubt on the claim that, since the end of the 1970s, the trade unions have taken the cause of migrant women workers to their hearts. As we explain below, the way in which a hasty compromise agreement was crafted and summarily imposed on the locked-out Gate Gourmet workforce was not entirely satisfactory. That it left the most vulnerable – older women and those with health problems – without the possibility of regaining their jobs indicates that the primary concern for the union was facing the accusation of illegal secondary picketing rather than representing the interests of all the workers involved. This raises questions about the nature of the compromise that was made and on whose behalf, and on what basis was an agreement reached that sanctioned these forced and selective redundancies. Some ten years later, many of the South Asian women who lost their jobs in this dispute are still suffering the after effects, not just in terms of their current income and employment situation but also with regard to their mental and physical health and their disillusionment with the UK labour movement.

The change in union treatment of the women migrant workers from South Asia and elsewhere between the Grunwick and Gate Gourmet disputes cannot be solely attributed to changing union priorities and practices; these were themselves a reflection of the changing legal and political environment in which unions operate in the UK today. It is also important to understand the very different context of these two disputes and the range of demographic, economic and political changes that have taken place in the UK and elsewhere, as the economy has been reshaped by the forces of globalisation. Particularly pertinent is the ongoing – and changing – migration flows from different parts of the world. In the 1970s, the rapid influx of South Asians displaced from East Africa – the so called 'twice migrants' – provided a cheap labour force for enterprises such as the Grunwick plants. Women workers who had no previous industrial experience were expected to be docile, and their relatively good education, mostly achieved through the medium of the English language, made this particular group of migrants very appropriate workers for this new kind of work, which involved not only the developing and printing of customers' photographs but also managing the mail order operation of this business. This could be seen as a modern industrial process linked to technology rather than manufacturing. It also entailed a good deal of administrative input – recording and chasing orders, dealing with money that was mainly sent in postal orders and cheques, and dispatching prints back to the customers. In other contexts, it might have been seen as skilled work, but given the availability of workers with the skills and aptitudes required – literacy, numeracy and the ability to work methodically and accurately – these migrant women could be employed as unskilled manual workers and paid and treated as such, echoing the ways in which women have been incorporated into the global workforce throughout the world (Elson and Pearson 1981).

In contrast to the high profile role of South Asian women in the Grunwick dispute, and in contrast to the political and scholarly accounts of the strike, the union tactics, and the protracted legal struggles, most other research on South Asian migration and diaspora tends to ignore women as workers in favour of an emphasis on their domestic and cultural roles. Women's roles in the public sphere, particularly as workers and economic sustainers of their families is frequently ignored, in favour of what is generally a stereotypical depiction of South Asian women confined to a restricted and problematic private sphere of the family and the community. Indeed, as we explain in Chapter Two, this view of women from the sub-continent is enshrined in UK immigration legislation which permitted the entry to the country of South Asian women to join their spouses on the grounds that they were dependent on the male head of the family, whilst limiting the equivalent possibility for men from the same region. Subsequent policy and political discussion has continued to focus on problematic migrant men, whilst women have been primarily portrayed either as domestic captives of patriarchal communities, or, in the increasing religiosisation of language and analysis, as downtrodden Muslims, and more recently, as helpmates of potential extremists.

Labour historians have recorded, but rarely highlighted the ongoing role of South Asian women in the wage labour force, and in the various important protests and strikes that have occurred over the last forty years. But instead of a narrative which celebrates the diverse and differentiated role of South Asian women workers over that time, there is frequently a resort to the default position of the heroic South Asian woman worker in the depiction of the Grunwick strike leader Jayaben Desai.

Moreover, the Grunwick strike remains the iconic representation of the way in which the trade union movement has diversified and opened up to migrant workers, a narrative which ignores the very different reality experienced by other women workers, including those in dispute with Gate Gourmet. These women experienced a very different relationship with the trade unions. In this book, we are committed to ensuring that the multiple voices of those who were involved in these two disputes are recorded, so that we can better understand the realities they faced, the way they responded to it and the different ways in their lives were shaped by these experiences. We are also committed to ensuring that there is a wider appreciation of the migration and work histories of these two groups of women workers; to this end we have produced a series of materials for schools and community groups, including a website with a downloadable comic which presents the events of the two disputes.[3]

The varied class backgrounds and migration experiences of different groups of South Asian women in the UK is explored in Chapter Three. Much of the existing discussion of Grunwick has presented that particular workforce as being representative of South Asian women who were, as Jayaben Desai frequently claimed, inspired by Gandhi's struggle for independence in India; this was what inspired her to lead the struggle at Grunwick for dignity and justice for her fellow workers. But the history of South Asian women workers who migrated to the UK from post-independence East Africa was complex. Indian migrants to colonial East Africa at the end of the nineteenth century and onwards supplied the bulk of the administrative and mercantile workforce there. The Indian community maintained a relatively privileged position in the post-independence regimes, expanding their commercial interests as their role in government and public administration was diminished by the rising educated African elites. When Africanisation was imposed – wherein countries such as Kenya, Tanzania, Zambia and Malawi sought to provide the African majority population with greater control over key areas of the economy and the government – there remained little or no option for the South Asian residents other than to either return to the subcontinent or migrate to the UK where they held subject citizenship. And when they moved, they took their class formation and experiences with them. The ex-Grunwick workers we interviewed recalled a range of paid work experiences in East Africa, though these were home or office based and did not include factory or other manual jobs.

Subsequent waves of South Asian migrants to the UK had different histories, which are also explored in Chapter Three. The women who formed the bulk of Gate Gourmet's workforce were direct migrants from the Indian subcontinent. Arriving in the UK in the 1970s and 1980s, many of their migrant journeys overlapped in time with those of the Grunwick women. However, this is where their similarities end. While the Grunwick women were older, mainly having migrated with their long established families, those who ended up in Gate Gourmet were younger, often daughters or new brides who had arrived in the UK as part of the increasingly restrictive family reunion framework of UK immigration legislation the 1970s and 1980s. Although they had been educated at local schools in India, their schooling had been undertaken in Hindi or Punjabi – most of them therefore lacked any fluency in the English language. Very few of these women had any previous experience of waged work, coming from middle-class small landowning communities in the Punjab, where increasing prosperity and local norms pre-empted the need for women to work outside the home to meet family subsistence needs. But they soon found that in the UK they needed to find jobs to contribute to the household budget, a role that came as a shock to some of the young women we interviewed, who were pressured by husbands, mothers-in-law and other relatives to earn money as well as carry out domestic tasks.

In the decades between the Grunwick and Gate Gourmet disputes, women of South Asian descent occupied changing positions in the UK labour force. This trajectory is explored in Chapter Four which investigates the options available for migrant women and how this changed over time. Based on interviews with women employed at Grunwick in the 1970s and Gate Gourmet in the 2000s, the chapter explores their perceptions of the kind of jobs they sought and secured, their achievements in terms of moving up – however slightly – the occupational ladder and securing better jobs over time. But we also discuss the struggles they engaged in, including strikes and other confrontations with management, during the decades before they came to work at Gate Gourmet which included those at Hillingdon Hospital in 1995 and Lufthansa Skychef in 1998/9. In Chapter Four, our analysis of South Asian women's labour histories in the broader context of their lives also allows us to problematise a key issue which has hitherto been ignored in previous analyses of South Asian women in Britain: the ways in which they managed to reconcile – or not – the dual demands of production (paid work) and reproduction (family responsibilities and domestic labour).

The labour market experienced by migrant women who arrived in the UK in the 1970s and 1980s was increasingly racialised and gendered. Chapter Four sets out the range of manual and low-paid jobs available to South Asian women who frequently had to take work which was far below their educational experience or other qualifications. This chapter also explains, in the words of the women themselves, the distress this caused them, as well as the difficulties they experienced in trying to meet the demands of their paid employment while at the same time fulfilling their responsibilities for domestic work and childcare at home. It also presents their direct recollections of the ways in which they not only endured, but also resisted, the indignities and discrimination they faced at work, and the strategies they developed to juggle their productive and reproductive work.

These issues are directly reflected in the ways in which the Grunwick women experienced their jobs and the labour process in which they were engaged, which is fully explored in Chapter Five. Their responses to the conditions at work resulted from both their class and work experiences, as well as from their gender, and were shaped by their migration journeys and subsequent settlement in the UK. Their walk-out from the Grunwick factory was the consequence of the outrage they experienced both in relation to the class position they had occupied prior to their migration to the UK and the lack of respect and indignities to which they were now being subjected. There were other workers who joined the strike to support those who were protesting at unacceptable management practices, even though they themselves had not directly experienced it. This primarily represented solidarity with other South Asian workers; more generalised class solidarity was established later in terms of the trade union membership and in recognition of the support from workers throughout the labour movement.

After the tightening of immigration restrictions the 1970s, the majority of South Asian and other migrant groups entered the UK as family members, with increasingly restrictive family reunion visas permitted by the UK Home Office. The demographic characteristics of the migrants therefore changed – most were family members of already settled male migrants, including many younger women, daughters, sisters or young brides. The labour market experiences of these later migrants differed from those of the middle-class, English-educated, African-Asian women employed at Grunwick, who were forced by family circumstances to enter a hostile labour market in order to contribute to the household's survival.

The 1980s and 1990s was a period of retreat and struggle for the British labour movement, exemplified by the Miners' Strike in 1984, which ended in defeat in spite of the mass mobilisation and resistance it engendered. As the post-1979 governments increasingly adopted a neoliberal stance that privileged the market over the social, and the individual over the collective, increasing inequality, restrictions on public services, welfare and social security were matched not just by yet further restrictions in immigration policies, but also by the sharpening of social divisions around race, ethnicity and class.

This was the Britain in which different migrant workers sought to make their lives and their homes in the late 1970s through to the 1990s. With the trade union movement increasingly on the back foot, many South Asian women workers found employment opportunities primarily in the low-skilled end of public sector employment – such as hospital auxiliaries – and in light manufacturing. The public sector was an important bastion of trade union membership and many migrant women working there joined workplace unions and recognised the importance of collective organisation to defend their rights at work. It is therefore not surprising that many of the women involved in the Gate Gourmet protest had experience of a number of previous industrial disputes, experiences which they brought to their Gate Gourmet employment.

What is surprising is that the celebration of South Asian women's industrial militancy in the UK is largely silent about these later actions. The strike at Chix bubblegum plant in Slough and the engineering factory Futters in West London, both in 1979, were examples of South Asian women's determination to fight for their rights. The successful strike against the deteriorating terms and conditions for the workforce following outsourcing of the cleaning services at Hillingdon hospital in 1985, was led by an South Asian woman shop steward representing migrant workers; they initially had to battle for recognition from their own trade union, and even then, there was no widespread trade union support. And, there was a dispute at the Lufthansa Skychef airline catering company at Heathrow in 1999 in which South Asian women played a prominent part. It is significant that none of these disputes have garnered the iconic status of the Grunwick strike, given the ongoing celebration of Grunwick as the tipping point in relation to the trade unions' recognition and incorporation of South Asian women's rights.

The post Grunwick period, and particularly the post Miners' Strike era saw increasing restrictions on trade union organisation, including the outlawing of secondary picketing. Furthermore, outsourcing and privatisation made it much harder for unions to effectively organise in many workplaces, as industrial tribunals increasingly replaced confrontational actions that withdrew workers' labour. Therefore, the lack of mass response to the Hillingdon, Lufthansa and other disputes is logical. But the exclusive celebration of the Grunwick dispute and the neglect of other industrial actions in which minority women workers have played a leading part downplays the significance of these later mobilisations. It is in this context that our study seeks to explore the different realities of the two disputes at Grunwick and Gate Gourmet.

Chapter Six explores the events of the Gate Gourmet dispute in the context of these changes to the industrial relations legislation as well as the changes to the labour market in the context of globalisation processes. It details the ways in which the Gate Gourmet workers resisted the steady deterioration in the conditions at work over a number of years, culminating in the standoff over the introduction of non-unionised agency workers on the production line. The support from their union was temporary and limited; the union negotiated a compromise agreement that entailed the compulsory redundancy of selected workers, including 'troublemakers' and a return to work for the remaining workers, who were required to accept new contracts with reduced pay and entitlements. Fifty-six workers resisted this agreement, and felt betrayed by their union.

In exploring South Asian women's experiences of industrial militancy at Grunwick and Gate Gourmet, we are seeking to apply a more nuanced, intersectional analysis to the events of the last forty years. We want to understand how social axes of identities of different groups of minority women workers such as their gender, race, ethnicity, diverse class positions, migration histories and family circumstances are mobilised and reproduced in migrant labour markets and shape particular political possibilities in response to exploitation at work. We are also seeking to challenge the representations of South Asian women that have become dominant in UK political discourse in recent years. When we embarked on this research, which was supported by the Arts and Humanities Research Council, the title of our project was 'Subverting stereotypes: South Asian women's political activism – a comparison of the Grunwick and Gate Gourmet strikes'. The stereotypes we wanted to contest related to the increasing religiosisation of minority identities in the UK – in which 'South Asian' has largely been replaced by 'Muslim', 'Sikh' or 'Hindu' in contemporary debates. The post 9/11 landscape also seemed to have erased the reality of South Asian women as workers, as industrial activists, and people who were seeking to take control of their identity; instead, we were bombarded with constant images of veiled women, subservient to dominant husbands and other family members, or as helpmates to Islamic terrorists. The religiosisation of identities has meant that the important differences between diasporic communities of South Asian origin no longer seemed to matter in these debates; and also that their history at work as well as elsewhere in the UK was largely being forgotten.

This book seeks to provide a more historicised account of the workers involved in the Grunwick strike, the Gate Gourmet dispute and the many other industrial conflicts in which women of South Asian origins have participated in over the last four decades. These women were part of a multigenerational migratory movement, stimulated by British colonial rule not only in the Indian sub-continent but also in the East African countries which were part of the British empire until the 1960s. It has become a truism to assert that it is necessary to take an intersectional approach to analysing social phenomena, examining how race, ethnicity, gender and class intersect both in the identities of individuals and in the trajectory of social and political movements and moments. The efforts to understand and explain the moments of resistance, such as the walk-out of the Grunwick strikers in 1976 or the response of the Gate Gourmet workers to being locked out of their workplace in 2005, must also be sought not just in the intersectional identity of the workers concerned, but also in the imperial, political and industrial history of the countries from whence they came.

Feminist analysis has increasingly been concerned with understanding the intersection of different aspects of women and men's identities and how they affect and are affected by their gender, and feminist activism has been built on the appreciation of the ways in which the personal and the political, the public and the private lives of women are intertwined. The focus in this book on the individual biographies – of family, work and community – of the South Asian women involved in Grunwick and Gate Gourmet is the basis of our exploration of what these disputes meant to them. These personal histories give powerful insights into how the women endured and resisted the legal, social and industrial structures of discrimination that faced them in the UK labour force at different times. This book offers 'the workers' story', and in doing so presents a more grounded understanding of the actions of the South Asian women involved.

NOTES

1. See https://grunwick40.wordpress.com/
2. The most widely circulated of these were the series of documentaries directed by Chris Thomas, which include *Stand Together* (1977) and *Look Back at Grunwick* (for Newsreel Collective). These contain footage from the Grunwick dispute as it unfolded over 1976-78. To mark the thirtieth anniversary of the Grunwick dispute, Chris Thomas directed another documentary in 2008, *The Great Grunwick Strike 1976–1978: A History* (for Brent Trades Union Council).
3. These resources are available at www.striking-women.org.

CHAPTER 2

Beyond the stereotypes: South Asian women workers in Grunwick and Gate Gourmet

The representation of the Grunwick strike as a tipping point, heralding a new era that recognised the role of South Asian women as workers and as industrial militants, needs to be seen in the context of dominant representations of South Asian women in the UK. Over the past three decades, the representation of South Asian women's experiences in dominant scholarly, media and policy discourses in the UK and has veered from invisibility in early anthropological accounts of South Asian diasporas (Tomalin 2014) to hypervisibility in recent media and policy debates which emphasise the 'problematic private sphere' and religio-cultural basis of violence against minority ethnic women (Ahmad 2003). Analysis of academic, policy and popular media discourses on South Asian women's presence in the UK enables us to map the contours of this representation. Based on South Asian women's narratives about their migration and settlement into the UK our analysis also counter-balances what has been termed as the 'cultural turn' in current academic social sciences, whereby themes of identity and culture have come to dominate studies of diaspora populations since the 1990s, ignoring material issues of work and economic survival strategies from the frame of analysis.

DOMINANT REPRESENTATIONS AND ERASURES

Early scholarship on South Asian migration to the UK sought to examine the causes and the process of migration, settlement and community formation in the diaspora and orientation towards the homelands. Much of this work relies primarily on celebratory accounts of male pioneers and privileges male voices as representative of the experiences of the entire communities (Anwar 1979; Dahya 1974; Eade 1989), thereby rendering invisible the gendered processes of migration for men and women and the particular experiences of women outside the domestic sphere (IMR 2006; Mand 2006; Sangster 1998). When women's lives were the focus of academic research, this focus was predominantly on the private sphere, demonstrating a preoccupation with women's roles in enacting and thereby preserving their culture and traditions within family, kinship and caste networks (Gardner and Shakur 1994; Warrier 1994). Sayyid (2006) argues that such representations reiterate earlier Indological imaginings, which were premised upon the opposition between normative Western practices and establishments against which South Asian ways of living appear as distortions and aberrations (Sayyid 2006, 2).

While the particular experiences of migrant women, their characteristics, the causes and patterns of migration, and the processes of adaptation in the receiving countries became increasingly studied from the early 1980s, there remains little scholarship on the gendered processes of South Asian migration to the UK. Some studies did focus on South Asian women's lives during this period (Ballard 1994), but they fell short of a gendered analysis of the migration process as inherently different for men and women, influenced by gendered interactions and practices imbedded in institutions and organisations (Curran et al. 2006, 210). Rather, this literature reinscribes South Asian women's location within the private sphere, despite the diversity in the employment profiles of British South Asian women in the UK. There is research on the low employment rates among some categories of South Asian women in the period, including recent migrants from Bangladesh and Pakistan; but there is relatively little focus on the working lives of South Asian women migrants from Punjab and East Africa who were active participants in the labour market.

Tomalin (2014) acknowledges the limitations inherent in the stereotypical representations of South Asian women in early ethnography which erase women from public spaces and risk essentialising the domestic sphere as an unremittingly repressive space, devoid of any possibilities of exercising agency. Analysis of women's role in community formation in the 1980s and early 1990s sought to understand the different and changing ways in which gender was (re)configured during and through the process of migration and settlement in the UK (Bhachu 1985; Ballard 1994; Shaw 2000; Werbner 1990). This approach resisted the simplistic assumption of 'the family, community and culture' as a repressive domain and recognised women's agency within patriarchal constraints by exploring the changes and contestations which shape re-articulations of culture in particular diasporic contexts (Ballard 2004; Baumann 1996; Bhachu 1985; Shaw 2000). Focusing on the dynamics of Pakistani and Indian Punjabi migration and the role that kinship networks, particularly marriage, played in facilitating migration, this recognition of the gendered dimensions of these processes makes clear the agency and centrality of women's role in maintaining and extending kinship by the smooth operation of complex ties of reciprocity, which strengthen transnational networks and thereby facilitate ongoing migration and settlement. Similarly, Bhachu's (1985) study of African-Asian Sikh women in West London emphasises the role of Sikh women as reproducers and negotiators of their cultural identity. She examines the position of women who are located within structural constraints of racism and patriarchy to argue that their experience of working in the UK enabled them to transform marriage practices. She stresses the role of women's employment for accumulation of funds for their own dowries, but her focus is on the impact of work on women's domestic life rather than exploring the social construction of minority women's identity and agency as workers.

Such representations that elide South Asian women's role in the economy and wider society also result when policy makers and media 'expect' to find women confined in the 'problematic private sphere', an expectation which then shapes and constrains the ways that they represent British Asian women (Tomalin 2014, 182). Post-war UK immigration policies reflected these gendered and racialised constructions of women, consistently assuming that the male worker was the primary migrant from South Asia. When immigration restrictions were first placed on Commonwealth nationals in 1962, the statutory provisions that enabled the right to family reunion followed similar gendered formulations of men's and women's roles within these communities, despite a steady growth in women's participation rates in the UK labour market. During the parliamentary debates on the immigration restrictions brought about in 1962, some Members of Parliament suggested replacing the word 'wife' by 'spouse', but the Conservative government of the day declined because '[i]n the Bill, as in our nationality law, we have assumed the husband is the head of the family and that the wife acquires his domicile' (Wray 2011, 43). The legislation stipulated that husbands could enter only at the discretion of immigration officers, not under statute, which meant that UK immigration authorities could block applications by South Asian men to join their spouses resident in the UK, based on the construction of such men as a threat to the job prospects of indigenous men. However the legislation permitted South Asian women entry, since they were considered primarily as dependants and in gender specific roles in policy formulations (Sachdeva 1993; Wray 2015), contrary to their lived realities as workers. Prior to the Immigration Act 1971, alien workers were written into the legislation as male and were permitted to be accompanied by their wives and children, but there was no corresponding right allowing women to migrate for work and allowing their family dependants to accompany them. Woman who sought to enter the UK for purposes other than family reunion, and unmarried women who sought to enter for the purpose of family reunion found that, in practice, they had to rely on the arbitrary administrative discretion of immigration officers (Wray 2015).

This conceptualisation of migrant women as non-workers continues to inform much of current social policy responses towards migrant communities in the UK and beyond. Analysis of the immigration policy and the materials for new immigrants in Canada, The Netherlands and Sweden reveals similar assumptions about gender roles and family life, consistently portraying migrant women as symbolic markers of the differences between immigrant and host cultures (Wilton 2009). An understanding of women's roles as cultural reproducers of communities has continued to underlie the ways in which many European governments, including the UK, envisage very specific roles for ethnic minority women. Following the disturbances in Bradford, Oldham and Burnley in 2001 and particularly since the so-called 'war on terror', policy discourses exhort minority ethnic women to educate their children and speak English at home to help them to integrate into the majority British society (Andall 2003, 3; Gedalof 2007; Yuval-Davis et al. 2005, and 2012). More recently, similar discourses inform calls for women to monitor family members in order to promote integration and to prevent the radicalisation of their children. For example, in 2016, the then Prime Minister David Cameron suggested a causal connection between the appeal of ISIS and Muslim women's lack of knowledge of English, claiming on the BBC Radio 4's Today programme that this made them 'more susceptible to the extremist message coming from Daesh' (Mason and Sherwood 2016). This was in spite of the fact that most ISIS recruits from the UK have been second generation migrants, fluent in English and in the use of social media technologies. Policy discourses in the UK continue to construct Muslim women of South Asian origin as custodians of a community identity that is counterposed to dominant constructions of 'Britishness'.

Similar expectations inform the nature and extent of state investment in resolving perceived 'problems'; in recent times, the focus of government policies has come to be directed at the social and economic integration of black and minority ethnic young men – particularly Muslim men. Within these policy debates, the unemployment of black and minority ethnic young men is cast as a social cohesion problem (e.g. see Cantle 2001), while the unemployment of minority ethnic women is largely ignored in public policy formulations (Mirza 2003). This differentiated explanation is maintained, in spite of academic research indicating that the unemployment of Bangladeshi and Pakistani women is partly a consequence of: cultural attitudes and traditional gendered expectations about responsibility for childcare (Aston et al. 2007); differential employment patterns such as high rates of home working (Allen and Wolkowitz 1987; Brah and Shaw 1992; Phizacklea and Wolkowitz 1993); as well as social exclusion (Dale 2002). When minority ethnic women come to the attention of policy makers, it is as vectors of the integration of their community rather than as active citizens and participants in the labour market in their own right.

The focus on South Asian women in academic literature and in policy formulations as reproducers of the cultural lives of their communities resonates with recent re-articulations of the centrality of culture within diaspora studies (Brettell 2000, 98). The parallel decline of academic interest in economic aspects of gender, as opposed to cultural aspects, would appear to have continued unabated since the late 1990s (Bradley and Fenton 1999). Confronting the intellectual and material problems posed by the 'cultural turn' in diaspora studies, Anthias (1998, 558) notes how ethnographies of diasporas have tended to emphasise origins over 'points of settlement' in constructing identities and solidarities. The cultural construction of migrant identity in diasporic studies is evident in the focus on languages, cognitive and normative frames, images, texts, myths and symbols of society and self ('symbolic culture'). In her work on gender and ethnicity in contemporary Europe, Andall (2003) argues that in new migration settings, 'culture' and identity tend to assume a new significance precisely because migrant groups are transformed into ethnic minorities. Writing about South Asian communities in the UK, Modood et al. (1997), for example, argue that ethnicity and religion have become key markers of identity as well as symbols of social and political resistance, and thereby impute to ethnicity a greater salience than other markers of commonality and difference. More recent scholars have challenged the primacy of ethnicity as a marker of identity, arguing that this assumption is rarely grounded in any historical or political economy perspective (Carter and Fenton 2010; Mattaush 2000, 181).

Based on an anthropological study of culture, community and identity in Southall, the 'most densely populated multi-ethnic ghetto of London', Baumann noted how ethnic minorities have been transformed in both popular and policy discourses into communities in *possession* of a 'culture' which is perceived by children as well as adults as a 'stable, collective, and distinctive' possession of communities (Baumann 1996, 34). In contrast, he termed the native-born white settled communities as the 'English without culture'. Baumann's research contested the paradigm of community studies focused on isolated communities and their 'autonomous', stable, homogeneous culture, arguing that migrants in Southall, West London were engaged in a process of meaning-making and rejecting the notion of 'culture as an ethnic heirloom' (1996, 109). However Baumann's focus is almost exclusively on what people say about their identities;

his otherwise admirable analysis fails to engage with the material and social structures of class formation and differentiation, or with migrants' lived experience of paid work and how this might shape differentiated formulations of culture.

Discourses on community often reduce ethnicity to culture and/ or identity and increasingly to a notion of religiosised, racialised, ethnic belonging quite separate from the centrality of class and work related experiences. This reification of culture and the emphasis on textual and cultural analysis to unpack migrants' conceptualisations of identity and belonging in countries of settlement seems to have resulted in a corresponding neglect of the material, of structural inequalities, of lived everyday experience of discrimination and of individual agency and social action to resist marginalisation and inequalities. The reification of culture is particularly relevant to the construction of gender within particular minority communities. Both the invisibility of women in some of the early anthropological accounts of the South Asian diaspora and the hypervisibility of South Asian women in recent policy and media discourses are premised on similar culturally essentialist representations of South Asian women – as predominantly passive, apolitical, limited to and by their domesticity, wholly determined by their (repressive) culture (Ahmad 2003, 43), and as forever victims (Mohanty 1988). Over the last decade and more, South Asian women have increasingly been depicted as 'as essentialised oppressed figures of victimhood and despair, in need of rescuing from their men' (Ahmad 2003, 43). Underlying these constructions is an increasing saliency, especially since 2001, of using the trope of religion in South Asian and Western geopolitical discourses, as well as within academic analysis and media commentary to convey an immutable cultural difference. Ahmad argues that such representations of South Asian women are limited in scope, 'fixed' within a wider construct that configures religious beliefs as homogeneous and unchanging, and offer little possibility of recognising the struggles and processes of empowerment of South Asian women through social or political agency (Ahmad 2003, 43).

Wilson (1978) made one of the earliest contributions to an alternative account of South Asian women's agency. She documented hitherto ignored aspects of South Asian women's migration and settlement and the challenges facing these women in the UK, including experiences of loneliness and culture shock, their experiences of marginalisation and oppression at work. She also demonstrated how women of South Asian origin exercise their agentic capacity despite all the constraints placed upon them. Locating South Asian women within an intersection of gender, race and colonialism, Parmar's work (1982) draws attention to the agency and political struggles of South Asian women in the UK, with a particular focus on their role in a gendered and racialised labour market. More recently, Takhar's (2013) research has drawn attention to South Asian women's activism as they have sought to create critical spaces within diaspora and feminist communities and have successfully influenced public policy on a range of issues including combating violence against women.

Central to this shift in research focus from the invisibilisation of women to acknowledging their agency is the challenge posed by a number of postcolonial feminists including Mohanty (1988), hooks (1991), Spivak (1998) and Brah (1996). Mohanty (1988) challenged the ways in which 'white feminism' has sought to represent 'the third world woman' as being in need of liberation, 'not in terms of their own herstory and needs but into the "progressive" social mores and customs of the metropolitan West' (Carby 1982, 114). The practice of homogenising minority women within the category of 'third world women' without locating them within a geographical and historically specific context serves to deny the specific experiences of difference (Brah 1996; Mirza 2009; Mohanty 1988 and 2003). Puwar and Raghuram (2003, 3) have questioned the use of the category 'South Asian woman' for its underlying assumption of an 'imperious sweep across nations and communities', arguing that any scrutiny of this category reveals that it 'represents an assortment of women who are more often than not positioned in contra-distinction to each other'. Brah (1996) also draws attention to the importance of 'challenging the homogenous and simplistic migratory histories' that are often ascribed to South Asian communities abroad. More recent research on particular categories of South Asian diasporas has explored their evolution as distinct diasporic entities, shaped by the intersections of different socio-cultural histories, migration trajectories, class and caste backgrounds, and subject to different economic and political situations in their places of settlement (Jayaram 2004, 17). The diverse configurations of gender in different South Asian communities have increasingly come to be recognised in a number of studies that unpack the heterogeneity of South Asian women's experiences in the UK (Evans and Bowlby 2000; Herbert 2009; Mand 2006; Puwar and Raghuram 2003; Ramji 2006).

Our work is a further contribution to the task of deconstructing the category of 'women of South Asian descent'. Drawing upon life stories of South Asian women workers in the UK, we utilise an intersectional lens to understand their location and agency in the UK labour market, with reference to their diverse histories of migration and settlement, (changing) class positions, different geographical origins, ethno-linguistic identity and castes. In doing so, we seek to move beyond simplistic constructions of agency and celebratory accounts of resistance that are uncoupled from the gendered, racialised and classed contexts within and despite which they are articulated and enacted. We see this as an attempt to destabilise the creation of a 'comforting story or narrative of the self' (Hall 1992, 277) in order to understand some of the contradictory ways in which women of South Asian origin recount and remember their agency in the UK labour market, and interrogate the appropriation of their actions by diverse political projects, including a range of trade unionist and feminist accounts.

TRADE UNIONS AND ISSUES OF GENDER, RACE AND ETHNICITY

The stereotypical representations and erasures discussed above have also informed the institutional practices, processes and responses of trade unions in the UK with regard to minority ethnic and women workers who have been their members. Virdee (2014) documents the processes whereby working people and their organisations in Britain played an active part in the construction of successive visions of a 'national identity' suffused with racist exclusions. The boundaries of this racist exclusion were contestable and shifted to successively construct particular groups such as Irish Catholics or Jews as 'outsiders', only to subsequently incorporate them into a vision of the nation that excluded other recent migrants, such as workers from the Caribbean, Asia and Africa. Gilroy (1992) and Sivanandan (1977a) argue that racism was an inherent feature of British trade unionism in the post-war era, whereby practices such as the 'colour bar' which excluded non- white workers from specified occupations, preserved the economic interests of the white working class through the exploitation of migrant labour. Virdee (2000) challenges 'black radical theories of trade union racism' by arguing that such racist practices were shaped by the particular economic, political and ideological conditions in post-war Britain, and along with Sivanandan (1977a), holds on to the possibility of inter-racial class solidarity developing in the future, an optimism that many would argue is belied by recent political developments in Britain subsequent to the 2016 EU referendum.

Despite the long involvement of black workers in working-class organisations in Britain (Fryer 1984; Ramdin 1987), trade unions in the UK have a long history of outright discrimination towards minority and women workers, and a demonstrated neglect of their specific needs. When post-war labour shortages led the British government to look towards the colonies as sources of labour, British trade unions articulated concerns that the foreign workers would be used to undercut wages and made the following demands: these workers should be required to join unions; the numbers of immigrant workers should be limited; and, in some cases, they demanded that the immigrant workers should be the first to be made redundant if jobs were lost. Some two decades after this, the TUC was still suggesting that immigrants should not have the same rights as the established workforce, a stance which reiterated trade unions' response to women's entry into the labour market during the two world wars (Cooper 2013). From the 1950s through to the 1970s, often with the complicity of their trade unions, the everyday practices of management together with those of shop floor union officials, reinscribed gendered and racialised hierarchies through constructions of particular jobs as 'skilled' or 'unskilled', and through exclusionary practices that relegated women and Black and Minority Ethnic (BME) workers to unskilled and low-paid work (Duffield 1988; Virdee 2014). These trade union practices and processes structured the gendered and racialised division of labour, as well as re-inscribing the stereotypes of migrant workers, particularly women, who were differentially incorporated into the labour market in the UK.

This discrimination in the labour market by employers, fellow white workers and trade unions was challenged by black and minority ethnic workers through self-action as well as by mobilising the support of their communities. One early instance of such resistance was the protest against the policy of the publicly owned Bristol Omnibus Company; the company refused to employ black and South Asian people as bus crew, a practice which was supported by the white workforce and unchallenged by the trade union (Jones 2015). In 1963, a local community group, the West Indian Development Council, encouraged a black man called Guy Bailey to apply for a job as a bus conductor and when the company refused to interview him despite his qualification, mounted a community boycott of the bus service calling for an end to the colour bar. This action, which drew national attention to the issue of racial discrimination, was supported by the local Labour MP Tony Benn and the then Labour Opposition leader, Harold Wilson, and the local Trades Council. Within two months, the bus company gave in and lifted the ban on non-white workers (Mizen 2016).

In the 1960s and early 1970s, trade unions colluded with a number of discriminatory management policies including: paying differential wages for black and white workers, and in many cases for men and women workers; barring certain groups of workers from promotion; and selectively making certain categories of workers redundant (Wrench 1987). Compared to their reluctance to support strike action which had its basis in discriminatory management practices, the trade unions of the day were far more supportive of strikes which were on the issue of union recognition (Duffield 1988, 72-87). Duffield documents powerful shop steward-led radicalism among the South Asian workforce in the foundries in the Midlands and beyond. This was the backdrop for the growing radicalism of South Asian workers in the 1970s , manifested in a number of industrial disputes such as those at Mansfield Hosiery in Loughborough in 1972 and at Imperial Typewriters in Leicester in 1974 (Dhondy 1974; Race Today 1974). In the latter, South Asian women workers, supported by community groups had to confront elements within their own unions as well as their discriminatory management. These strikes, together with the Grunwick dispute, are widely recognised as key factors that impelled the TUC towards policies recognising discrimination in the workplace and their responsibility to act in response to this discrimination (Sullivan 2012).

The first of these strikes began in October 1972 at the Mansfield Hosiery Mills Ltd. This strike followed unresolved grievances about a series of discriminatory practices by the management including the reservation of the better-paid knitting jobs for white workers. Initially the mainly South Asian women workforce were denied support from their union but, with the support of a number of community groups they prevailed. According to Virdee (1999: 137) 'it was only when the strikers occupied the union offices that the union finally made the strike official'. The Race Relations Board eventually found that this trade union, the National Union of Hosiery and Knitwear Workers, 'connived with management to prevent Indian workers' advancement in training' (Race Today 1972, cited in Smith 2017, 148). This dispute also sheds light on the complicity of the Race Relations Board, the TUC, the Loughborough Community Relations Council, the TGWU and the Runnymede Trust in discriminatory practices (referring to their initial refusal to back the strikers) , in contrast to the support that the workers received from their own community, which helped them to sustain their action (Bunsee 1974). After twelve weeks, the strike resulted in a partial victory, and led to the South Asian workers receiving training to be knitters, a category of work which had previously been exclusively white, and the workers were able to form a shop committee consisting of fifteen representatives, of which eleven were South Asian.

In May 1974, over 500 South Asian workers went on strike at the Imperial Typewriters factory, in protest against the lack of opportunities for promotion for South Asian workers and against unpaid bonuses. The Imperial Typewriters strike of 1974 was similar to that at Mansfield Hosiery in a number of ways: there was a lack of support from the trade union and from the strikers' white co-workers, in the face of discriminatory managerial practices and in contrast to the support the strikers received from the wider community. However, on this occasion there was also the additional threat of the fascist National Front organising against them. The strike began with a walk-out by thirty-nine workers, including twenty-seven women,

who assembled parts into complete typewriters. The women were
paid £18 a week compared to the £25 that the men received;
additional bonus payments were paid to workers who met target
production for the day. However, South Asian workers were set a
higher production target than white workers, which made it harder
for them to receive the bonus (Wilson 1978, 56-58). As in previous
disputes, the South Asian strikers did not receive any support from
their union, the TGWU, which went on to actively oppose them.
Frustrated at the white shop stewards' failure to recognise the
everyday racism that structured their working lives, the South Asian
workers demanded their own shop stewards to negotiate equitable
treatment in matters of pay, bonuses and everyday working conditions such as lunch and toilet breaks, which were allocated on a
differential basis between white and South Asian workers. When
this demand was rejected by their union, this resulted in the walkout
by South Asian workers. Smith (2018, 152) documents how the
Strike Committee pushed for a number of short-term demands and
refused to return to work other than on the basis of '(1) absolutely no
victimisation (2) continuous employment [and] (3) [the] democratic
election of shop stewards'. The TGWU representative for Imperial
Typewriters criticised the unofficial measures being taken by the
South Asian strikers and their apparent disregard for the 'proper
disputes procedure', stating that the strikers 'have got to learn to fit
in with our ways' and then claiming, 'the way they have been acting
… means they will close factories and people won't employ them'
(Smith 2018, 153). Despite the lack of support from their union, the
strike was sustained by widespread support by community organisations, but the strikers ultimately had to return to work having won
few concessions.

Both strikes were notable for being led by South Asian workers
against discrimination in mixed workplaces with divisions of labour
radically structured by race (Cooper 2013). Smith (2018, 149) documents how the striking workers at both Mansfield Hosiery and
Imperial Typewriters positioned their struggle as 'not a fight against
the white workers but a struggle for equal job opportunity'. In the
context of exclusionary practices directed by their trade unions
against non-white workers, both sets of workers felt it necessary to
construct their struggles as part of the broader struggle for workers'

rights, rather than as a response to racist discrimination. The Mansfield workers described themselves as part of 'one brotherhood in the struggle for the improvement in their working conditions', (Patel 1973, cited in Smith 2018, 149), while the Imperial Typewriters Strike Committee claimed in one of their strike bulletins, 'we did not regard our dispute as a fundamentally a racial one [sic.] but as a workers' dispute' (Smith 2018, 154), despite this being an action that was not supported by the white workers. Phizacklea and Miles (1987a, 117) note that these disputes should clearly have demonstrated even to the most short-sighted and reactionary trade union leader that racism was rife within trade unions' own ranks. A subsequent report to the TUC warned that discrimination such as that faced by the Mansfield workers was 'not an isolated case' and risked pushing immigrant workers away from the labour movement and towards forming their own trade union organisations (Smith 2018, 149-150).

The first challenge to discriminatory practices within trade union bureaucratic structures was articulated by rank and file trade union members at the 1969 TUC Congress, where some delegates called for positive action by trade unions to combat discrimination and to support a legal response by the government to prevent discrimination. However, the TUC General Council prevented the motion from receiving majority support (Fine and Holgate 2014). From an initial position (1960s to mid-1970s) which held that special policies to address the needs of black workers would discriminate against white union members, from the late 1970s and particularly into the 1980s, the TUC began recognising racial discrimination as an issue that required specific action, although measures such as positive action to tackle discrimination took longer to materialise (Wrench 2004). This gradual shift towards the incorporation of black and South Asian workers into the trade union movement was signalled by the establishment of the TUC's Equal Rights Committee in 1975, and the first TUC Black Workers' Conference in 1984. These initiatives took place largely in response to: organisational pressure exerted by black and South Asian trade union members; the external pressure created by the rise of far right groups such as the National Front; and the fear that non-response by trade unions would push black and South Asian members away from mainstream trade unions. This was also in the context of increasing support for black and South Asian workers' cause from some white activists (Fine and Holgate 2014; Wrench and Virdee 1996; Wrench 1987), including socialist internationalists who were seeking to forge a wider class solidarity that challenged racism (Virdee 2014).

The trade unions' inability to address the needs of women and black workers has been attributed to a combination of factors that arose from the unrepresentative structures and decision-making processes of the unions themselves (Cockburn 1995; Dickens 1997). The issues raised range from early trade union ambivalence or hostility towards tackling racism and discrimination at work (Phizacklea and Miles 1987a; Wrench 2004), exclusion strategies of unions against black and women workers (Dickens 1997; Wrench and Virdee 1996), reluctance of unions to take on issues specifically affecting its women members (Davis 2010; Phizacklea and Miles 1987a; Wrench 1987), and the unrepresentative nature of the union decision-making structures which effectively were dominated by white men (Dickens 1997; Kirton and Healy 1999; Kirton and Greene 2002). This latter is a charge that holds to this day.

With notable exceptions (Holgate 2005; Healey et al. 2004; Kirton and Greene 2002), there is little research that explores the particular experiences of minority ethnic women as members and shop stewards in trade unions. It has also been argued that the gendered occupational and organisational structures of both workplaces and unions have served to reinforce patterns of gendered segregation and discrimination and have marginalised the priorities of women members (Cox et al. 2007). Consequently, strategies of separate organising have also been explored in the context of the trade unions' neglect of issues of gender and the lack of representation of women in union decision-making structures and practices in the UK (Colgan and Ledwith 2000; Parker 2002).

In contrast to previous industrial disputes such as those at Mansfield Hosiery and Imperial Typewriters, at the Grunwick factory, divisions and hierarchies between white and migrant workers based on race were less significant at the shop floor level. There, the racial segregation of the workers operated *within* categories of migrant workers, through differential roles for South Asian and Caribbean workers – while any white workers were likely to be deployed in supervisory roles. Perhaps it was this difference from previous disputes – which had been based on different wages for white and migrant workers in similar roles – that in part, contributed to the success of a unifying struggle for union recognition at the Grunwick dispute.

With changes to union membership and a momentum created by a more diverse union base, as well as policy imperatives from above, a more engaged approach by trade unions to questions of race and ethnicity and gender has emerged since the 1980s (Davis et al. 2006; Wrench and Virdee 1996). But we should be cautious about overestimating the efficacy of this new approach; Martinez-Lucio and Perrett (2009a), following Alleyne (2002), challenge the stereotyping of ethnic minority union members. They express concerns that the new trade union approach to migrant and minority ethnic workers seems to be based on an essentialist notion of collectivity embedded within ideal constructions of 'community', which results in assumptions about the common interests of these workers. This is reflected within much industrial relations analysis, which tends to assess black and minority ethnic workers in terms of their deviation from the accepted norms of white worker practice, though the latter are rarely burdened with assumptions about common and collective interests based on their 'culture' or 'community'. The Gate Gourmet dispute was also widely represented by both the mainstream media and by union leadership (Woodley 2007) as an outcome of different repertoires of industrial militancy which were brought into the dispute by minority ethnic women workers. More accurate narratives of the South Asian women strikers at Grunwick as well as the sacked Gate Gourmet women workers – who have spent their entire working lives in the UK – tell the history of their engagement with their union and the particular events of both these disputes and thereby allow us to challenge this construction of their actions as unconventional and outside the norms of accepted union practice.

UNDERSTANDING WORK AND LIFE HISTORIES – BEFORE AND BEYOND GRUNWICK AND GATE GOURMET

The research that we draw on in this book was carried out between 2007 and 2009, and involved life history interviews with five of the then-elderly Grunwick strikers, and twenty-seven Punjabi women workers who were sacked by Gate Gourmet. In addition to the interviews with the workers, our research was also informed by interviews with three senior officials in the TGWU (now UNITE), direct observation of the proceedings of several cases on this dispute, heard at the Employment Tribunal in Reading, and an analysis of the full judgements of the seventeen Employment Tribunal cases heard between November 2006 and June 2008. There is a large quantity of secondary literature on the Grunwick dispute, as well as a range of political and journalistic accounts (Dromey and Taylor 1978; Levidov 1981; Rogaly 1977; Rossiter 1977, Wilson 1978) and video productions including documentaries by Chris Thomas (1977; 1978; and 2008), Deep Sehgal (2003), and Steve Sprung (1985). In contrast, there are few published accounts of the Gate Gourmet dispute. In general, however, the range of sources we were able to draw upon has provided a unique perspective on the ways in which these different groups of South Asian women workers experienced the role of their trade union in the genesis, trajectory and official conclusion of their dispute.

Utilising life history methods enabled us to move away from an incident-centred analysis of the two industrial disputes, to one where these particular acts of industrial militancy can be located within workers' lives as a whole. Castree (2007) argues for a more holistic perspective on work, exploring people's experiences of their working lives within the wider nexus of home and community that they inhabit. We would add that beyond a broader focus on the social structures and relations within which workers are embedded, a holistic understanding of particular moments of industrial militancy in their working lives requires an approach that encompasses their past and ongoing experiences of paid and unpaid work (McDowell, 2013 and 2016). Further, in the case of migrant workers, understanding workplace experiences and aspirations also requires an insight into the workers' ongoing links to their home countries, the particular contexts of those home countries and the workers' relationships with those people they have left there. The Gujarati and Punjabi women we interviewed spoke to us about their experiences of migration and settlement, their family lives and roles in relation to the paid and unpaid work that they undertook, their labour histories as they moved jobs over the years, experiences at work including the everyday labour processes and work practices, workplace relations, and conflict and resistance at work. Life history methods opened up the space for women to talk about their experiences of work in the context of their lives as a whole, enabling analysis of the power relations and the larger structural constraints posed by the intersecting inequalities that shape their mobility, identity formation and incorporation into the labour market in the UK. Life history interviews brought into clearer focus the specificity of women's lives and experiences at the intersections of various axes of disadvantage and privilege structured by (changing) class positions, caste, gender, race, ethnicity, education and the women's status as migrants, as well as their subjective experiences of work.

In the case of the Grunwick dispute, the singular account of its leader, Jayaben Desai, has hitherto frequently stood in for the experience of all the women strikers, in media accounts from the time, and even more so in subsequent representations of the dispute. This was because of her high public profile during the strike, and perhaps also because of the obscurity of the other strikers, whose relative lack of proficiency in English might have deterred the researchers and journalists from seeking them out. Given that Jayaben Desai's account of the Grunwick dispute had been told and retold countless times in the UK, in stories that were burnished through repeated rendering, we chose to interview her in Hindi, in the hope of bringing forth submerged accounts and hitherto unvoiced memories, not least because Jayaben and the four other women that we interviewed who had participated in the Grunwick strike were in their 70s and 80s at the time of our research.

A principal objective of our research was to document the voices of a range of women involved, given that ownership of the memory of the Grunwick dispute has been primarily claimed by trade unions, as exemplified in the celebrations in the fortieth anniversary year of the beginning of the strike. In contrast, the Gate Gourmet dispute continues to be ignored in the mainstream media, and there is little appetite for the participants' alternative accounts of it. Although some of the leaders of the dispute had spoken to journalists before, in our interviews, these Gate Gourmet workers were able to render a detailed account of their lives and their involvement in the dispute for the first time.

As Riessman (2008) argues, the interpretive approach of narrative analysis is very well suited to studying identities as well as 'critical life events' such as experiences of migration and settlement, and of acts of industrial militancy. Analysis of life history data and semi-structured interviews entailed a process of continuous engagement with each transcript, in order to identify significant concepts within each woman's narrative, and to compare across narratives, identifying emerging themes. Equally important as the content and the themes, were the contexts within which they emerged in the telling of the narrative – the lived and affective accounts of women's experiences, the way the narratives were organised and the work that stories perform at a social and cultural level.

The central features of this approach include: identification of key events in the life story, with particular attention to temporality and sequence of events; the causality attributed to different events and the connection/link that participants attribute to these events; the structure of the narrative; exploration of what particular life-events meant for the participant at the time as well as what they mean at the time of the interview; the agency of the participant within their story; and the socio-cultural context of the story. Oral histories are not based on the notion that memory is an accurate portrayal of the past, and it is widely acknowledged that there are both subjective and objective elements to such narratives. As Herbert (2009) has argued, repetition of specific accounts of important events in the past also serves to assert positive aspects of individual and collective identities. Rather than working out 'what really happened', our task here was to explicate how social realities and identities are built, following Passerini's (1989, 197) observation that 'all autobiographical memory is true: it is up to the interpreter to discover in which sense, where, and for what purpose'.

Apart from the Grunwick strike leader, Jayaben Desai, who was happy to be named, the names of the other women have been changed to protect their identities. Pseudonyms in keeping with naming conventions associated with particular regions and religions have been allocated to the interviewees. We use long verbatim quotes from the women workers, and where words or phrases are marked by quotation marks *within* their quotes, this indicates that those utterances were in English in an interview that was otherwise in Hindi.

Though Gujarati was the first language of all the Grunwick strikers as was Punjabi for most of the sacked Gate Gourmet workers, Hindi was a strong second language for all of them. We have indicated with a 'G' or 'GG' after each interviewee's name whether she worked at Grunwick or Gate Gourmet.

Focussing on the disputes enables us to explore the agency of these two groups of South Asian women workers, to understand their engagement in mainstream trade union practices and to bring to the centre voices that remain marginalised. We recount their stories of involvement in industrial militancy as a counterpoint to widely expressed surprise at South Asian women's presence on picket lines, which has persisted despite the long history of South Asian women's labour activism in the UK. Their stories are a contrast to familiar orientalist constructions of their dissent – both in mainstream media and some trade union accounts (McDowell et al. 2012) – as exotic, impulsive and somehow unusual compared to the 'norm' of the white male worker.

The research process described in this chapter marks a different approach not just to analysing the disputes at Grunwick and Gate Gourmet, but also to understanding the realities of South Asian women workers' lives in the UK over the last four decades. This serves to contextualise the hard fought struggles undertaken by the women involved, in the context of their own histories of migration, family and work. But it also offers a distinct perspective on the interconnectedness of work and family issues – what we can call production and reproduction – which should be the basis for understanding the decisions and actions undertaken by these women, and the ways in which their trade unions succeeded – or failed – to appreciate their ambitions, principles and priorities. The interviews with our research participants also provide new understandings of the ways in which these two industrial disputes played out in the very different political and economic contexts of the 1970s and the 2000s.

CHAPTER 3

South Asian women in the UK: Histories of migration and settlement

As we argued in the previous chapter, our focus on South Asian women's working lives and their participation in industrial disputes in the UK presents a counterpoint to the stereotypical representations and erasures of South Asian women as waged workers from historical accounts of South Asian diasporas and from popular and media constructions of 'the South Asian woman'. In this chapter, we analyse the experiences of migration and settlement of two different groups of South Asian women who arrived in the UK between the late 1960s to the early 1980s, from newly independent countries in East Africa on the one hand, and the Indian Punjab on the other. These women migrants participated in the UK labour market as they sought to build a better life for themselves and their families and to secure their children's futures. Subsequent chapters explore their experiences of entering a gendered and racialised labour market in the UK and their struggles and strategies in their quest for respect, dignity and better rights at work. It is our contention that understanding particular moments of militancy in these women's labour history – and especially their participation in the Grunwick and the Gate Gourmet disputes – requires the location of women's agency in the context of: their particular histories of migration and settlement; their class backgrounds and changing class positions; and the constraints and opportunities posed by their gendered location at the intersections of the workplace, the home and the community.

SOUTH ASIAN MIGRATION TO POST-WAR BRITAIN

In order to recognise diversity and difference, it is important to provide an account of the different waves of migration from the subcontinent. Though South Asian presence in the UK can be traced back to the beginning of the seventeenth century (Visram 2002), the first settler communities of any significant size were documented from the early nineteenth century onwards, in Cardiff, Liverpool and the East End of London (Ansari 2006, 143). These early settlers included a range of transitory and permanent migrants, and were diverse groups from different regions of South Asia, including: members of Indian royal and aristocratic families who came for education purposes and for leisure trips; professionals such as doctors, lawyers and merchants; students; nursemaids and travelling nannies (known as *ayahs*), who accompanied British families returning from India; and sailors (*lascars*) from Sylhet (in present-day Bangladesh) and Mirpur (in present-day Pakistan), who were not re-employed on return journeys or who jumped ship to escape maltreatment, and settled in port cities (Visram 2002).

More significant numbers of migrants from South Asia began to arrive and settle in the UK during the post-Second World War period of labour shortages, in which many men came to the UK under the British Nationality Act of 1948. This Act guaranteed free right of entry to British subjects and Commonwealth citizens. The shortage of labour in the UK coincided with high levels of poverty and lack of employment opportunities for the large labour force in the ex-colonies, and independence and partition inevitably increased instability in the sub-continent – particularly for those groups that had had strong links to the former colonial regimes. From exporters of raw materials, these ex-colonies were to become exporters of cheap labour, fuelling the post-war growth in Britain (Sivanandan 1976).

In keeping with their long established culture of migration – 5 per cent of the total Sikh population live outside their homeland (Tatla and Singh 2006, 33) – the earliest phase of post-war migration to the UK drew large numbers of men from an agrarian society in Punjab that was predominantly rural, patriarchal and hierarchically structured along caste rules. The majority of Punjabi migrants were from a landowning caste, the Jat Sikhs, whose members had been previously employed in the colonial army or the police force (Tatla and Singh 2006). The preponderance of Jat Sikhs among those in the colonial army and police can be attributed to Victorian 'scientific' notions about race and masculinity, which informed the nineteenth-century conceptual categorisation of Sikhs as a 'martial race' by the British, who actively sought members of this caste for military service (Rand 2006; Streets 2004). Jat Sikhs are estimated to represent 60 per cent of the population of Punjab, and constitute between 70-90 per cent of the population of the Doaba region in rural Punjab, which is where most of the migrants to the UK originated from, dominating the South Asian migration stream in the 1950s. The transnational mobility of Jat Sikhs, who are also the politically and socially dominant caste in Punjab, reflected the material resources that they could command on account of their caste-specific history of land ownership and transnational intra-caste migration networks. Migrants from Punjab also included a sizeable minority of middle- and low-ranking artisan castes like Ramgarhias, and landless labourers from ex-untouchable castes including Chamars, also known as the dalits ('the oppressed'). Similar to all migrants and irrespective of their caste and occupational status in Punjab, upon arriving in the UK Punjabi migrants found work in the lowest rungs of the employment hierarchy in unskilled manual jobs and engaged in night or shift work, as these fields were unpopular with local white workers.

The areas where Punjabi migrants settled included: West London, where they secured jobs at the new Heathrow Airport and the light manufacturing industries in surrounding areas; in Northern towns, especially West Yorkshire, where they worked in textile, steel mills and heavy manufacturing industries; and in West Midlands in iron foundries, light engineering and transport industries. Duffield (1988) suggests that apart from labour shortages, the reason for their concentration in some of these regions and industries was the weak unionisation and the consequent low wages there. Subsequent migrants secured jobs and initial support through their social networks with those previously settled in the UK, creating a multiplier effect in particular regions and industries that followed the caste configurations of previous settlers. The initial impetus for migration was to accumulate savings and to return home, an imperative that entailed long hours and multiple shifts and living predominantly in multi-occupancy all-male households in order to minimise their living costs.

During this period, anti-immigration sentiments in the UK began to be mobilised by Conservative MPs such as Cyril Osborne and various racist groups including the newly formed National Front (Brah 1996, 23; Sivanandan 1976), which eventually resulted in the passage of the Commonwealth Immigrants Act 1962. This Act restricted the free movement of workers from the Commonwealth. Citizens of the UK and its colonies whose passports were not directly issued by the UK government now became subject to immigration control, with the exception of those with passports issued at a British High Commission in an independent Commonwealth country or a British Consulate, who remained free from immigration control. The 1962 Act also increased the required residence period for Commonwealth citizens applying for registration as Citizens of the UK and Colonies, from one to five years, and employment vouchers were now required to gain entry into the UK. Following these changes, the 'myth of return' dissipated (Anwar 1979) and most workers from South Asia began to settle on a long term basis in the UK, whilst the fear of further prohibitive immigration controls led many to send for their families. This made the South Asian settlement more permanent and more varied (Anwar 1979).

It was primarily during the 1970s that women and children from Punjab began to migrate to join their fathers and husbands, with a view to indefinite settlement in the UK. Given the class/caste origins of these migrants, economic imperatives to buy a home and to send remittances to extended family shaped these Punjabi women's entry into the UK labour market. These Punjabi women found employment in labour-intensive and low-paid sectors such as food, light manufacturing and garment industries, including home-based work. Wilson (1978, 48) notes the exploitative nature of such work where lack of proficiency in English combined with gendered pay differentials to relegate these women to the 'bottom of the heap'. During this period schools were experiencing a significant increase in the number of South Asian and as well as other black children from the former colonies in the Caribbean, leading to demands by some white parents that the intake of non-white children in particular schools should be restricted. 'Bussing' of these children to schools in other areas began as a localised practice in late 1963 and became national policy in 1965 (Brah 1996, 22-23). In the context of these anti-immigration campaigns, with considerable racism in education, housing and in employment, a new phase of migration to the UK took place in the late 1960s and early 1970s.

British passport holders of Indian origin were long settled under the British empire in countries in East Africa including Kenya, Uganda and Tanzania, and a small minority of them could trace their origins to the indentured labourers recruited primarily from Punjab in the last decades of the nineteenth century for building the Kenya-Uganda railway in East Africa. Though a majority of these labourers returned to South Asia once the period of their indenture was over, the few thousand who remained were joined by subsequent flows of voluntary passenger migrations (Twaddle 1990, 160). A majority of Indians in East African countries originated from Gujarat and were Hindus belonging to the landowning Patidar caste, but, in general, South Asian migrants in East Africa were a heterogeneous category comprising of a sizeable minority of Punjabis, primarily Ramgarhia Sikhs and smaller numbers of Jat Sikhs (Bhachu 1985; Mand 2016), as well as Muslims (from Gujarat as well as from latter-day Pakistan), Parsees and Ismailis from other parts of Western provinces in India (Twaddle 1975). South Asians came to occupy a middle position in the tripartite colonial hierarchy organised in East Africa, between the British colonial rulers at the top and the African majority at the bottom. This racial division of labour resulted from the policies of the colonial state which facilitated the migration of South Asians to take up commerce, middle-level administrative roles in the colonial bureaucracy and petty trade, while the Africans were restricted to agricultural labour. A significant share of commercial trade in Kenya and Uganda was in the hands of South Asian settlers by the 1940s. But behind this common characterisation of the tripartite hierarchy, there lay important distinctions in the different East African countries where the South Asians settled. For example, in Kenya, they were more likely to be employed in the civil services, while they dominated trading and commerce in Uganda and Tanzania (Mattaush 2001, 65). Twaddle also counters the myth of a monolithic South Asian community of wealthy traders and businessmen, arguing that – at least in Uganda – a sizeable population of South Asians were middle-level government employees and artisans of modest means (Twaddle 1975).

After independence in the 1960s, each country adopted different policies towards South Asian residents to counteract their economic dominance. The 'Africanisation' policies of countries such as Kenya, Tanzania, Zambia and Malawi were intended to ensure that the African majority population acquired greater control over key areas of the economy and the government. Legislation was passed restricting the choice of residences, trade and employment for non-citizens. For example, trade in certain commodities such as staple foods was widely restricted to citizens only. In Tanzania, the nationalisation of banks and other financial institutions particularly affected the livelihoods of the South Asian community, who owned the vast majority of finance-related businesses. Following Kenya's independence from Britain in 1963, South Asians were given two years to acquire Kenyan citizenship to replace the British passports that most of them held. However, there was a low take-up of Kenyan citizenship among residents of South Asian origin, a pattern that was repeated in other East and Central African countries after independence. Faced with declining economic opportunities and security, many East African Asians who held British passports chose to migrate to the UK by the end of the 1960s. However, although they were British subjects, they were not always welcome in the UK and faced widespread discrimination in matters of housing and employment.

In 1968, a new Race Relations Act came into force in the UK, making it illegal to refuse housing, employment or public services to people because of their ethnic background. But in that same year, with growing immigration of East African Asians, Conservative Party MP Enoch Powell made his infamous 'rivers of blood' speech arguing that the government must be 'literally mad' to allow mass immigration from Commonwealth countries and predicting that this would lead to violence in Britain's cities (Hillman 2008). Against the backdrop of increasing racist attacks against South Asian and other black migrants the Commonwealth Immigrants Act of 1968 was designed to restrict black immigration to the UK, and was passed through the Houses of Parliament and received royal assent within a mere two days. So, in the same year as the first legislation criminalising racial discrimination, this Act institutionalised racial discrimination into immigration law by removing the right of entry of British passport holders unless they had a substantial connection to the UK, defined as having a parent or grandparent born there. By differentiating between those citizens with close ties with the UK who were free to enter, and those citizens who had no such ties and were therefore subject to immigration control, this Act specifically excluded most British East Africans, whose connection to the UK was through British colonial rule. The 1971 Immigration Act strengthened this exclusion by reaffirming the concept of 'patriality'. Only those with a work permit for a specific job with a named employer, where it could be argued that the skills required were in short supply, were allowed to enter the country, thereby placing the UK in the rare position of denying some of its nationals entry into their country of nationality. Together, these and subsequent immigration acts were designed to enable white British citizens to enter the UK while excluding South Asian or black British citizens (WING 1985).

Asians living in Uganda had no choice but to leave after General Idi Amin seized power there in a military coup in 1971. On 4 August 1972, he ordered all Asians to leave the country within ninety days. Thousands left Uganda with no property and no more than the permitted £55 in cash. The British government responded to pressures from anti-immigration groups by creating the Uganda Resettlement Board, which delineated the UK into 'red' and 'green zones' and was designed to steer Ugandan Asians away from existing areas of minority ethnic settlement such as London, Leicester and Yorkshire. The Leicester City Council even posted an advert in the *Uganda Argus* newspaper telling Ugandan Asians not to come to Leicester, which was deemed to have reached a migration saturation point. But it is widely believed that the advert had the opposite effect, and served to signpost Leicester to potential migrants as a desirable destination; new migrants sought out places with established communities of Gujarati East Africans, and this drew them to London and Leicester.

About 27,000 Ugandan Asians came to the UK (Parekh 1997), while smaller numbers went to Canada, India and Kenya. While many Asians in Uganda already held British citizenship, others were granted it after they lost their Ugandan citizenship. In 1968, there were 345,000 Asians resident in Kenya, Tanzania, Zambia, Malawi, and Uganda. By 1984, according to the Minority Rights Group (1990), their numbers had fallen to about 85,000, with just 1000 remaining in Uganda. Correspondingly, the number of Asians from Africa who were resident in the UK rose from about 45,000 in 1971 to about 180,000 in 1981 (Anwar 1998, 5).

Herbert (2012) argues that the East African Asians have changing, contested and often ambiguous links to India. This challenges much of the current literature on South Asian diasporas, which foregrounds the link to India and a 'mother' country as a defining feature of this specific East African Asian diaspora (Singh 2003). As multiple movers, who were forced to migrate or who moved due to coercive circumstances, these migrants have maintained close connections with other East African Asians who settled in different parts of the world, a connection in which a collective memory of East Africa as the homeland, and the trauma of leaving plays a central role (Herbert 2009). Despite their identification as Indian rather than African in the British context, Murji (2008) points to the profound impact of Africa on these twice-migrants' language, food and identity. Focusing on the Punjabi East African Asians – who were in a small minority compared to the Gujaratis – Bhachu (1990) notes the distinction between them and direct migrants from Punjab. She observes how they perceived themselves as urbanised and sophisticated, that they tended to socialise with other East African Asians, and that they maintained these connections through marriage within this community, rather than seeking marriage partners among direct migrants from Punjab. Drawing on her research with twice-migrants settled in Canada, Rahemtullah (2010) similarly argues for a more nuanced approach to thinking through the complexities of affiliation and self-identification in diasporic spaces. Direct migrants from Punjab, in contrast to this, have maintained close ties with their homeland, which has created a remittance economy and avenues for further migration through family reunion following marriages between British Asian men who seek brides from Punjab, and smaller numbers of Punjabi men who migrate abroad to marry.

Although the twice-migrants were urban educated, from middle-class backgrounds, they initially had to accept work in low-paid jobs and they struggled to gain better pay and rights. Herbert

(2009, 21) argues that their fluency in the English language plus their business acumen and familiarity with urban and bureaucratic institutions, as well as the particular circumstances of migration as entire family units, enabled them to make long-term commitments to settle indefinitely in the UK, to invest in property and business, and to seek educational opportunities for their children. These twice-migrants have prospered over the past forty years and have now largely regained their wealth and the middle-class status they left behind in East Africa. They are frequently celebrated as a 'model minority', perceived to have successfully integrated and prospered in the UK (Mattaush 1998), to the extent that by the fourth Labour Force Survey in 1979, 'African-Asians' were no longer considered a 'disadvantaged group' (Modood et al. 1997, 342).

The 2001 census records a home ownership rate of 82 per cent for Sikhs; this is the highest rate of all religious categories, including Christianity, and this suggests an upward economic mobility for this community.[1] However, given that a majority of Punjabi migrants to the UK are Sikh, and predominantly Jat Sikhs, the agrarian caste history of this group means that land ownership is an important marker of identity for them, and was a marker of their dominant socio-economic status in Punjab. Tatla and Singh (2006) argue that this might explain the imperative for property ownership among this community, though this was also driven by their experiences of racist exclusion from private rental and social housing. In contrast to the economic success implied by home ownership, the labour market experiences of Sikhs in the UK suggests that their early experiences of employment in low-status and low-paid jobs has continued for the Punjabi communities in the UK, though to a lesser extent than the experience of Pakistani and Bangladeshi workers (Brown 2000; Dustmann and Fabbri 2005, 445). Research indicates that Sikh women are most likely to be working in low-skilled jobs – almost one in ten was working as a process, plant or machine operative in 2004, compared with approximately 3 per cent of women in other groups (ONS 2004). During this period, a total of 45 per cent of employed Sikh women worked in distribution, catering and manufacturing industries, compared to 30 per cent of all employed women. This indicates a gendered dimension to the occupational profile of Sikhs in the UK given that the male Sikh representation in manufacturing sector was in line with the national average. At the time of the Gate Gourmet dispute, Sikh women were grossly over-represented in this sector, which is representative of their continued concentration in low-waged, inner-city factories (Tatla and Singh 2006, 160-1).

WOMEN'S NARRATIVES ABOUT MIGRATION, SETTLEMENT AND ENTERING THE LABOUR MARKET IN THE UK

The South Asian women workers in the two disputes at the centre of our research belonged to two very distinct groups of South Asian migrants – the twice-migrant East African Asians and those from direct migrant Punjabi families. We found both commonalities and differences in the migration journeys of the two groups of women we interviewed, separated as they were by time, class backgrounds, country of origin, the nature of their migration and the reasons for migration. But there were far more commonalities in their experiences after settlement; in the British context they faced similar constraints in matters of housing and in employment due to their gender and race. Some differences also emerge in the narratives about their employment histories both prior to migration and about their entry into the labour market in the UK.

Gujarati women tended to migrate with their entire families in the period between the late-1960s and the mid-1970s from primarily, though not exclusively, urban backgrounds in countries in East Africa. Though the term 'twice-migrants' is used for East African Asians who came to the UK to indicate their prior migration histories as they moved from India to countries in East Africa, and then to the UK, two of the Grunwick strikers we talked to were thrice and four-time migrants, as they moved between countries in East Africa upon marriage, or returned to India for a brief period before migrating to settle in the UK. Jayaben Desai recalled her own family's experience:

> When I heard the news on radio about the new immigration law, we had to act quickly. We had thought about going before, but we thought he [husband] would go first, find a job and find a place to live and then we would all join him. I said, 'You have planned and planned, but not done anything and now this law

will come into being'. He said, 'I will go to Bombay and I have a British passport, so nothing will affect me'. He went to the High Commission and asked them about the new law, and they told him that he would have to stand in a queue to enter Britain. So he got a ticket and got on a plane. I got a telegram saying he had left! He had just taken a tiny case with him for an overnight stay in Bombay to assess the situation, and he ended up going to London! (Jayaben, G)

As British passport holders, many East African Asians had the right to travel freely prior to the Commonwealth Immigrants Act of 1968, and made the decision to migrate to the UK to rebuild a better life for their children, fearing that this option would close with restrictive immigration policies. Others from urban middle-class backgrounds came to the UK directly; as discussed previously, in East African countries, upon independence, there were constricting opportunities for Indians because of policies of Africanisation. Under threat of expulsion from Uganda:

When they started throwing out the Indians from Uganda, we had to leave our business and everything there and come here. I came with the children and my husband joined us after a month. We had four cars at home – we had to give them away to the drivers, there was no time to sell them. We were only allowed to bring £55. We got our clothes and some personal possessions. And we had to work when we came here and start all over again. Those were very difficult days. The children were very young – they used to keep asking, 'I want this, I want that', and I used to feel very sad – we had nothing, how could I buy them what they wanted? (Nirmalaben, G)

Contrary to popular perceptions, many wealthier migrants held some financial assets in other countries or were able to transfer at least some of their financial resources prior to migration, particularly where they were from countries other than Uganda. However, most Gujarati women reported a setback to family finances because of the relocation, and having occupied the middling rung in the colonial hierarchies in East Africa – having servants and a big home was mentioned by the majority – they experienced a profound dislocation in their class and social status, which loomed large in their accounts of that period in their life. Herbert (2009) argues that such memories which separate their narratives into an idyllic period 'before' migration and a period of struggle and transcending difficulties 'after' migration capture important moments in the expression of their collective history, and serve to communicate a profound sense of loss as well as a story of survival. And inevitably these memories are filtered through time and aging in the four decades following their migration.

The migration patterns of the Punjabi women who we interviewed during the Gate Gourmet dispute followed a somewhat different route from the Gujarati women, and took place over a longer period. Though small numbers of women had migrated in the late 1960s and a few families had left in the context of the separatist movement in Punjab in early 1980s, most of the women we interviewed migrated during the 1970s. While some women came to the UK as children to join their fathers settled in the UK, the majority were marriage migrants who arrived in the UK as fiancées and as new brides of Punjabi men who were already settled in the UK.

A smaller number of women came to the UK as teenagers following 'adoption' by relatives, with the intention of working and settling in the UK. They often went on to marry Punjabi men in the UK, or went back to Punjab to find a spouse who subsequently migrated to join them. There were several reasons why single women took this route, despite the fact that migrating as a single woman would appear to have transgressed the patriarchal norms that prevailed in rural Punjab in the 1970s. The presence of relatives already settled in the UK and the prospect of shared living arrangements in their households served to dispel some of these concerns. The nature of the immigration laws also shaped some of the strategic decisions made by the women and their families. The UK immigration legislation was based on the presumption of a single male – the head of the household – migrating for work, and his wife and children migrating to join him (Wray 2015). In some families, where all the other children were over eighteen and beyond the age of adoption, or were too young to be separated from their families, parents sent daughters who were almost at the age where they could undertake paid work, to be 'adopted' by a relative settled in the UK. Tatla and Singh (2006, 53) document the creative ways in which the early migrants subverted the immigration control and claimed extra dependents in order to facilitate the migration of their relatives. Parents expended considerable money to enable travel, and sometimes to bear the initial expenses of settlement with relatives, following which women were expected to support themselves through work, and often to send remittances home. Young women in this situation – most of whom were aged fifteen to eighteen – but sometimes older, although their 'passport age' would have put them under eighteen – seldom went to school in the UK.

As one woman in a situation like this recounted, life in the UK was harder than she expected:

> The work was hard and things began to deteriorate at home too, with my uncle and aunt. I did enjoy cooking and all that. But I felt like, it was as if they had got me here almost as a servant. To be honest with you, that's how it felt. (Parjot, GG)

When one such woman had the opportunity to return to India for a holiday, she was reluctant to come back to the UK but was persuaded to do so by her family:

> I went to India and I didn't want to come back. Everyone there said, you are making a mistake, you should go back. I did not want to come back, but I did it for my father. You see, he had artificial legs. In those days, the limbs you got in India used to be very heavy. He suffered a lot. I felt that if I was here, I could bring him here to get him treated here. It was not possible to afford it if you lived there. So I came back and worked here for a year and half, and then got my parents here and they made him the legs here, and it was so good! So light, so easy to walk on. His life changed when he got that. It was very expensive. Whatever I had earned so far, I spent it on his legs. (Jasmeet, GG)

Women in circumstances like these do not figure in mainstream academic or media accounts of migration from Punjab; they are imagined exclusively as dependents, and their migration is conceptualised as family reunion, though the reality may be somewhat more complex and multifaceted.

Women's narratives about their migration generally reflect a binary trope of expectations and excitement before the move and disappointment and difficulties upon migration. When asked if they had actively sought out a match with a non-resident Indian, contrary to commonly held constructions of Punjabi women as eager to migrate abroad, most women we interviewed suggested with an offended air that they were, in fact, initially reluctant to marry so far away from home but eventually came around to the idea. This disavowal of their agency in their accounts to us is surprising, and contrasts with other accounts in their interviews with us and elsewhere (Herbert 2009), which in contrast emphasise their agency. Portrayals of their initial reluctance to marry abroad could have been presented as a counterpoint to the dominant constructions of Punjabi women as eager to migrate or as adhering to gendered norms that disapprove of expressions of eagerness in matters of marriage by women.

In interviews, women recounted their expectations of marriage, which generally centred around an ideal middle-class life, widely associated in the popular imagination with life in the UK. This version of the UK included accounts about the glamour and ease of life, and the access to consumer goods such as washing machines and other labour saving domestic appliances, which were beginning to be available to the middle classes by then. Some marriage migrants cherished the possibility of setting up households with their husbands, away from the constraints of a joint family and free from the competing demands on their husbands' affections from the mothers-in-law who wished to retain influence over their sons (Singh and Uberoi 1994). After outlining their hopes and dreams about migration, most women also contrasted – with varying degrees of self-deprecating laughter – the initial period of shock and sometimes disappointment as they talked about a period of intense adjustment.

These women's narratives recalled the social isolation they experienced upon migration, as they were unaccustomed to the contrived and pre-planned nature of social interactions within diaspora communities in the UK, necessitated by the distances between households and people's busy schedules as they balanced multiple shifts at work.

I was so excited about coming here, but it was very different from
what I had expected. In India, you have friends nearby, you visit
people whenever you feel like a chat. It's not like that here. All
you do is go to work, come home, and then go to work again.
And also, at work, there is a lot of 'pressure', which I did not
expect. No one tells you about that when they come to India with
stories about how life is abroad. If you want to visit someone, you
have to call them up and check if they are free, and then if they
are busy, you have to wait till they have the time. It's not like that
in India, you can pop in whenever you want. (Satinder, GG)

Two women who migrated from middle-class families in larger
cities compared the relatively relaxed norms surrounding women's
behaviour in metropolitan India in the 1970s and 1980s, with the
gender segregation and gendered expectations they encountered in
the UK. The assertion of such norms has been explained by feminist sociologists who have explored the manifestations of ethnicity
as it intersects with gender ideologies in the particular context of
diaspora communities. Here, women are positioned as markers of
communal ethnic identity and as the custodians and transmitters
of ethnic values (Anthias and Yuval-Davis 1993). The women we
talked to recalled the difficult process of adjusting to the practices of
the Punjabi diasporic community, which was primarily from rural
agrarian communities and structured by hierarchies of caste and
patriarchal cultural norms such as gender-segregated socialisation:

[In India,] I used to go to college, go and see films with boys and
that seemed normal to me. Among Punjabis here, it was a big
deal if you were seen out with a boy, men and women even sat in
different rooms when people socialised. And back there we used
to cycle all over the place, go and see films in mixed groups – my
friends, my brother's friends. I missed all that when I came here.
I wanted to go back and considered it several times, but then my
parents had spent so much money to send me here, so I had to
make the best of it. (Puneet, GG)

Though there are regional variations within particular communities, arranged marriage in North India commonly follows structural

patterns of kinship and marriage practices such as female hypergamy, whereby women marry men of the same or a higher social status or sub-caste, often giving large dowries to get higher-status groups to accept their daughters as wives (Milner 1994; Parry 1979). It has been argued that the direction of transnational marriage flows also mirrors gendered norms about hypergamy, whereby non-resident Indians are constructed as a particularly desirable match and women from India marry 'up' the transnational hierarchy. Constable (2005, 15), writing about 'mail-order brides', terms this process 'spatial hypergamy'. Such marriages also enhance women's status within their natal families, open up routes to future migration of kin and may enable them to realise aspirations of social mobility (Chaudhuri et al. 2014). For communities with a strong history and culture of migration, and given the ever-tighter immigration controls in the UK since 1962, transnational marriage remains one of the few viable routes for migration, as documented by Mooney (2006).

However, women who migrated to marry, often found their expectations of hypergamy upon marriage thwarted by the reality of global geographies of power. Like many migrants, the women who participated in our research experienced a profound dislocation in their accustomed class, lifestyle and social status. Kofman and Raghuram (2006, 296) argue that women who relocate through family migration experience a higher degree of downward mobility than men do. For many Punjabi women we interviewed, this downward mobility was due to the mismatch between their social and class status in India and that of their husbands in the UK. Though a proposal from a similar status family or a factory worker with lower levels of educational qualifications may have been unacceptable were he in the Punjab, many parents were willing to overlook class, status and education in pursuit of the opportunity for international migration for their daughter (Ballard 2004, 12). Qureshi (2016) documents this pattern whereby Punjabi men in the UK frequently marry women in India who are more educated or qualified than them.

> When my aunt used to visit, her daughters used to talk about here as if it was this wonderful place. They used to wear such wonderful clothes. So I thought it must be great here. I thought it would be a 'dream'. We gave a lot of dowry as well – money

and a lot of things – you know how things are, you have to give, whether they ask or not. My parents thought I was going to have a good life, so they wanted to set me up. But when I came here, it was a different story. The house was in disarray, there was dirt everywhere, the carpets had holes in them, it was all very shabby. I was very disappointed. (Simran, GG)

A common refrain in the narratives was the distance between the dominant constructions of life in the UK as told to people in India and the reality, which fell far short of the image presented by the earlier migrants. Taylor (2013) explains this in the context of the importance of the culture of migration among Punjabis, and argues that for Jat Sikhs, migration has come to be the most important marker of social status, eclipsing even land ownership. Drawing upon Hochschild's (1979) concept of emotional labour, Taylor characterises this re-presentation of life in the UK as part of the repertoire of 'emotion work' carried out by returning migrants, whereby they perform 'surface acting' to convey their success and contentment from overseas migration and conceal the difficulties and contradictions it entails from their Indian Punjabi audiences. This emotional management helps them to attain or maintain high *izzat* (honour) via the Punjabi marker of success in overseas migration.

As well as class-related displacement discussed above, a particular set of difficulties and contradictions that the returning migrants attempted to conceal included racism in the housing market. This was encountered by both Gujarati twice migrants and Punjabi direct migrants and made renting difficult. As Jayaben Desai recalled:

We used to rent two rooms in someone's house – there was so much condensation that water used to drip down. And there was no heating, so we used to light this paraffin heater. There was smoke everywhere. We used to keep it at the doorway, and once it fell and caught fire. I managed to put it out – thank god! The house could have caught fire that day! That's how we used to live. They did not rent to us in those days because we were Asian. And we had two children. Our children were so well behaved but they had that 'impression' of us that they would not rent their house to you. We rented off this Asian family who must have come here earlier and managed to buy a house. They were Kumhar – Prajapati (lower caste). And imagine – we had to live in their house, we even shared a kitchen! … That's why we wanted to save money and buy our own place. (Jayaben, G)

Most of the women we interviewed recalled that their families rented from other migrant families, particularly those of Indian or Pakistani origin. Some women recounted living arrangements that entailed several families renting one of two rooms each in a larger house. Renting and living together with families from across religious and caste divides was perceived as particularly onerous for some respondents, whose caste privileges were undermined through such shared living, as it entailed sharing toilets and cooking or eating together. Tatla and Singh (2006) argue that in the case of Punjabi migrants, caste distinctions were also weakened by sharing a canteen in the workplace and working together. However, though caste configurations changed through the process of migration (Brah 1996), and caste distinctions in public spaces weakened, caste was still an important factor in private settings.

Coming to the UK as entire family units enabled creative economies of the household by Gujarati migrants, who were able to pool their resources and rent, or later buy, a house for the extended family, and subsequently buy further property to separate into nuclear family units.

We had this tiny flat – above a shop – which had three rooms. The four brothers (husband and his brothers) got together and bought the shop and this place above it. We were thirteen people in that house, in those three rooms. Two wives, four brothers, the father-in-law and mother-in-law and the children. I had one child then. Later we rented a room in a house nearby. But it was hard. It was very, very cold, and I found that hard. We had a coal fire. That's all. We stayed like that for a few years. Slowly we managed to save up and bought another place. We bought our separate house in 1971, but they continued to work together in the shop. (Naliniben, G)

For Punjabi migrants who came from poorer backgrounds and lacked such resources, the aspiration to home ownership took longer to materialise. Women's entry into the labour market took place in the context of economic imperatives, such as educational aspirations for their children and the need to accumulate savings for home ownership. Both Gujarati and Punjabi women recalled their experiences of entering paid work as difficult. The Gujarati women had worked before migration but usually in home based activities in their relatively protected situations in East Africa, and for the majority of the Punjabi women this was the first time in their lives that they had been in paid employment.

ENTERING THE LABOUR MARKET IN THE UK

In sharp contrast to the dominant construction of South Asian women as defined by their domesticity and confined to the home, all the women we interviewed were active participants in the labour market as they sought to support their families and eke out a living as migrants in what was often an unwelcoming country.

Previous research has explored the gendered segregation of roles in East Africa and the class dimension of this segregation, whereby South Asian women from affluent families were unlikely to work outside the home. Echoing the findings of Herbert's (2009, 26) research with Ugandan-Asians in Britain, respondents framed this as a positive facet of their middle-class lifestyle in their countries of origin:

> Life was good in those days. We were well off. I used to cook, manage the kitchen, that's all. For other work at home – cleaning, washing up, we had domestic help. (Lataben, G)

Most of the Gujarati migrants were educated in English to GCSE or A level, while a few had undertaken further education or training. All of the Grunwick workers we interviewed had experience of paid work in India or in East Africa. One woman had been employed as a typist in Tanzania, while another had worked briefly as a teacher in India. Although one woman had given up paid work after she married, the rest continued to work after marriage, though any paid work had to be accommodated with their domestic responsibilities through home-based work such as sewing or tutoring. As Jayaben recalled:

> The teacher I had while I was in India had moved to Africa and become the head of a girl's school. When he heard that I was here and I had done a three year course in sewing, he said, 'Come to my school, I need a teacher there'. I asked my husband, 'Should I go?' He said, 'When the money comes in, you will like that and so will I, but what will happen with the kids? Who will look after them? If you want to work', he suggested, 'why don't you work from home? You can start sewing classes at home if you want to work'. I liked that idea, so I started working from home. (Jayaben, G)

Contrary to popular perceptions of a homogeneous category of affluent Asians engaged in trade and commerce in East Africa, there was considerable diversity of income and wealth among African Asians (Mattausch 1998). In the absence of socialised welfare, losses in a business venture or the death of the primary earning member of the household could create hardship and poverty (Brah 1996, 31) and these were the catalysts for some women's entry into paid work. Two of the women recounted a childhood where their family faced financial difficulties:

> My life was very hard. We were six brothers and sisters. When my father was thirty-five, he died in a car accident in Kenya. I was sixteen then – I had just taken my GCSEs. I was good at sewing, so I started working from home then, to survive. My mother also started working then. She used to tie the tassels on the edge of saris, from home. We had to work, whatever little money we had, got used up very soon. My brothers and sisters used to go to school, and we had to pay their fees. Education wasn't free there, there was no, like, welfare. My brothers and sisters were all younger than me, so the responsibility for all of them fell on me. So I worked like this for four years to support my family. (Nirmalaben, G)

Although it was common for Gujarati women in East Africa to undertake home-based paid work such as sewing and tutoring, one woman who was from a less affluent family worked outside the home as a secretary. Another 'respectable' occupation that women could undertake was teaching – they would never have considered manual work, which many found themselves forced to accept once in Britain.

N: After marriage I went to Tanzania and worked there for two years as a typist in a company, and I also used to take phone calls as a receptionist.

Q: Was it common in your community for women to work?

N: Girls had started working in those families by that time – it wasn't as backward as during my mum's days. Women went out and worked among our community, doing office work, never in factories. But there was no other choice [in the UK] because though I had completed my education in English, my spoken English was not very fluent at that time. (Naliniben, G)

The success of East African Asian community in Britain has been attributed in part to this propensity of East African Asian women to undertake paid work in their countries of origin in the post-war period, which enabled them to bring crucial skill-sets with them to Britain (Brown 2007, 49; Mattausch 2001, 66). Compared to the Gujarati women from East Africa, the Punjabi women employed by Gate Gourmet were less likely to undertake paid work prior to migration. The minority who did, were in occupations such as home-tutoring, while three of the twenty-seven Punjabi women we interviewed had previously been employed as teachers in government schools. Most of these women were also educated to GCSE or A level, and a few were graduates or had interrupted their university studies to marry. For more than one worker, the life history they narrated was laced with particular bitterness at recalling their low-status jobs in London, which did not align with their self-identification as middle-class or as a skilled worker. After obtaining consent and preparing to start the interview with Guneet, a Punjabi woman who had worked at Gate Gourmet, she interrupted in order to explain her feelings:

> First let me tell you something. All of us who have come here from India are from 'good' families. Well off. We all have land back home. It is our circumstances that have brought us where we are. It so happens that life brings us here – you know, the glitter of life here draws us here, and once we are here it's not bad, but it is not possible to go back. (Guneet, GG)

A common refrain in women's construction of their early lives was of their agency in continuing their education beyond the level that was normative in their communities. When describing their jobs in India prior to migration, the women who worked were also keen to emphasise that they took up paid work despite dominant gendered expectations about women's roles, and asserted that their work had *not been* in response to any financial need – unlike several of the East African Asians:

> I was the first girl in my village to go so far away to work – to another village, teaching at a government school. My brothers did not like that. They used to say, 'Our father is the headman of the village. We have a truck business. What will people say? That we send our girl to work and eat off her labour.' But my thinking was different. I had grown up hearing tales from the village women – that so-and-so's husband does not work, he mistreats her, and things like that. They had made an impression on my mind from a young age. I had decided that I want to work so that if I ever got married to such a man, I should have some means of independent living. My parents were dead against it as well. But I argued with them, persuaded them and managed to work for a year and half. They used to say to me, 'We don't need the money'. I would say, 'Neither do I. But I want to work'. (Amanjot, GG)

In common with narratives of African Asian Gujarati women documented by Herbert (2009), the women we interviewed drew upon aspects of their life histories to emphasise their active agency in their lives prior to migration, and in their migration, which is at odds with dominant masculinised migration narratives which are based on constructions of the male pioneer and breadwinner. Such accounts of agency also featured in women's labour histories, which are discussed in the following chapter.

Although they came from middle-class backgrounds, East-African Asians were able to bring only limited financial assets when they came to the UK as entire family units, and they subsequently worked together to regain their middle-class status, to re-establish themselves and to educate their children. Direct migrants from Punjab came from relatively less affluent backgrounds, but a majority of the women were from landowning families that had the means to facilitate the migration of family members. The poverty and financial hardship they faced in the UK upon migration created pressure on the women to contribute to the family finances. In the cases of some single women, they both contributed most of their wages to the extended family they lived with and sent remittances to family members back home. Some women also recounted positive experiences of marriage migration, and framed their entry into paid work in positive terms as a counterpoint to the loneliness they experienced during their first few months as a new bride in the UK:

> You know, I had heard that people give new brides a hard time when they get them here, that everyone has to work here. Everyone. Before we married, my husband had reassured me that if I did not want to, I wouldn't have to work. But when I came here, there was no one at home, everyone went off to work and I used to stay at home all the time, all by myself. I felt so lonely. We lived in Southall at that time and my in-laws used to tell me to go out and see the place. I used to look out of the window, but it was hard to go out by myself. Then one day I had enough, I told my husband that I wanted to go to work. (Harjot, GG)

Two women who were in abusive marriages remembered the heavy pressure they faced to contribute to the family income through paid work. They recalled their shock at having to seek employment very soon after they had arrived, having never undertaken paid work before. This was on top of undertaking all the domestic work in their new home, which they were unaccustomed to doing in their natal homes because of their previous class position:

> The week after the wedding, he [husband] started talking about it – 'Why don't you go to work?' I wanted to work, there was nothing to do at home, there was no one at home. I just had that one room and kitchen to myself, the rest of the house was locked. It was too cold to sit out in the garden. What is there to do all day in one room? (Jasminder, GG)

Most women secured jobs in places which employed a predominantly migrant workforce, having learnt about these jobs through family and friends. Literature on South Asian migration – and the broader scholarship on gender and migration – recognises the significance of informal networks based on norms, reciprocity and trust in providing access to resources, including jobs (Mand 2006; Shaw 2000; Werbner 1990). Reliance on social networks to secure jobs was also a consequence of the racism that women experienced when responding to job advertisements in newspapers and in notices on shop-fronts.

> Sometimes when we went, they used to look at us, and then say 'There is no work, we have already given it to someone else', if they did not want to give it to us. (Lataben, G)

In some cases, the networks also resolved the problem of the hurdles that some women faced because of their lack of proficiency in English, which made completing written job applications a daunting process.

> It was difficult because we could not speak the language either – so that made it very hard for us to find jobs. We could not fill out forms. (Nirmalaben, G)

Informal networks also signalled that a workplace employed what some women termed 'people like us' – and thus got around the need to complete job applications. A few women narrated with pride their experiences of responding to job advertisements and going for an interview for a job where they had no networks; in their narratives, these experiences were constructed as exceptional and part of a broader narrative about their agentic capacity. One consequence of relying on these community based networks was that both twice-migrant Gujaratis and direct migrants from Punjab were confined to employment that reinforced the gendered and racially segregated labour markets prevailing in the UK.

CONCLUSION

Despite variation in their particular experiences, some commonalities can be traced in the patterns of inequalities experienced by Gujarati African-Asians who settled in North London and Punjabi women in West London. Both groups of women entered the labour market in the UK soon after their migration, and were only able to obtain low-paid employment with limited prospects. Although most of the women had been educated beyond secondary school level – the direct migrants from Punjab were educated in the Punjabi language and most migrants from East Africa had studied in English medium schools which followed the English curriculum, which was a matter of pride for them – a combination of gendered deskilling, reproductive responsibilities and gendered social networks meant that their entry into the labour market could only be into the 'Three-D' jobs – dirty, dangerous and degrading work (IPPR 2006, 11). This was an experience common to migrants then as well as in more recent times (Portes 1998; Waldinger and Lichter 2003).

The Punjabi and Gujarati women who migrated to the UK and subsequently went on to participate in the Grunwick and the Gate Gourmet disputes came from very diverse backgrounds in relation to: their class, rural or urban location prior to migration; the circumstances which shaped their migration decision; the patterns and purpose of migration for family reunion or for relocation as entire family units; educational attainment; and their previous experience of paid work. However, as racialised minorities, their narratives also highlight the commonalities in their experience. Both groups experienced changing social status and class dislocation upon migration, as well as racial discrimination in the housing market and the consequent imperative for home ownership. There are also particular commonalities in their early labour histories of entering paid work in the UK.

Subsequent chapters will explore the nature of the women's incorporation into a gendered and racialised labour market in the UK, which relates to the centrality of paid work to their identities. These chapters will therefore analyse the struggles and strategies of these workers as they tried to manage their productive and reproductive roles, and sought to move away from jobs that did not resonate with their notions about their place in society. Alongside the survival strategies that they instituted, these chapters will also explore both the everyday and the exceptional resistances and struggles waged by these women to evade managerial control, restore dignity to their work, improve their pay and conditions and gain workers' rights.

NOTES

1. As discussed, Punjabi migrants to the UK are predominantly Sikh. The existing statistics on labour force participation disaggregates according to country of origin *or* according to religion, thereby making it difficult to make valid comparisons. Both Punjabi direct migrants and those East African Asians who self-identify as Indian would be categorised under the label 'Indian', but have very different experiences.

   The category 'African-Asian' is not uniformly utilised, and likewise, the category 'Sikh' does not capture the experiences of Hindu Punjabis with whom the Sikhs share many characteristics. To complicate matters yet further, the category of African Asians comprises mostly Gujaratis, but includes a small minority of Sikhs, whose experiences are very different to those of direct migrants from Punjab. Hence the category of 'Sikhs' will also include the relatively small numbers of East African Asian Sikhs. These statistics however, do provide approximate indications of how these communities have fared since their migration to the UK.

CHAPTER 4

Women in a gendered and racialised labour market: Everyday accounts of resilience, struggle and resistance

The women who participated in our research started their working lives in the UK in a range of manufacturing sectors including food and film processing, electronics, packaging and garments. The Punjabi women also took on service sector jobs such as cleaning, working in the hospitality sector and picking vegetables in farms – jobs that were particularly low-paid, low-status and entailed hard manual labour over long hours. More recent experiences of work for both the Grunwick and the Gate Gourmet workers have included working as cashiers in the retail sector, opportunities which had not been available for them in the early years following their migration to the UK, when such jobs were largely the preserve of white British women. In the later stages of their working lives, some of the ex-Gate Gourmet workers have also worked in the care sector. The following sections explore women's accounts of entering the gendered and racialised UK labour market, the ways in which they managed to juggle their productive and reproductive roles as well as their experiences in their workplaces. Many of the women recounted experiencing harsh and exploitative conditions at work, but they also spoke about what work meant to them and their families.

THE GENDERED AND RACIALISED LABOUR MARKET IN THE UK

During the 1970s, the employment patterns of women from different ethnicities varied significantly across different sectors, indicating that they were being incorporated into a clearly gendered and racialised labour market. For example, the Labour Force Survey data for 1979 (the year after the end of the Grunwick dispute) indicates that compared to the 25 per cent of the employed, British-born, white women who worked in manufacturing, the corresponding figures were 58 per cent for Indian, 45 per cent for African-Asian, 54 per cent for Pakistani and 50 per cent for Bangladeshi women (Dustmann and Fabbri 2005, 445). Like other groups of migrant workers, South Asian women were incorporated into the UK labour market on the basis of assumptions about their docility and capacity for 'hard work', which constructed them as 'passive, inhibited and exclusively family-centred' and 'ideal sweatshop fodder' because of their 'limited understanding of employee rights' (Wrench 1987, 179). These notions were reproduced in the 1970s and 1980s by the media and even some trade unions.

It was on the basis of assumptions such as these that South Asian women were actively sought by the management at Grunwick, who distributed leaflets at South Asian owned shops and workers' houses during the mid-1970s. The hierarchies of workers that employers construct on the basis of stereotypes have been recognised as factors that shape the 'migrant division of labour' (Waldinger and Lichter 2003; Wills et al. 2010). It is within such discourses about the suitability of particular bodies and personalities for different categories of work, and the categorisation of workers' capacities as 'good', 'bad', skilled' or 'unskilled', that South Asian women, alongside other categories of migrant workers, found their options in the labour market greatly restricted (Carter et al. 1996; McDowell 2009).

Given their middle-class backgrounds, the African-Asian Gujarati women who went on to work at Grunwick experienced a profound class dislocation upon migration to the UK. Although the Punjabi women came from less affluent but nonetheless landowning families, they also had no previous experience of waged manual labour. This meant that they also perceived an acute sense of dislocation in their social status in the UK, which was particularly reflected in their working lives.

A Gujarati woman who had migrated from East Africa remembered the pressures women faced to undertake paid work:

There was no question of whether you wanted to or not – you had to work, so you did. And wherever you found work, you had to take it. It wasn't that you were educated, so you only wanted certain kind of jobs – we had to work in factories and that's how we brought up our children. That's life […] Of course I felt sad. (Lataben, G)

There were common tropes in both the Grunwick and Gate Gourmet women's narratives that conveyed this dislocation, many of which were structured through binary accounts of their expectations of life in the UK and the rather different reality of the manual work that they found themselves doing. The expectations of the lives they had imagined for themselves when they got to this country often drew upon the positive constructions of a middle-class life that had been circulated by relatives visiting from the UK.

Many of the Punjabi women from Northern India had similar stories:

I didn't know much about England, but I had a few relatives who lived abroad and when they visited, I saw the fancy clothes they used to wear and I thought, 'How nice! They must have a good life there'. The way they talked about it, it seemed that their life was easy. They would say that they had to work outside home, but they would convert the money they earned into rupees, and it seemed that they earned an enormous amount for very little work. (Leena, GG)

While women remembered the displays of status and affluence by visiting relatives, they reported that they were unaware of the nature of the work that would be available for them upon migration. A recurring theme in women's narratives about their first jobs in the UK was the hard work that manual labour entailed for those unaccustomed to it, whether this was recounted as a positive testimony to their capacity or as a difficulty that had to be endured:

You tell the people who read this that those who come from India are not afraid of 'hard work'. They come here, work hard and settle here. (Rajdeep, GG)

The discourse of the 'hard worker' utilised by employers (alongside that of 'cheap labour') in their constructions of migrant workers (MacKenzie and Forde 2009) was also reiterated by the women themselves to celebrate their capacity for work. While most women co-opted this discourse in their narratives about work to construct themselves as an able and committed workforce by comparing themselves with white women who, for example, took cigarette breaks, a few Punjabi and Gujarati women also reflected on the contexts that drove South Asian women to work harder than was the norm, thereby creating pressure on other workers:

> I remember this paraffin factory where you had to make the parts – like wicks and things like that – the money was better at £10 a week, but the work was harder because we had to do it with our bare hands and we had a quota for each day. If we did not meet it, they would dock our wages. I found it hard to meet the quota. But there were some of our women who could work very hard, so they did. The white women who were there told them not to go so fast, as everyone else found it hard to keep up. But they needed the extra money, so they carried on. Then gradually, the managers increased the quota and it almost became impossible to meet the target. In places where there were our [Asian] and white people, some of our women worked very hard, I think that made it hard for everyone in the long run. Maybe they were desperate for the money, they were scared of being sacked, so they put everything into it. And when things got harder, the white people started leaving. And I saw this happen in other places as well. (Meeta, GG)

In the context of their research on low-paid migrant workers in London, Wills et al. (2010) argue that migrants' self-identification as 'hard workers' can be understood as a response to the dominant negative and contradictory constructions of migrants as lazy, taking jobs from the native-born and claiming benefits. But the way they were dealing with the class dislocation they confronted was also part of the story.

A few women who migrated to the UK following adoption by relatives began work in businesses run by those relatives, and their accounts about their entry into paid work were quite varied. Two women recounted periods when the difficulties and dependency associated with living with relatives at home were compounded by the harsh conditions at work. In contrast, three Punjabi women gave positive accounts of their entry into paid work:

> For me, the first year of working life went by easily. It was family business, so I spent the hours laughing and fooling around with my cousins. It was like being at home. It did not really feel like 'hard work'. We [cousins] were young and working together was fun. If you work for others, you are tied to the work. (Harjot, GG)

However, for most women, the dislocation in their class status following migration was most acutely perceived through lived experiences of the hierarchies in the gendered and racialised workplace, where most of the managers were white men. For both Punjabi and Gujarati women who had previous experience of work in better status jobs, primarily as teachers, home-based tutors and as secretaries, comparisons with their earlier working lives made for a stark reminder of the reversal in their status:

> I started work within two weeks of coming here. My work in India was good, and here it was a servant's job – working under people. As a teacher, I got a lot of respect there, but the job here was just a job for money. I suppose every job is for the money, but there was more to teaching than just money. When I used to walk down the street in my village in India, people used to greet me and I got recognition and respect due to my job. Here the work is that of a labourer, it gives you the money to fill your stomach. That's all. (Daljit, GG)

One key marker of middle-class status in India is not having to undertake menial work – even within one's own home. In this context, having servants is an important aspect of an Indian middle-class lifestyle (Dickey 2000; Froystad 2003, 2005; Ray 2000). Women routinely referred to their lack of familiarity with routine household tasks such as washing dishes and sweeping, tasks that would have been undertaken by servants prior to migration. Many women also noted the hardship of undertaking the domestic labour associated with running a household single-handedly, where they might previously have lived in extended families and undertaken these tasks alongside other women in the household.

> Whatever our background – even if we have grown up with servants – when we come here, we have to work hard and become a servant ourselves. (Rajdeep, GG)

In most middle-class households in India, a part-time lower-caste servant is commonly recruited for the sole task of cleaning toilets, a job that is traditionally associated with the lowest of castes: the scavengers and other ex-untouchables. In this context, having to clean toilets in a public space was remembered as particularly demeaning, a theme that echoes the experience and representations of other categories of migrant workers (Marciniak 2008; McIllwaine et al. 2006):

> I had all these hopes that it must be marvellous here, the houses must be wonderful! When people came from here, they used to talk about the things they had, the machines that wash your clothes, your dishes – it was like London is an amazing place. But it is not what it sounds like, at least you have house-help there. You can get most of the work done by others. And if your finances are good, you can even buy these goods. You have to work hard here, but that's OK. I could deal with that. But the worse thing is when you have to clean the toilets. We had never done this kind of job! I felt terrible. (Puneet, GG)

None of the Gujarati women who had come from East Africa recounted such experiences, probably because their previous experience of paid work, English-education and social capital helped them avoid the most demeaning and low-status jobs available to migrants. But for some Punjabi women the only jobs they could find in the area around Southall where they settled was as cleaners in hospitals and at the airport. This work symbolised for them a period when they had few options, and most women moved on to other 'better' work as soon as they could; although this was not necessarily better-paid work it was work that was not considered similarly tainted.

In India, domestic work including cleaning has been traditionally associated with lower castes (Raghuram 2001, 1), though particular categories of domestic work such as cooking may be constructed as suitable for middle or upper caste workers on account of caste-specific concepts of purity and pollution associated with vegetarian food preparation and consumption. Based on her research with domestic servants in a North Indian city, Froystad (2003) argues that alongside gender, caste is central in constructions of domestic work, and caste hierarchies are reinscribed through the labour process, a point which has been frequently overlooked in other analyses. However, caste-based association with particular forms of work such as cleaning is beginning to be destabilised in the particular context of the growth of 'professional cleaning services' in the globalised labour market in India (Mirchandani et al. 2016). These traditional links are being undermined by migration, education and new labour technologies, as workers reframe cleaning as a 'professional' occupation in particular contexts where this work requires use of equipment, such as gloves and cleaning agents. Some of the Punjabi women we spoke to who recollected their jobs as cleaners in the 1970s and 1980s drew upon similar constructions to describe work such as cleaning toilets, and they thus differentiated it from similar jobs in India which would have been performed by lower caste workers:

> It was different here, we had gloves and did not have to touch anything with our bare hands. (Sukhwant, GG)

Conceptions of dirty work also informed women's accounts about working in a laundrette, handling people's soiled clothes. Laundering is associated in India with the dhobis (washerfolk), an ex-untouchable caste; washing clothes was traditionally their occupation, but most middle-class families now have domestic servants and may use washing machines. Women's distaste for this work stemmed from these caste-based associations, and a few women recounted how they moved to other categories of work within the laundrette such as ironing laundered clothes or they moved jobs as soon as they were able to.

I worked at a laundrette in Birmingham, packing clean clothes. I preferred that to the earlier job, handling dirty clothes. (Manjot, GG)

The stigma associated with 'dirty' work was also overlaid with racialised, gendered dimensions of such work. Parjot was acutely aware of other people's perceptions about her national identity and associations with such low-status work – as work that 'these Indians' do:

It was dirty work. Everyone used to look at us, like, these people – we were mostly Indians there – they do cleaning jobs … I felt very bad from inside. I liked the idea of working, but not this kind of work, cleaning toilets. What kind of job is that? I used to think I would do something different. In India, we have people who come to clean our toilets. And here I was, doing this kind of work. I asked myself again and again, why did I come to this country? Why was I doing this job? I wanted to leave the job, but I had to wait till I found something else. (Parjot, GG)

Working with other new migrants from Punjab in a cleaning job at the Heathrow airport, Parjot was upset at the misrecognition that she perceived on account of dominant constructions of such work as intrinsic to Indian migrants. In contrast, she stressed how alien this work was to her and to others like her, and a temporary consequence of the constraints she faced in the labour market.

Another category of unacceptable work that featured in several women's accounts about their labour histories was handling meat while they worked in catering or food processing industries.

M: My first job was at tray-set, you know, the meals on flights? My neighbour used to work there, and she told me about it. I was not used to standing all day, so I found that difficult.

Q: Tell me what it was like on your first day there.

M: What can I say? For someone who had never worked before, it will be hard. I found it hard to touch meat, as in our community [or caste], we don't eat meat. My hands used to tremble when I had to handle meat. I often used to feel sick. And when I was like that, my friends used to take over and exchange their work with mine, so I managed to get through that. (Meeta, GG)

Implicit in women's accounts of their disgust at handling meat ('in our community, we don't eat meat') were caste-based associations with such work as well as taboos about meat consumption. Despite the long and widespread popular food cultures of meat consumption among a wide variety of castes including upper castes in India, there is a strong caste-based association with vegetarianism in the popular imagination. Such associations have been valorised in recent Hindu nationalist mobilisations against beef consumption, which invisibilise the longstanding beef-eating culinary traditions that exist among different Hindu castes (Jha 2002). In this contemporary context, handling and preparing meat is perceived to be a predominantly Muslim, and in some regional contexts, a lower caste occupation, not least because of the manual nature of such work. Writing about the cultural politics of meat-related commodity production in India, Robbins (1999) argues that the production and preparation of meat and its consumption, or the restraint from these practices, continue to be deployed as a marker of status. Research has also investigated the embodiment and experience of disgust among members of upper castes towards meat-eating itself, and, more broadly, towards meat-eating communities in India. This feeling is also exhibited by upwardly mobile castes, who are encouraged to repudiate their own low caste practices of meat consumption in expressions of hyperbolic vegetarianism (Ghassem-Fachandi 2010; Robbins 1999, 411-413).

Apart from the inherently stigmatising nature of their work, women also recounted the demeaning treatment meted out to them by their managers and supervisors, in workplaces where the management comprised of predominantly white men and the majority of the workforce was South Asian women:

The managers were horrible. They used to shout at us all the time, ask us to work faster, pick faults in our work. They were all white managers and all the workers were our women. In India, we had people working for us in the fields and here we had to work for others. I found it very difficult. (Manjot, GG)

While most women identified race as a significant factor in the treatment they were accorded at workplaces, as characterised by these hierarchical relations between white managers and South Asian workers, gender was also implicated in the mistreatments to which these women were subjected. Parjot, who went on to work at Gate Gourmet, recounted her experiences whilst working at the Heathrow airport, cleaning planes, where her immediate managers included Punjabi and white men:

P: The attitude of the managers was not nice.

Q: Could you tell me more about it? What was not nice?

P: How do I tell you? [Sighs.] Like, they used to say that we have not done the job, even when we had, and after we had signed the paper. [Pause.] It was a toilet cleaning job. Even if we had completed the job, they used to harass us by creating dirt in the toilets, you know, going there to do – you know what I mean – making it dirty again.

Q: Why do you think they did that?

P: Because they were men, and they wanted to harass us. Because they were in a position of authority, they wanted to make it harder for us. (Parjot, GG)

Several women remembered the emotional hardship they endured on account of their reversal in social status:

It was hard, I felt pain inside me. When the supervisors said anything the way they often do – [shouts in a gruff manner] 'Do this, do that' – tears would well up in my eyes. My life had turned upside down. I had servants there and here I was, working in a place like this. (Rajdeep, GG)

It was in the context of the combination of the low status of the work, the heavy workload, long hours (necessitated by the low wages) and the demeaning treatment by managers that most women stressed that this work was a mere survival strategy, soon to be replaced by work that was more commensurate with their capacities, and their expectations about social status, wages and working conditions. This was the case even though any subsequent work was still within the gendered and racialised constraints of the labour market.

However, many women also sought to challenge the negative experiences that they suffered in the workplace, either by offering narratives of explanation or by reframing their experiences in different lights. Research on workers whose jobs do not offer typical qualities associated with workplace dignity, documents the processes whereby these workers go about constructing positive work identities (Hodgson 2001; Lucas 2011). Some women gave positive accounts of their early working lives recalling it as a period when they made sacrifices for the betterment of their family and when they endured hardships which enabled them, and particularly their children, to build a better life in Britain:

> We made the move for the children. People do so much for their children. Once we had come here the work had to be done, and however painful it was, I did it. This is what life brings! (Rajdeep, GG)

Other strategies included reiterating the hard work and the long hours of the work, in combination with assertions outlined earlier that such hard work was beyond the capacity of native-born workers. This, the women argued, was why employers sought South Asian women as workers. Some women, unlike those quoted above, restated but simultaneously rejected the indignity associated with cleaning and other manual work, by drawing attention to the different meanings associated with the same work in India and in Britain, and asserting that all jobs are important and valuable (Lucas 2011). Some also asserted their resistance to or reframing of poor treatment by management:

> In this country everyone works. Work is work. No one looks down on you – even the bosses don't always treat you like you are a servant. It's different in India – if it was the same here, we wouldn't have been able to work in these places. But if anyone does treat us like that – tries to show that they are superior to us

because they are managers and is rude to us, we can deal with that as well. We are not uneducated you know. (Guneet, GG)

Some women who were engaged in caring work, sought to reclaim dignity and a sense of positive selfhood by emphasising the intrinsic rewards of the job, rather than dwelling on the pay or the designations of such work as 'dirty work' because of its associations with other people's bodies:

I started working within the first week I came here. I worked at an old people's home, owned by a family friend. I liked the work. Of course, money was the main issue, but I did enjoy the job as well. These old people, some had no children, some had no visitors, it felt like I was doing something good. When you have nothing, if someone talks to you nicely, it's like you have gained the world! They were very affectionate towards me, and I also became very attached to them. I was a 'hard worker', right from the beginning. (Kamalpreet, GG)

Studies have shown that care workers often counter negative associations with their work by drawing upon their caring inclinations, their altruistic motivations, relationships with users (as in Kamalpreet's comments) and by identifying a 'familial care logic' to emphasise the emotional rewards rather than the low pay associated with such work (Atkinson and Lucas 2013; Palmer and Eveline 2012). Hebson et al. (2015) suggest that the primacy that care workers afford to the intrinsic rewards of the job provides an alternate framework to the gendered and class-based processes that limit the 'field of possibilities' they face. The ways in which these women constructed the significance of their work as individuals is informed not just by the objective conditions of the job, but the ways in which it interacts with their gendered, class and caste-based experiences both pre- and post-migration. They were very clear about the ways in which their working lives in the UK had been shaped by the gendered and racialised labour market they entered, and the socio economic constraints that they faced.

WOMEN'S NARRATIVES ABOUT MANAGING PRODUCTIVE AND REPRODUCTIVE LABOUR

There exists a rich body of literature from diverse perspectives, which explores the processes through which people respond to what Jarvis (1999) terms the 'infrastructure of everyday life' as they cope with the demands of home and work. The linkages between production and social reproduction of the family through domestic and caring work, have been explored in the context of challenges and changes such as: unemployment and industrial restructuring (Pahl 1984); women's increasing entry into the labour market (Hochschild 1989); and the privatisation and subcontracting of the welfare state. Much of this literature is on 'coping strategies', recognising the agency of workers and their families within structural constraints, and negotiations of and transformations to gender in the face of these changes in the labour market (Crompton 1999).

Migrant women workers are often obliged to deal with the competing demands of earning money for their families in their destination countries and sending remittances to their families at home. They also have to devise strategies to secure the caring and domestic work necessary for social reproduction, particularly childcare and the education of children both in their countries of origin and destination (Andall 2000; Anderson 2000; Parrenas 2001). One focus of this research on the reproductive migration of women has been on 'transnational mothering' or 'global circuits of care' (Ehrenreich and Hochschild 2003; Yeates 2005 and 2009), whereby female migrants from the global south move to developed economies to work in the domestic and care industry, whilst sending remittances to their countries of origin, to provide for their own children's care by other women, generally female relatives. There has been comparatively less – though growing – attention to the processes and strategies through which migrant families strategise to manage domestic work, childcare and paid employment in their new situations, often without easy recourse to support from kin and community networks (Bonizzoni 2014; Datta et al. 2007; Doyle and Timonen 2010; Dyer et al. 2011; Pearson and Kusakabe 2012; Wall and José 2004).

Early accounts about South Asian men's experiences of migration, settlement and work in the UK were characterised by a failure to analyse and understand men's roles in managing productive and reproductive responsibilities (Kalra 2000), a silence that largely prevails to this day. The assumption in this literature is of a male breadwinner model, whereby social reproduction was the exclusive domain of women, but this pattern is challenged by the women who participated in our research. These women had to manage simultaneously both paid work and unpaid domestic labour; they talked about the complex and diverse strategies they deployed in order to maximise family income whilst retaining responsibility for housework and childcare, strategies that often entailed negotiation and balancing of work and family roles within the nuclear or extended family.

The ways in which these women managed their work and childcare responsibilities were shaped not just by their individual circumstances but also by the intersection of gender, race and class which included particular domestic and labour regimes. The constraints faced by these particular Gujarati and Punjabi women workers echoed those documented by Wall and José (2004, 604). They are constraints commonly faced by first generation migrant families and include the nature of their work in low-income occupations with long and atypical working hours, poor housing conditions, and the inability to afford formal care services, although in any case those services would seldom cover the long and varied care needs of children. The constraints on these women also reflect strong gendered conceptions of domestic and caring work. Another recent study of migrant workers in the service sector in Greater London (Dyer et al. 2011) documents how gender identity, class, earning potential and visa status/citizenship impact on migrant workers' care strategies.

The first challenge recounted by the women we interviewed was their exclusive and sole responsibility for domestic work upon migration. In line with broader social norms, the women accepted responsibility for domestic work following marriage and had indeed been socialised into this role. However, given their class backgrounds as discussed above, most women were from middle-class and/or middle ranking peasant families, so they were accustomed to fulfilling (at least some of) their domestic responsibilities through supervising the work of domestic servants, and also to sharing this responsibility with other female members of the extended household. In the absence of such networks, and reflecting on their class dislocation upon migration, many women recalled their shock at the scope of domestic work expected from them, particularly when contrasted with the dominant expectations of a middle-class lifestyle associated with living in the west.

> There are plenty of people who spread all sorts of wrong notions about life in the west. My uncle, who was in Canada used to exaggerate – it was like you just press a button and the house will get cleaned! That's how they talked – 'We have all these things and you don't have to do anything'. I was astounded – things pick themselves up and clean themselves – how can that be?! When I came here and asked my husband about it, he laughed. He said, 'I'll show you which button to press to clean the house – it's called the wife!' And he handed me the Hoover. (Gurinder, GG)

Many women recounted that domestic appliances, like vacuum cleaners and washing machines, were presented as labour saving devices that compensated for the absence of servants, a perception that research refutes (Bittman et al. 2004). For some recent migrants, the presence of this technology that was meant to ease the burden of domestic labour actually served to add to their difficulties. One young woman we talked to was adopted by her uncle and aunt who sponsored her migration to the UK largely so that she could contribute to their household economy through her unpaid and paid work. She was expected to do this in addition to sending remittances to her biological parents in Punjab. She recounted her difficulties in meeting all of these responsibilities:

> Within the house, when your aunt, uncle don't take time to teach you, things can be hard. They used to say, 'Don't you know how to do anything?' These things – like washing machines – we didn't have them in India, how could I have known? It was the same at work. Only when people are willing to teach you, can you learn. Even a prime minister learns to talk in front of so many people by and by, he is not born with that ability, is he? (Parjot, GG)

Most women entered the labour market soon after migration, and had to quickly find ways to manage the competing demands of paid work and their domestic and caring responsibilities:

> I had never worked outside there, only the work in the house. But here, it became, well, 'double'. I had to do the full eight hours or more outside the house, and then there was the housework on top of that. (Kulvinder, GG)

Rather than seeing the way women had to meet the demands of both domestic and paid work as a balance, Wall and José (2004) argue that these competing demands required active management, even if the outcome was less than satisfactory for the individuals concerned. However, Datta et al. (2007) reject the widely used conceptualisation of 'coping strategies', arguing that in more recent contexts, the experiences of migrant workers in London's low-pay economy is framed by the widespread social and economic exclusion that migrants face. They similarly reject the term 'strategies' and instead draw upon de Certeau's (1984) concept of 'tactics'. This reframing draws attention to the range of reactive, fragmented and fragile arrangements that enable these workers to get by rather than get on, sometimes on a day-to-day basis, such that a small change in circumstances can lead to the collapse of carefully constructed arrangements (Dyer et al. 2011). Reconciling responsibilities for production and social reproduction is an ongoing challenge for migrant workers in many parts of the world. Drawing upon their study of African-origin immigrants in France and Portugal, Chinese immigrants in Finland and Moroccan immigrants in Italy, Wall and José (2004) identified five ways in which migrants manage work and care: extensive delegation of care (formal or informal); negotiation of care within the nuclear family (partners or older siblings sharing the care responsibilities); mother-centeredness (mothers cutting working hours); child negligence; and finally, the superimposition of care upon work (bringing children to work).

Some of the ways in which the women we interviewed managed work and care were similar to those documented by Wall and José. Several of the Gujarati and Punjabi women we spoke to were sacked each time they became pregnant as maternity leave provisions were not available when they started work. Even after the introduction of the first maternity leave legislation in 1975, many women had to work under short term contracts that were designed to evade these new rights. Women's temporary withdrawal from the labour market was a common response to childbirth, particularly when alternative strategies were unavailable.

As documented in other research (Jarvis 1999; Wall and José 2004), the scope and density of social and kin networks were significant in shaping household and individual strategies to manage productive and reproductive work. The most common means to manage unpaid and paid work was through extensive informal delegation of care to kin within what has been described as the 'tangled web' of reciprocal networks (Jarvis 1999). Gujarati East Africans, many of whom migrated as entire family units were likely to be embedded within close kin networks particularly in the early years following migration, when they lived in extended family units whilst they accumulated resources. This arrangement enabled Gujarati women to manage work and home life, and it potentially gave them greater mobility in the labour market as well. This is illustrated by the experience of one of the Grunwick women we interviewed, Ilaben, who migrated to the UK with her husband and children and was later joined by her mother and brothers; she was able to move between jobs in her search for better pay and conditions and take up opportunities for overtime without having to negotiate complex childcare arrangements.

> I had my mother living with me, so I never had to ask for anything. You know, any time off when the children were ill or when they need to be picked up from school or something. My mother used to manage all that, so I could always go and come back on time and do everything that was needed at work. That's why, I think, I had less difficulties wherever I worked. (Ilaben, G)

This kind of intergenerational childcare by parents and parents-in-law relies on geographical proximity, which was available for only a minority of the first generation migrants from Punjab. For the Punjabi women who did have extended networks of kin, the demands of work and family were often managed differently to the

Gujarati East African women – though still through reciprocal care provided by the women in the family:

> My sister-in-law and I found cleaning jobs at the airport, where my mother-in-law worked. She used to work nights, I used to work days because we had to look after the little ones as well. All the children used to be together, and we used to take turns to look after them. (Parjot GG)

In other words, for most Punjabi women, familial childcare was delegated through networks of reciprocity among horizontal rather than inter-generational relationships with sisters, sisters-in-law and cousins.

Some women managed to sustain a multiple-jobs schedule that entailed a portfolio of part-time work, shift work, with additional overtime when possible, as well as full-time jobs for periods when a visiting relative could take over childcare. These complex arrangements were all managed around domestic responsibilities.

> I used to drop the girls off to school and go to work, and my sister used to look after them at weekends. And that helped a lot. I used to leave them at home, sleeping, when I left for work. From 6.00am to 8.00 a.m. I worked at the Sainsbury's, stacking shelves. Then I would get the bus home, get them ready for school and drop them off, after which I would work at the local hospital from 9.30 a.m. to 2.30 p.m. so I could pick the children up from school. I had this Gujarati neighbour – we used to talk a bit over the garden fence – she told me about this part-time job where she worked. So I got this cleaning job at the airport in the evenings – from about 5.00 to 10.00 p.m. (Simran, GG)

Other strategies included temporary job-lending to retain jobs through each pregnancy and through the first year after childbirth, whereby women sought to transfer jobs to relatives – mainly sisters and sisters-in-law – thereby cementing kinship networks and negotiating shared childcare between households.

> I could not work at that time, I was about to have my baby. My sister was looking for a job, so I said to them [my employers],

'Give her my job, she will work like I did. And I will come back
after I have my baby'. I was a good worker, so he agreed to hold
the job for me and took my sister on my recommendation. I left
two weeks before my daughter was born. (Sukhwant, GG)

The importance of wider, non-kinship social networks in providing
access to jobs for newly arrived South Asian migrants in the UK has
been widely documented (Mand 2006; Shaw 2000; Werbner 1990),
but these networks were not utilised to provide regular childcare as
time was a scarce resource for most migrant families. In most cases,
women only drew upon such wider networks to cover unexpected
and short gaps in their arrangements.

For many first generation migrants who did not have extended
kinship networks, therefore, one possible solution was to 'box
and cox' whereby , the working hours of husband and wife were
arranged sequentially in order for one or other of them to be able
to cover childcare. Such arrangements required complex adjust-
ments to organise their often changing schedules to collect/drop
off children at school, or to work alternate shifts so one parent was
always at home if needed for younger children. While this was not
universal practice, where it did occur it demonstrates that gender
roles amongst even first generation South Asian migrants could be
more flexible than is often assumed:

> We bought a shop and the house was above it. The children were
> young, and it was difficult, with the school and everything. I
> used to run the business when the children were in school. He
> [husband] used to work in a bank, and at the shop in the evenings
> and weekends. The children were upstairs, so I could keep an eye
> on them while I worked there. My husband used to help at home.
> He was different – it wasn't like he would dump everything on
> me, we used to share the housework. (Nirmalaben, G)

Another couple worked at the same factory, which helped them
co-ordinate their work and care with relative ease:

> We used to do the opposite shifts. We used to have her in the car
> with us, and leave our shift fifteen minutes early – the manage-

ment had agreed to that and they cut our pay accordingly – so we could hand over to each other and whoever was on that shift could start on time. We would have a few minutes to exchange some words, to tell each other if the child had eaten and things like that. Those few minutes in the car, they were the time we had with each other in this marriage. Because we worked opposite shifts, he would be sleeping when I came from work, or the other way round. Well, that was all that was left of a husband and wife's relationship, the few moments in the car exchanging information about your child! [Laughs bitterly.] (Kulvinder, GG)

However, despite these different cases, it was generally women who were expected to 'adapt' their work schedules to the childcare responsibilities, not least because men earned more than women, which worked alongside cultural expectations and practices. Wall and José (2004, 617-8) draw attention to the role of gender inequality within the household in shaping work/care strategies, particularly for women who migrate to marry, and who are also simultaneously disadvantaged by gender inequalities in the labour market for recent migrants. In this context – where care was negotiated within the nuclear family in the absence of intergenerational or cross-generational kinship networks in the UK – it was primarily women who held multiple jobs or undertook the night shift, leaving men nominally responsible for childcare during the night when the children were likely to be asleep and the domestic tasks minimal. Women's childcare responsibilities had to be managed alongside domestic work, which left many women with very little or fractured time for rest, and none for leisure.

Gurinder's experience illustrates the way women managed the dual responsibilities of work and family, at great cost to their own wellbeing:

G: I worked at nights, and looked after them in the day.

Q: And when did you sleep?

G: Whenever I had the chance! It was like, give them lunch and then put the TV on, set them up with some water and snacks, and catch a couple of hours of sleep. A bit after the shift ended, before the kids woke up. And that's how I managed. We bought a shop in 1984. So I also had to help in the shop between doing all this. It was hard, but I somehow managed. At weekends, he used to say he needed a break, so I had to go and work in the shop while he had his 'weekend'. I never got one, did I? That's how the next few years went by. (Gurinder, GG)

Feminist analyses of women's work highlight the benefits that women derive from their work, but also the costs for them, including long hours, struggles with complicated childcare arrangements and the 'second shift' of housework after paid work that is by no means unique to migrant women workers (Hochschild 1989). Like Gurinder, many women in our study reflected on the particular stresses of combining paid and unpaid work in a context where they could not rely on a wide network of family to share the caring responsibilities and were restricted to low-paid shift work, contrasting life in the UK with a romanticised memory of life in Punjab. Amarjot explained how shift work took a toll on the affective dimensions of her relationship with her husband:

I had such a happy childhood free of stresses – I still think about that time of my life and miss it. Here, life is full of worries – you have to work all the time. There are times when I do the morning shift and my husband does the evening shift and we don't see each other for three to four days. If there is something in my mind that is bothering me, I have to plan when I can find time to tell him about it. There are so many times that you have to swallow your words because we don't have the time to sit down and talk to each other. If it's a heavy matter, you have to consider whether he has enough time to take that in. He has just come back from work and has four hours to sleep before he has to get up for an early shift tomorrow, I'd better not tell him in case it keeps him awake. (Amarjot, GG)

Women had to deploy other strategies where husbands refused to share childcare or domestic responsibilities even if the working patterns of husband and wife could have allowed this. Researchers (Datta et al. 2007; Wall and José 2004) have documented how migrant women who are particularly constrained by the absence of any reliable kinship networks, the lack of cooperation by children's fathers and the demands of low-paid work in the form of long hours and multiple jobs often have to resort to what Wall and José term 'child negligence' whereby children are left alone at home, looked after by other younger children or by unqualified 'childminders'.

> When I was at work, he was at home – he had given up work – but would not look after the children. He'd leave them and go out to see his mates. I would call up from work and speak to the children as often as possible to see that they were OK. One day, when I got back home, the police and the social workers were there because someone had called them to say that the children were left alone. Luckily for me, my brother-in-law happened to be there that day and told them that the children were with him and my sister, so I was saved. They came a few times to check, and then stopped coming. (Simran, GG)

In this situation many women decided to undertake home-based work in the early years after the birth of their children. Jasminder found that this was her only viable option after other arrangements had collapsed:

> I stopped work as there was no maternity leave then, and when he was six weeks old, I returned to work while I paid someone to look after him. It was hard, she used to give him milk, that's all. But she would never change his clothes or his nappy and he used to come back in a horrible state. We lived in a rented place, we needed the money. So I bought an industrial sewing machine and began to work from home. Doing piecework. At least I could spend some more time with my son. (Jasminder, GG)

As is so frequently the case with research that gathers women's accounts of their lives, there were inevitably a few accounts of domestic violence, and a number of women spoke about what it meant to hold down a job and at the same time live with the impact of violence on their daily lives. Their memories of their working lives were inseparable from the violence within the home, while these circumstances amplified the difficulties of managing their reproductive and productive labour. For two women who were in abusive relationships, home-based work was the means through which husbands sought to maintain control over their wives, whilst benefitting from their paid and unpaid work. Rajdeep recalled how she was set to work on an industrial sewing machine soon after the birth of her second daughter:

> **Q:** When she was born, did you get much time off before you had to work?

> **R:** Not even a day! [Tears running down her cheeks.] I was sent home from the hospital the same afternoon, and had to start working on the machine that evening and do all housework as well. The violence resumed on the same day as well. I had a daughter, that's why. (Rajdeep, GG)

Some of the previously mentioned research in the field of women's paid and unpaid labour examines the impact of gendered power imbalances within families on the nature of the strategies women have deployed to manage paid work and social reproduction (Wall and José 2004). Researchers on violence against women in the US have also begun to document the impact of domestic violence on women's capacity to sustain work as well as men's control over women's earnings (Borchers et al. 2016; Sanders 2014; Stylianou et al. 2013). However, there is little exploration of the processes through which women's productive and reproductive labour is controlled and exploited in the context of abusive relationships.

Formal childcare was the least common option among the women we spoke to, primarily because of the high costs of such care relative to their low wages, and because of the inadequate quality of the care where they were able to secure it at a price they could afford. Only one woman in our study totally withdrew from the labour market for several years because of the additional caring responsibilities arising from her son's complex needs, which made delegation of care unsustainable:

> Sometime after my second son was born, I gave up the homework because everyone in family blamed me for the way my older son

was. He did not talk much, he was 'slow' and they said that I was busy with the sewing and did not give him enough attention or speak to him enough, which is why he turned out the way he was. I also blamed myself. Now I know why he is like that, that it is not my fault, but my relatives still blame me. I feel angry but that is the way it is, we have to put up with people's attitudes. (Devinder, GG)

Punjabi and Gujarati women who entered the labour market in the UK from late 1960s to the early 1980s utilised an array of complex care arrangements to manage the competing demands of paid work and domestic and caring work. Particular circumstances such as the availability of intergenerational support and presence of wider kinship networks shaped their choices. For women who had additional constraints due to domestic violence or additional needs arising from a child's disability, their arrangements proved to be rather more fragmented, reactive and fragile, akin to what has been characterised in recent literature as 'tactics' rather than 'strategies' (Datta et al. 2007). Their narratives point to Dyer et al.'s (2011, 687-688) observation that the precarious nature of migrants' work-life balance is symptomatic of the way they are 'dehumanised through being constructed only as workers, having no families or family needs', which 'reinscribes class-based and racialised hierarchies of labour' (Dyer et al. 2011). The strategies documented above were shaped by the prevailing gendered norms within the women's communities as well as the nature of the labour regimes where migrant women were allocated low-paid jobs with long and atypical hours.

EVERYDAY EXPERIENCES AT WORK: RESILIENCE, REWORKING AND RESISTANCE

In the context of their subordinate location in the labour market and the constraints imposed by the imperative to earn money, the women we spoke to recounted the ways in which they conducted their working lives in order to manage the exploitative conditions at work. This included a combination of strategies – or more ephemeral and reactive tactics – in early jobs to recuperate and build resilience in the face of everyday indignities and harsh working conditions.

Their aim was to get by, rather than to get on, and they deployed strategies that were aimed at mitigating particularly onerous aspects of their working conditions at individual levels; but, at times, they also participated in more collective efforts including organised action aimed at resisting exploitative labour practices.

During the early stages of their working lives, women generally found themselves in jobs where they recognised exploitative conditions but could do little to change them, a situation which is well illustrated by the quote from Meeta at the beginning of this chapter. For want of other options, women's most common responses in the early stages of their paid work were geared towards recuperation and resilience. Kulvinder, who had overstayed her visitor's visa on account of troubles in Punjab in the late 1980s and did not have the requisite documents for official employment, recounted her experiences of working in a farm in the early 1990s:

> We packed leeks and lettuce in a farm beyond Slough. The farmers used to send buses to pick us up. Men harvested the crops, while the women did the packing. The money was very little, the work was very hard – sometimes it was as much as fifteen hours a day, more than twelve hours most days, six days a week. And for all that work, we earned not much more than £100 a week – £1.50 an hour. People who had just come from India used to work there – those who had no NI number. If you had the NI number, why would you work at a place like this?' (Kulvinder, GG)

Women also recalled the range of strategies employers utilised to exploit migrant workers; the employers were secure in the knowledge that their employees had few other options for work:

> I was at the bakery as a 'casual' – they did not make me permanent. The system was that you worked for thirteen weeks then they laid you off for a week, then you started again for thirteen weeks, so that they would not have to give you sick pay and all that. (Simran, GG)

Simran was pregnant, and aware that she would have to leave work in a few months, so she decided to put up with the conditions.

Though women characterised their treatment as exploitative, they were wary of jeopardising their jobs by challenging management control. Kulvinder who was first a vegetable picker, then a packer at a vegetable farm recounted some of these practices in the packing work she did on the farm she described above:

> If you slowed down a bit, they would divide you up into two teams and then create a 'competition' between you and try to increase 'production'. They also used to, I suppose what they did was cheating, really. If someone was slow, they would tell them that they would pay them piecework rates for each crate so they had to increase their speed. And in those days I was young, I used to be quick, and when they saw how I worked, for the people who worked fast, they would tell them that their pay was on an hourly basis! Only those who were not 'settled' [had irregular immigration status] worked there. (Kulvinder GG)

The practices Kulvinder describes in the mid to late 1980s have been documented by Rogaly (2008), who notes the hyper-exploitative and intense workplace regimes in British horticulture in the 1990s through strategic use of piece rates by employers seeking to drive down wages. Kulvinder then found work at a shoe shop in Southall for the same wage but the work was less strenuous, and she felt she was treated with respect there. After a few more moves, once she obtained her documentation, she found a salaried full-time job at a food packing factory with better conditions, including paid leave. Other women recounted similar labour market trajectories:

> Shall I tell you what my first job was like? You worked hard all day, and frantically counted all the time in your mind – how much money have I made? Can I make some more? Can I work faster? That's how piecework was. Then I had enough of it, and shifted to ironing department in the same place. I managed to make good money there, but it was hard work. So I moved to a warehouse job. (Rajdeep, GG)

The women who spoke to us reported high levels of labour mobility as they were constantly on the look-out for better jobs, often securing new jobs through their social networks and moving for relatively small gains in terms of pay, conditions or less stigmatised occupations. Some literature on migrants suggests that they may be relatively tolerant towards substandard employment conditions, due to a so-called 'dual frame of reference' (Waldinger and Lichter 2003, 179) whereby they assess the situation relative to the conditions and options encountered 'back home'. However, other studies document the ways in which migrants have deliberate strategies around temporary employment in often oppressive low-wage labour markets which often involves moving across different jobs to try and improve their precarious lives (Alberti 2014; Datta et al. 2007; Forde and Mackenzie 2009). The labour histories of the women we interviewed commonly included home-based work or piecework in the initial period after migration and a move towards more 'standard' employment (with the attached rights and protections) once they had gained knowledge and understanding of how the job market operates in the UK, learnt some English or gained particular skills. But for some women, 'poor work' characterised most of their labour market experiences in the UK and was at odds with their imagined identities as career women.

One Grunwick striker, Naliniben, remained bitter about her moves from one low-status, low-paid job to another in search of only slightly better wages and conditions, both before and after her experience in the Grunwick dispute. When we interviewed her, though past retirement age, she still worked at a supermarket till. Having worked as a secretary in East Africa, her abiding regret was that, upon migrating to the UK, she had to give up her dreams for a career concomitant with her expectations about her status:

> When I came here I should have applied for a typist's job here. But I didn't. I was a fool not to apply for it. Because I was not confident in speaking English, though I had studied English, I could write in English. I thought if I speak in front of others, they will laugh at me. So I took on a job as a machinist. (Naliniben, G)

Juggling the responsibility of home and work, Naliniben never managed to find time for the English language classes or vocational training that would have furthered her occupational aspirations.

Following the pattern that Kofman et al. (2000, 106) document, through an account laced with disappointment and unfulfilled hopes, she articulated the greater emphasis that she placed on the 'life-chances of the next generation', rather than her own career trajectory.

Writing about migrant workers in London's low-paid economy, Datta et al. (2007) note that for some workers, low-paid work may be constructed as a temporary measure necessary because of constraints such as lack of documentation or as part of a longer term strategy to gain educational qualifications to pursue a career. However, they argue that the reality of migrant workers' exclusion from the labour market, as well as the wider contexts within which the migrants work – including their domestic responsibilities – have a profound impact on their workplace experiences, aspirations and attitudes, and on their responses to the constraints they face.

Some sociologists of work have characterised such moves in the labour market – 'mobility power' – as a form of resistance to degrading work (Alberti 2014; Hagan et al. 2011; Smith 2006) that defies employers' assumptions about migrants' availability and willingness to work under poor terms and conditions (Forde and Mackenzie 2009). However, the effects on the employer are hardly discernible, and these tactics entail no challenge to prevailing employment practices or structures. We would argue that in the absence of any efforts – individual or collective – to challenge working conditions and change them, these occupational mobility strategies are little more than survival mechanisms aimed at securing individual interests and getting by.

In accounts about the later phases in their labour histories, women spoke about their struggles to evade managerial control, to secure dignity and respect in the workplace and to gain better pay and conditions. By examining the longer working lives of these two groups of South Asian women, rather than just focusing on their employment at Grunwick or Gate Gourmet, we can come to a better understanding of the centrality of work for them, the complex story of how they sought rights at work and derived a sense of dignity, support and solidarity. Two women, who entered the labour market relatively unconstrained by financial imperatives to work, recounted such agentic behaviour in their very first jobs:

Q: So tell me more about the work. How did you first find the job?

G: To tell you the truth, initially it was hard. I had to pack the rolls, the bread. The bread was ok, but the roll was tricky – the tray used to move like this [shows how fast it moved with a gesture] – here now, gone the next second. I kept missing it and it would fall off. My manager was nasty to me, he used to keep saying things, like criticising me. I put up with it for two days, then on the third, I said, 'I can't take this anymore. I'm leaving'. As I was heading towards the locker, this other manager saw me. 'What's the matter?' he asked. I told him that I was leaving, that this manager was very rude to me – 'If you want to get work out of me, you have to treat me with respect', I said. So this manager said, 'Come with me. Don't walk off just like that'. He asked me to show him where I was working and I showed him. He said to my line manager, 'Are you stupid, placing her here? She has to receive four weeks of training first, only then can she do this kind of work. Let her work behind there.' 'Sorry, sorry', said my manager. And that was that. I felt very good. (Gunwant, GG)

Harjot, who lived with her in-laws and so had no housing expenses and was able to count on their help with childcare, framed her entry into paid work as a choice rather than a necessity, as she was 'fed up with being tied to the home, to the children'. Her first job was at a knitting factory, doing piecework. She also recalled her early history of resistance at work, which was similar to Gunwant's:

The first four weeks were good, you learn during that period. So you get a fixed amount of money, however much work you do. From then on you used to get paid according to the work you did. One day, I could not get the machine to work properly, so the stitches kept getting dropped. I told my manager to help me out. It was not that I had to work, you see, I also wanted to enjoy my work. She told me that she was busy. I asked her again, and when I asked the third time and she did not come, I told her, 'If you do not have time, I do not have time either. I am going home. When you find the time, you can phone me to get me back to work'. She was not helping me learn. Why waste my time at the machine all day? She then came and apologised, and helped me out. (Harjot, GG)

The accounts of these women – exceptional as they were in asserting their agency by threatening to quit their very first jobs – are constructed to convey a sense of themselves as capable workers who might find themselves in low-paid jobs, but for whom the emphasis was on the learning and the respect that they derive from their work. Smith (2006) draws our attention to the implicit potential for conflict in workers' quitting strategies, and the destabilising impact on labour processes of workers' 'mobility power'. This mobility power of workers is manifest in the time involved in network-building, the resources used to plan and explore job moves and the use of mobility threats to create strategic rewards (Smith 2006, 391; also see Alberti 2014). Harjot and Gunwant's capacity to make this strategic use of threats relating to their mobility was shaped by the multiple axes of differentiation based on gender and class, and supported by the presence of collective resources and networks such as access to child-care and by relative financial stability at home.

Such strategic uses of 'mobility power' as leverage can be characterised as agentic efforts to rework existing conditions to their advantage, and, as in the above cases, to secure requisite training and support. Katz (2004) characterises this as an intermediate category of agency – 'reworking strategies' – positioned between those practices that have the primary intended effect of autonomous initiatives, recuperation and resilience, and those intended to resist, subvert or disrupt conditions of exploitation and oppression. Though such reworking strategies arise from a critical consciousness and an understanding of the power imbalances present in the employment relationship, workers do not seek to challenge or transform existing employment structures. Bernstein (2016) argues that reworking strategies are deployed to enhance workers' individual and collective opportunities and improve or ease their circumstances within the confines of the existing employment structures, without attempting to change underlying power imbalances.

Once they secured standard employment, most of the Punjabi women we interviewed joined trade unions and engaged in various individual and collective actions, with or without the support of those unions, to challenge managerial control and secure better conditions at work. The history of their industrial militancy was long and varied prior to their actions at Gate Gourmet. In contrast, for all the African-Asian Gujarati women we interviewed, Grunwick was their first standard employment, and they subsequently went on to join trade unions.

Both Punjabi and Gujarati women recounted everyday struggles as they challenged practices that reinscribed power imbalances between themselves and their managers, demanded respect and won small victories that served to improve conditions at work for themselves and for others. The Punjabi women we interviewed recalled some of their previous experiences that shaped the nature of their industrial militancy at Gate Gourmet:

> I found a job at terminal four, working with about eight of our women making sandwiches. There was a bonus of £10 a week for doing the work well, and we were to take turns to get it. But our supervisor never gave us the money. Her friend would get the bonus occasionally, but never us. We asked her why, and she replied, 'Because you do not do the work properly'. I felt so angry when I heard that. I spoke to my friend about it, we even exchanged angry words with the supervisor who threatened to throw me out of the job. My friend was scared of losing her job, and she asked me to let it be. But I was not scared. I don't know why, maybe because I knew I was right, I had that confidence. One day when she was on leave the senior manager came by, so my friend and I, we told the manager whatever we could, in our broken English. From then on, we all got the bonus. (Parjot, GG)

By the time of the Gate Gourmet dispute in 2005, most of the Punjabi women who worked there had accumulated long and uninterrupted histories of trade union membership and several women had represented the interests of their co-workers as shop stewards.

> G: It was my first proper job. We were all in the union in that place. T&G [TGWU]. I was outspoken, so I decided to stand for shop steward.

Q: Did you discuss this at home?

G: No what is there to discuss? It's not a general election! So I came to be elected. There was a manager there – an Indian. He started 'telling off' a woman on the floor, in front of everyone. That was not right. So I said, 'Come to the office'. I then said 'What right do you have to tell her off in front of everyone?' He apologised! For an Indian man to say sorry like that is a big matter, that too to an Indian woman! I was delighted. [Laughs] (Guneet, GG)

Going over this interview transcript, we can now see how certain stereotypes about South Asian families might have shaped our surprise at this account of her agentic behaviour as we probed Guneet about her decision to stand for shop steward, only to be put in our place for any presumptions we might have held about the constraining role of her family.

A few Punjabi women had taken part in successful industrial disputes in the West London area at Hillingdon Hospital and at Lufthansa Skychef, and one had participated in both. The Hillingdon dispute erupted in 1995, a year after the outsourcing of cleaning services at Hillingdon Hospital to Pall Mall Cleaning, when the workers were offered new contracts, effectively forcing wage cuts of between £25 and £35 a week on people who were already receiving very low wages.[1]

> They gave us ninety days' notice and asked us to sign the new terms. About six of the cleaners signed it, but about fifty of us did not. On the last day – it was my day off, but I still went to see what was going to happen – everyone was standing outside, assembled together. They said, let's do 'demonstration'! And off we went! (Sharanjit, GG)

Fifty-five mainly South Asian women members of UNISON refused to sign the new employment contract and went on strike, at which point they were sacked. After five subsequent years of struggle, during which they eventually gained the backing of their trade union, the strikers finally won the dispute when an employment tribunal ruled that they should receive compensation and be reinstated:

The results were all over the TV and radio. I was home that day and someone called up and asked me to turn the TV on. We immediately assembled at the hospital. I felt very proud. It was such a long strike, but we saw it off till the end. It took us nine trips to the court. We got backdated wages for four years, after deducting the wages that I had earned from working part-time at this other place. And there was also the redundancy money. It felt great! (Sharanjit, GG)

In 1998, following a breakdown in negotiations on flexible working practices at Lufthansa Skychef, 270 TGWU members went on an official one-day strike, and were sacked only a few hours into it. This proved to be Britain's longest official industrial dispute at seventeen months and ended when Lufthansa offered to reinstate the workers or pay compensation to them, the day before new legislation was due to be introduced, under which the sackings would be illegal (BBC News 2000).

I was there for two years when a strike started there in 1997. There were mostly Indian people there, mostly women too. They had the same issue of increasing the workload without increasing the money. We were members of the union, and went on strike. But even this was not the first time I had been in a strike. I had been in two strikes at other factories before – one lasting a day and another two weeks. So I had experience of these things. But the Lufthansa strike lasted months – we used to go to the head-quarters of the airlines and demonstrate, we were very active for months. We eventually won and I got £7500 in the settlement. (Manjot, GG)

DIGNITY AND STRUGGLES AT WORK – A WORKING LIFE PERSPECTIVE

Overall, the way the women represented their early years as workers focused on the hardship they endured doing jobs that no one else would or could do and emphasised the exploitation and indignity they suffered at work. Their accounts about their later years, however, were more about their struggles for their rights and their resistance to those exploitative labour processes. Beyond these dominant themes of exploitation and resistance, women also talked about what work meant to them. What emerged from their narratives was a largely positive construction of work on account of the conviviality, banter and friendships with other women workers. Women also spoke about the empowering nature of paid work:

> When I went to work, I got money. Even if your husband is very good, it is hard to have to ask for money for every small thing. Also, in this country, staying at home also gets boring. When I came to this country, I had no one here. When you go out, you make friends, people you know by yourself, not through your husband. I did make friends among women in families that were known to my husband's family – but when you talk to them – you know, things that are in your heart – you can't tell them everything, can you? Your own friend is someone you can reveal everything to. (Dhanwant, GG)

A lot of feminist analyses of women's work in the 1970s and 1980s tended to construct women's work outside the home as positive and empowering in enabling them to overcome isolation, renegotiate their position within their families and to play a self-determinative role as active agents who shape their own lives (Westwood 1984; Westwood and Bhachu 1988; Whitehead 1981). These arguments resonated with women's narratives about the meaning of work for their senses of self, as well as it having more practical associations:

> I came to realise my value. I felt that the kind of work that they think men can do, well, I could do that as well. I could stand and work all day as well. If I had stayed there, I would have worked at home, but had to ask him for money for everything I wanted. Even if I wanted to visit my mother or go out, I had to ask for the bus fare. I had to, like, justify it. Sometimes we would argue, he would say, 'Why do you need to go? You went last month'. It was all a tussle over the money. Now that both of us work, I feel I earn as well, the money goes into the bank and I can take it out if I feel I need to. (Kulvinder, GG)

However, while the constraints related to low-paid work with no prospects of advancement were common experiences of many categories of women workers, these pressures were particularly amplified for those migrant women discussed above who had been deskilled and demoted in class terms. In the context of these constraints, some women – particularly those who had worked in higher-status occupations or careers prior to migration – dismissed any suggestion like Kulvinder's, that work might be meaningful to their identity or sense of self.

> I cannot say what difference work made for me, yes, for my family we were able to save a bit more. For me, the job was not the kind where you could feel good about yourself, was it? What sense of achievement can there be in chopping vegetables. I did manage to build up some savings, but nothing apart from that. (Leena, GG)

More negatively, for five of the women, work became yet another dimension of the control and abuse that was perpetrated against them within their intimate relationships. These women who recounted experiences of domestic violence also spoke about how their experiences of violence within the home shaped their encounters at work:

> He wanted the money, so he sent me to work, but was forever suspicious of me when I was at work. I came and went to work with a colleague, but he did not believe that I did so. He would keep going to her house and checking with her. I was under so much pressure, I would sometimes burst into tears at work and the other workers would enquire, 'Are you OK? What's the matter?' But I would just wash my face and resume work. (Gurinder, GG)

For these women, the abuse they experienced affected their everyday working lives, as well as their home lives, and the benefits of paid work eluded them as they had to hand over their wages to their husbands and were given little money to meet their basic needs. They recounted walking long distances to work or going by without a meal whilst at work, as they were not given any money to access transport or utilise the canteen facilities.

There was a time when I used to get up at 4.30 a.m. to go to work and work till late at night. I used to work the night shift, and he used to lie at home drunk when he was meant to come and pick me up. I would be standing at the bus stop, waiting, but he would not come to pick me up after I finished my shift. I was scared being out at that time, but it had to be done. I worked hard all day, and when I got my wages, I had to hand it over to my father-in-law. That's how it was. You won't believe how much he used to give me – £1 a week towards my expenses. There was no money to take a bus, so I had to walk to work. It took half an hour to walk there. (Simran, GG)

For women who were facing domestic violence, however, their work-place could provide them with opportunities to socialise outside the constraints of a controlling relationship, enable them to hide away some money through strategies such as working through their lunch hour, and find out about support services.

I had to do everything at home before I went to work – cook, clean, wash clothes by hand. I had to work hard, but I was glad to go to work. It was as if I had been freed from a cage and could spend some time with the girls. It felt good – I enjoyed the work. I was young, it was not that difficult for me. But most of all, I was glad to get out. The atmosphere at home was such that anything was preferable to it. It felt like freedom. (Simran, GG)

Three of the women interviewed had utilised the support of their co-workers to eventually leave abusive relationships, and their paid work was central to the lives they had rebuilt and to their sense of the journey they had undertaken.

CONCLUSION

An analysis of the Punjabi and Gujarati women's narratives about their lives demonstrates the commonalities as well as the differences in their experiences of migration and settlement, the significance of their previous and changing class positions, and in their early histories of incorporation into a racialised and gendered labour market in the UK. What emerges is the centrality of paid work to the identities of South Asian women in the UK and to the material position of their families following migration. The women emphasised the themes of dignity at work in relation to caste-based social norms, (changing) class positions, and particularly in the context of their everyday social relations at work. Despite and within the constraints of low-paid and low-status work, the working histories of the women signalled individual strategies of mobility as they sought better jobs in terms of pay and conditions, looking to manage their productive and reproductive roles, and as they pursued work that resonated with their notions of their place in society and the respect that they felt was their due. Women also recounted with pride their ongoing individual and collective resistance to managerial control and their industrial militancy in response to exploitative working conditions.

Also, as we have seen, several of the Punjabi women who went on to work for Gate Gourmet had taken part in industrial disputes during the course of their working lives, which included the notable victories secured at Hillingdon Hospital and Lufthansa Skychef. The narratives of the Punjabi and Gujarati women workers indicate the important role played by their socio-economic backgrounds and history of migration and settlement in shaping their sense of self at work and at home, and the ways in which they developed a keen sense of what constituted exploitation or unacceptable working conditions, and also when and how they decided to take action against this.

NOTES

1. A detailed account of the origins and the first year of the dispute is available in the record of debates at the House of Commons (see HC 1996).

GRUNWICK STRIKE COMMITTEE

WHAT ARE WE FIGHTING FOR?

1. The right to belong to a Union.
2. The right to have our Union recognised.
3. The right not to be dismissed for having joined a Union.

SCARMAN SAYS:

1. "They successfully resisted an attempt by the Transport and General Workers' Union to secure recognition in 1973. . . . They have sought up to this day to maintain their non-Union shop."
2. We are satisfied that it was made "abundantly clear to those who remained at work that the company did not want a Union".
3. "In the conduct of industrial relations in this country, and no matter what the legalities are, it is the exception rather than the rule for employees who are dismissed during the course of a strike not to be re-engaged after the dispute is ended."

WHAT ARE WE FIGHTING AGAINST?

1. £25 for a 35-hour week for clerical workers and £28 for a 40-hour week for process workers when the strike began.
2. Compulsory overtime at short notice.
3. An abusive and tyrannical régime—as Laurie Pavitt, the MP for Brent South, said: "A sweat shop with a management which could have been lifted straight out of the Dickens' era."

SCARMAN SAYS:

1. "Prior to the strike, pay was at the lower end of the rates of pay found in the by no means highly paid industry of photo-finishing."
2. "There was on other occasions a lack of human understanding" in dealing with "applications for relaxations on overtime working".
3. In the mail order department, where the strike began, "the threat of dismissal must have been an anxiety for many in the workforce" and "the annual turnover of staff in the department (was) as high as 100 per cent—a disquieting percentage".
4. Since the strike began, pay has increased by 25 per cent—"we make the obvious but necessary comment. The presence of the Union and the protracted nature of the dispute must have been important factors in the company's decision to improve rates of pay and other benefits".
5. "The company by dismissing all the strikers, refusing to reconsider the reinstatement of any of them, refusing to seek a negotiated settlement to the strike and rejecting ACAS offers of coniliation, has acted within the letter but outside the spirit of the law. Further, such action on the part of the company was unreasonable when judged by the norms of good industrial relations practice. The company has thus added to the bitterness of the dispute, and contributed to its development into a threat of civil disorder."

SCARMAN RECOMMENDED REINSTATEMENT, IMMEDIATE LIMITED RECOGNITION AND THE ESTABLISHMENT OF COLLECTIVE BARGAINING IN GRUNWICK. WE PUT OUR HAND OUT. NOW GRUNWICK HAS SNUBBED THE FINDINGS. THIS DISPUTE IS A DUNKIRK FOR THE TRADE UNION MOVEMENT. WE HAVE THE POWER—WITH THE WILL TO USE IT, WE WILL WIN!

London Caledonian Press (T.U.) Ltd., Watford, Herts.—57265

The Grunwick Strike Committee outline their demands.
Held at the TUC Library Collections, part of Special Collections at London Metropolitan University.

A painting of the Grunwick picket outside Dollis Hill tube station. © *Dan Jones*

On the Grunwick picket line in 1976.
© *TUC Library Collections, part of Special Collections at London Metropolitan University.*

Appeal to the public to boycott Grunwick's photo processing business in winter 1976. *Held at the TUC Library Collections, part of Special Collections at London Metropolitan University*

Grunwick picketers protesting low wages.
© *TUC Library Collections, part of Special Collections*
at London Metropolitan University.

The Grunwick strikers in 1977 – getting weary as the dispute goes on. © *TUC Library Collections, part of Special Collections at London Metropolitan University.*

The Grunwick strikers in 1977 challenging NAFF's support for owner George Ward. © *TUC Library Collections, part of Special Collections at London Metropolitan University.*

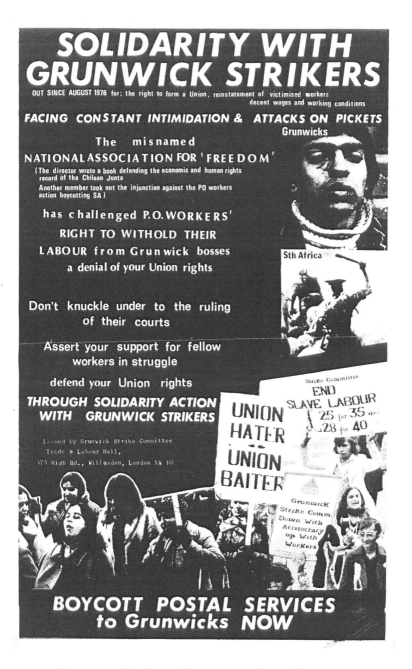

SOLIDARITY WITH GRUNWICK STRIKERS

OUT SINCE AUGUST 1976 for; the right to form a Union, reinstatement of victimised workers decent wages and working conditions

FACING CONSTANT INTIMIDATION & ATTACKS ON PICKETS

Grunwicks

The misnamed

NATIONAL ASSOCIATION FOR 'FREEDOM'

(The director wrote a book defending the economic and human rights record of the Chilean Junta

Another member took out the injunction against the PO workers action boycotting SA)

has challenged P.O. WORKERS'

RIGHT TO WITHOLD THEIR

LABOUR from Grunwick bosses

a denial of your Union rights

Sth Africa

Don't knuckle under to the ruling of their courts

Assert your support for fellow workers in struggle

defend your Union rights

THROUGH SOLIDARITY ACTION WITH GRUNWICK STRIKERS

Issued by Grunwick Strike Committee
Trade & Labour Hall,
175 High Rd., Willesden, London NW 10

UNION HATER UNION BAITER

Strike Committee
END
SLAVE LABOUR
{ 25 for 35 hrs
28 for 40

Grunwick
Strike Comm.
Down With
Aristocracy
up With
Workers

BOYCOTT POSTAL SERVICES to Grunwicks NOW

As the support for the strikers grows, the Strike Committee calls for mass solidarity action by trade unions. *Held at the TUC Library Collections, part of Special Collections at London Metropolitan University.*

Taken from www.striking-women.org, a web-based resource about migration, women and work, workers' rights, and the story of South Asian women workers during the Grunwick and Gate Gourmet industrial disputes. *Sundari Anitha and Ruth Pearson* © *University of Lincoln.*

GRUNWICK STRIKE COMMITTEE
APEX & TGWU

MASS PICKET

MONDAY 17th OCTOBER
6.30am onwards and on every morning thereafter

**Please report to the
Strike Committee Headquarters
Brent Trades and Labour Hall, 375 High Road,
Willesden, London, NW10**

This is the final chapter of this bitter and historic dispute. The right to organise is under attack from George Ward and his powerful backers. Show by your numbers on the mass picket that you will not let them defeat Trade Unionism.

1. Our industry is an under-organised jungle. Grunwicks cannot be defeated by cutting off supplies alone. Pour in resolutions to Union EC's, particularly those of the EEPTU, GMWU, the UPW, and the TUC, calling for co-ordinated action to cut off essential services—water, electricity and post—to the company.
2. Ask your Union-sponsored or local MPs to demand action from the Government.
3. Please donate regularly and generously to the Strike Fund.
4. Boycott the film processing services of GRUNWICK, COOPER AND PEARSON, BONUSPOOL, TRUCOLOUR and MONKOLOR.

AN INJURY TO ONE IS AN INJURY TO ALL!

**GRUNWICK Strike Committee, Brent Trades and Labour Hall,
375 High Road, Willesden, NW10**

The Strike Committee calls for the resumption of mass pickets. *Held at the TUC Library Collections, part of Special Collections at London Metropolitan University.*

Gategourmet

WARNING OF DISMISSAL

10 August 2005

A large group of workers have been dismissed today for taking part in unballoted industrial action.

Since you are not on shift as required, we believe you may also be taking part.

I warn you all that you have 20 minutes to get on shift and work normally otherwise the company will conclude that you are taking part in un balloted industrial action as well.

If you do not do this you will be dismissed with immediate effect with no right to appeal.

Hans Boesch
Director of Operations
Gate Gourmet London Ltd.

Gate Gourmet warns workers on the afternoon shift that they have twenty minutes to report to work before they will be dismissed. *Donated by a sacked Gate Gourmet worker.*

A cartoon in Schnews, Friday 2 September 2005. © *Schnews*

STRICTLY PRIVATE ADDRESSEE ONLY

Gate Gourmet London Limited
Heathrow South

Human Resources Department
Scylla Road
Heathrow Airport
Hounslow
Middlesex
TW6 3YF

Telephone: (020)8757-6032/3
Telefax: (020)8757-6034

Dear

This letter is to confirm that you were dismissed at approximately 16:00 hours this afternoon for participating in unballoted industrial action.

Please note that you will not be paid for today's shift when you were taking part in the industrial action.

Please be aware that the company is currently reviewing whether it will make deductions from your final wages to pay for the penalties that the company has incurred as a result of the disruption.

Your final salary payment and P45 will follow shortly.

You are not entitled to appeal against your dismissal.

Yours sincerely,

General Manager

Gate Gourmet issues dismissal letters on the day of the lock out.
Donated by a sacked Gate Gourmer worker.

GRADUALLY, THE COMPANY STARTED MAKING CHANGES TO THE TERMS AND CONDITIONS FOR THE WORKERS AND THE MANAGEMENT BECAME INCREASINGLY HARSH. THE WORKERS RESISTED THE CHANGES.

LET'S TRY INCREASING THE SPEED OF THE CONVEYER BELT. WHY DO WE HAVE 3 WOMEN DOING THE JOB, LET'S TRY IT WITH 2 WOMEN INSTEAD.

THIS IS IMPOSSIBLE!

ON 10TH AUGUST 2005, WHEN THE WORKERS RETURNED FROM THEIR MORNING TEA BREAK...

WHAT ARE THESE PEOPLE DOING WORKING IN OUR PLACE?

WHERE ARE WE SUPPOSED TO WORK?

THE WORKERS ASSEMBLED IN THE CANTEEN TO DISCUSS WHAT HAD HAPPENED. THEY WERE JOINED THERE BY SHOP STEWARDS FROM THEIR UNION.

THIS IS YOUR MANAGER SPEAKING. RETURN TO WORK RIGHT NOW OR YOU WILL BE SACKED.

BY THE NEXT DAY MORE WORKERS HAD BEEN SACKED BRINGING THE TOTAL TO JUST OVER 700.

THE UNION HAS REACHED AN AGREEMENT WITH GATE GOURMET – BUT NOT ALL OF US WILL GET OUR JOBS BACK!

LOWER WAGES AND REDUCED OVERTIME RATES. THE COMPANY HAS MANAGED TO GET WHAT IT WANTED ALL ALONG!

NO MORE

144 WORKERS WERE SELECTED FOR REDUNDANCY BECAUSE THEY WERE OLDER OR HAD HEALTH ISSUES. THIS TIME, THE WORKERS ALSO LOST THEIR CASE FOR UNFAIR DISMISSAL AT THE EMPLOYMENT TRIBUNAL.

Taken from www.striking-women.org, a web-based resource about migration, women and work, workers' rights, and the story of South Asian women workers during the Grunwick and Gate Gourmet industrial disputes. *Sundari Anitha and Ruth Pearson* © *University of Lincoln*

≡Gategourmet

Embargo of 00.01 Friday 16th December 2005.

GATE GOURMET ACHIEVES 'FULL AND FINAL CLOSURE' ON AUGUST DISPUTE

The deadline for former Gate Gourmet staff to sign compromise agreements in order to receive a voluntary compensation payment passes today.

Eric Born, managing director of Gate Gourmet UK and Ireland, today urged the remaining former workers to sign compromise agreements before the close of business today as the events of August 2005 achieve 'full and final closure'.

In November Gate Gourmet voluntarily extended the deadline for signing up to these compromise agreements to 16th December 2005. There is now only one day for the remaining staff to sign the compromise agreements. There will be no further extension beyond this date.

As of midday Thursday nearly 200 former Gate Gourmet workers had already signed compromise agreements and this number is likely to increase through Friday. As a result most will receive compensation payments. Others have been offered re-engagement with the company.

All the workers were dismissed for participating in the illegal wildcat strike in August 2005. The company is not required by law to make any compensation payments or to offer to re-engage former employees and is doing so voluntarily. Gate Gourmet can only make these offers once a compromise agreement has been signed by the individual.

Eric Born, Managing Director of Gate Gourmet UK & Ireland, said:

"For Gate Gourmet today marks full and final closure on the events of August 2005. We will have reached agreement with all those former staff prepared to accept a voluntary compensation payment or an offer of re-engagement.

"In the remaining few hours of today I would urge all those who are due to sign to do so rather than miss out on the payment they could receive. I don't want any family to lose out on a compensation payment which Gate Gourmet is voluntarily prepared to offer them.

Gate Gourmet announces 'full and final closure' of the dispute through its compensation agreement, which avoids any mention of compulsory redundancies. *Donated by a sacked Gate Gourmet worker.*

OUR DISPUTE IS NOT OVER!

We were sacked by Gate Gourmet eleven months ago on August 10 but over a hundred of us still refuse to sign the Compromise Agreement and we are now proceeding with our Employment Tribunals.

Our T&GWU leaders, previously refused to pay us hardship money and stopped it on January 6.

Last week, they informed us that they would pay another month's hardship money for February 2006!

We say if you can pay for February, what about March, April, May and June? WHAT HAS CHANGED?

Instead of treating us so contemptuously, we think our union leaders should be proud of our stand against such a ruthless boss. Our stand forced Gate Gourmet to publicly apologise last month and state that some of us **were wrongly sacked.**

WE HAVE BEEN PROVED RIGHT TO STAND FIRM –
Other employers are now copying Gate Gourmet and bringing in cheap labour to replace the normal trade union workforce.

We believe that this rotten Compromise Agreement should NEVER have been agreed to by TGWU leaders nor by TUC General Secretary, Brendan Barber.

We call on you, the leaders of the trade unions, to tell our TGWU leadership to back us and make our dispute official.

There is serious hardship among our members and we want our hardship money restored and all the back months paid

We also invite you to our one year's anniversary march & rally SUNDAY AUGUST 20 Marching through Southall followed by a rally, Indian Food, plus live entertainment

PLEASE GIVE US ALL YOUR SUPPORT

Gate Gourmet Locked Out Workers, 27 Old Gloucester Street, WC1N 3XX
Tel: 0797 45 49 537

Workers reject the Compromise Agreement negotiated by their union and call for continued support in June 2006. *Held at the TUC Library Collections, part of Special Collections at London Metropolitan University.*

Sacked workers organise a demonstration in Southall on the first anniversary of their dismissal in 2006. This was organised with help from the WRP (Workers Revolutionary Party), who had been supporting the strikers since some fifty-six workers rejected the Compromise Agreement. *Held at the TUC Library Collections, part of Special Collections at London Metropolitan University.*

Cartoon mocking the stereotype of South Asian women's domesticity.
© *Vishavjit Singh, Sikhtoons.com*

Sacked Gate Gourmet workers at the May Day rally in London in 2008. © *Sundari Anitha*. See image at http://www.leeds.ac.uk/strikingwomen/gategourmet/gallery

CHAPTER 5

'We are the lions, Mr Manager': The Grunwick dispute

As we demonstrated in earlier chapters, there was nothing in the previous working and life experience of the Gujarati women who migrated to the UK from post-independence East Africa which might have signalled that they would become industrial militants, nor that they would be willing to risk their jobs and livelihoods in what turned out to be a long struggle for dignity at work and the right to join and be represented by a trade union. But this is what came to pass in 1970s London. When a group of workers, led by the now renowned Jayaben Desai, walked out of a photo processing laboratory in the hot summer of 1976, in protest against arbitrary and humiliating management, their immediate aim was to defend their dignity and their rights. But this struggle later came to be centred on the right to union recognition and on collective bargaining as a means to this end. After ten months on strike, the workers' cause was taken up by the wider trade union movement, with mass solidarity picketing from other unions, anti-racist organisations and feminist groups. Following early successes through secondary solidarity action however, the TUC retreated from mass picketing. Instead, it moved towards reconciliatory efforts through mediation services and the government appointed Scarman Inquiry, despite the fact that this inquiry had no enforcement powers behind its recommendations. The picketing was reduced to accommodate these procedures, and eventually, under pressure from the Labour government of the day, the TUC effectively withdrew their support for the Grunwick strikers (Dromey and Taylor 2016; Rogaly 1977). In June 1978, the Grunwick strike committee was left with no option but to announce the end of the dispute, in the context of what they denounced as a betrayal by their union leadership.

The Grunwick strikers were predominantly Gujarati Hindus of East-African origin who had arrived in the UK between late 1960s to mid-1970s from urban, English-language-educated and middle-class backgrounds. At the time of the Grunwick dispute, they were mostly in their twenties and thirties; aged forty-three when the dispute started, Jayaben Desai was one of the older women workers at Grunwick. Although all of the Grunwick strikers we spoke to had previous experience of paid work in countries in East Africa or India, in keeping with their class status, this had been in 'respectable' occupations such as teaching, secretarial work or home-based work, as discussed in previous chapters. Upon entry into the labour market in the UK, they found that they had to accept the low-status and low-paid factory work that was available to migrants. Given that the majority of the Grunwick workforce was comprised of marginalised and relatively powerless women from minority and migrant backgrounds, who had endured an increasingly arbitrary management and control regime for some time, there are a number of key questions which must be asked: why did the dispute erupt and take the form that it did? How relevant are the workers' migrant identities and experiences to the ways in which they responded to the conditions in their work-place, and the ways in which changes were being imposed on the labour process? To what extent did their gender, class and ethnic backgrounds intersect to catalyse industrial action?

A range of texts have been produced dealing with different aspects of the Grunwick dispute (Dromey and Taylor 2016; Levidow 1981; McGowan 2008; Rogaly 1977; Wilson 1978), including studies of: the ways the strike was organised; the tactics used; the role of the trade union movement; changes in strategy; and the ultimate defeat and legacy of the strike. However, it is notable that none of these accounts bring forth the voices and perspectives of the striking women themselves. By locating their participation in the strike in the context of the larger lives and histories of these migrant women workers, our account enables us to understand and better interpret the causes of their industrial militancy through an intersectional lens. This incorporates the roles of gender, race and class in shaping the striking women's agency. Drawing upon life history narratives of five of the original strikers, as well as contemporary accounts in newspapers and government documents such as the Scarman Report and documents including Special Branch files released under the thirty-year rule, we offer a more comprehensive analysis of the causes, trajectory and the legacy of the Grunwick dispute.

THE LABOUR FORCE, THE LABOUR PROCESS AND WORKING CONDITIONS AT GRUNWICK

Examining the management strategies at Grunwick makes clear that the objective was to continuously reduce labour costs by lowering the unit cost of production, at the same time as increasing the productivity of labour – what has been termed the 'cheap labour' strategy (Elson and Pearson 1981). The recruitment strategy utilised at Grunwick was based on an intention to hire workers who exhibited all the classic characteristics of cheap labour – for example, labour that was immediately available, that cost little or nothing to recruit, people who were willing to accept low hourly and weekly wages, offered ultimate flexibility in terms of hours, overtime and seasonal demand, and who were assumed to be docile, and therefore unlikely to resist continuous efforts to increase their productivity.

According to George Ward, the joint owner of the firm, the original workforce at Grunwick's St John's Wood premises in North West London was mainly white. But as the company expanded to premises in Willesden and Wembley, it hired a 'truly multiracial workforce' (Ward 1977, 30) where the staff – including temporary workers, who were mainly students hired to cope with the seasonal peaks in work in the summer months – were West Indian, African, Indian and Irish. However, the Scarman Report (1977, 5) notes that by the time of the dispute, the workforce was predominantly South Asian, and comprised mostly of women. Recruitment was by word of mouth, using the networks of existing employees. Indeed, once the dispute had begun, Ward continued to hire 'relatives of those still working; he then geared up for the summer 1977 peak of the holiday snapshot market by recruiting workers from entirely outside the community of East African Asian refugees including Chinese students' (Levidow 1981, 132).

In the view of Jayaben Desai, who became the strike leader, the
recruitment of South Asian workers was part of a deliberate strategy:

> They got more work out of us. Asians had just come from Uganda
> and they all needed work. So they took whatever was available.
> Grunwick put out 'papers' [leaflets]: 'come and we will give you a
> job. We give jobs to everyone'. Door to door. When I went, a friend
> of mine followed. And soon they were full of Asians. (Jayaben)

The Grunwick recruitment strategy was similar to that of firms
operating within segmented labour markets (MacKenzie and Forde
2009, 144; Piore 1979), which sought to attract migrant workers
already in the national labour markets or to recruit directly from
abroad. This was based on employer stereotypes of migrants as
'good workers' with a 'positive work ethic' unlike the local labour
alternative. As suggested above, the recruitment policy at Grunwick
was informed as much by these positive constructions of migrant
workers as it was by a knowledge of their vulnerable position in the
labour market as newly arrived migrants from East Africa. In spite
of George Ward's celebration of his multiracial workforce, the terms
and conditions of those migrants' employment at Grunwick were
firmly limited to the bottom of the labour market.

George Ward's resistance to his workforce having any trade
union involvement, which might have formed the basis for them
to negotiate better conditions, was evident from a previous unsuc-
cessful dispute for union recognition at Grunwick in 1973, when
two workers who had joined the TGWU were made redundant.
Sixteen workers went on strike in support of the sacked two but the
company successfully resisted the attempt by the TGWU to secure
union recognition for the workers (Scarman Report 1977, 9).

Jayaben Desai had first started to work for Grunwick at its
Wembley premises in 1974, and recounted how the composition of
the workforce changed between 1974 and 1976, an observation that
was also made in the Scarman Report:

> I just had to put leaflets in an envelope. That's what I did at the
> beginning. That was easy. And we never took tea breaks, did not
> take smoking breaks, so they got a good level of production. And

gradually they started shifting the workers and replaced the white workers with Asian ones. (Jayaben)

When this this management strategy to shift the workforce took place, South Asian workers at Grunwick experienced it as an affront to their dignity when they saw white job-seekers turned away. Wilson (1978, 64) cites a Grunwick worker who felt slighted by constructions of the work as undesirable for white women who could secure better-paid, less arduous jobs:

> Imagine how humiliating it was for us, particularly for older women, to be working and to overhear the employer saying to a young English girl, 'You don't want to come and work here, love, we won't be able to pay the sort of wages that'll keep you here', while we had to work there because we were trapped.

In 1976, Grunwick employed 500 workers, mostly migrant women, especially in labour-intensive departments such as the mail-order department (Scarman Report 1977, 5). When the new Chapter Road plant in Dollis Hill was opened in April 1976, Jayaben Desai was relocated there to the department that handled the incoming and outgoing mail, a vital part of the mail order printing and photo processing business. The new premises housed this mail order department and the computer department, run by a Malcolm Alden, who was one of the harsher managers, according to accounts from the time. Although his responsibility was to supervise the automated system for producing invoices, he was housed in a glass walled office where he could watch over the (female South Asian) workforce. These workers were employed to manually process orders and payments for films, which were delivered at an increasing pace all through the peak summer holiday months.

Jayaben vividly recalls Alden's management style, which she argues was designed to produce insecurity; her view was corroborated by the Scarman Report (1977, 17) which described Alden as 'a tough manager determined to maintain a high level of productivity'. Jayaben recalls how the pressure of work escalated as the company expanded, and Alden sought to increase productivity through an authoritarian management style:

The manager there was a complete swine – his name was Mr
Alden. He was a [general] manager first. Then, when production increased, they made him a production manager. After
they purchased the Dollis Hill property, he had this wonderful
room there. You had a hall and on one side and on the other
the payment department, where I was. The payment department
was separate from the others. And the managers were in a glass
cabinet. They could see us, and if they called us in to their office,
the rest of the workers could see them, but could not hear what
was going on. Such was their gameplan. We used to work out of
fear. (Jayaben)

The pressures on the workforce were partly a consequence of
the nature of Grunwick's business, which hinged on processing
customers' photos at low cost and with a quick turnaround; this was
important for meeting new consumer demand for instant photos
from holidays in the UK and abroad, a consequence of increasing
real wages and holiday entitlement since the 1960s. However, the
method for this drive for efficiency and competitive performance
was achieved was key. Management had two options: investing in
automating different parts of the production process to increase
productivity, or reducing unit costs by employing a cheap, flexible and productive workforce. According to Levidow (1981, 139),
the automation that was undertaken was 'lopsided'; 'the chem-
ical processing and accounting phases [had] been subjected to an
extreme automation that reduces its workers to machine minding'
while the clerical handing of film remained 'a menial, highly labour
intensive routine. The computerisation of accounts facilitates the
rapid retrieval of information about money paid and owed by each
customer, without clerks poring through file cabinets potentially
under their human control'. This resulted in the subordination of
the clerical work of handling the film, especially the mail order film
which needed to be sorted and billed, to the automated stages, and
allowed management to vary the staffing and the pace of clerical
work, according to seasonal demand (Levidow 1981, 139-140).
This made this department the bottleneck – or pressure point – for
keeping up with the high turnover necessary throughout the peak
summer months. Levidow noted that Grunwick had secured its lead

position in the market for domestic mail order photo processing by offering a cheap and rapid mail order service for colour prints – with a turnaround time of three to four days compared to ten days to three weeks for other firms, a quality of service that was recognised by the consumer magazine *Which?* (Ward 1977, 24).

The nature of the semi-automated labour process, together with the structure of the workforce, and the ways in which management control was exercised with a view to maximising the flexibility of labour to match the increasing and time-controlled demand, explains why the dispute at Grunwick occurred in the mail-order department rather than elsewhere in the production process. As Jayaben recalls, the culture at Grunwick was one of fear:

> They adopted a technique that increased production. They used to make this list of the workers. Those who had produced the most, their name would be at the top. And those who produced the least would be at the bottom. This affected everyone 'mentally'. I understood how this worked, but others did not always understand. They were fearful that if their name was at the bottom, they would get the sack. In the summer, the demand was high, so they employed more people. When they did not need so many people in September-October they used to make up excuses to sack people. Everyone was scared. So they started to put in more work to stay on top of the list. (Jayaben)

As Jayaben here highlights, one of the ways in which the management sought to maximise productivity was through constant threats of dismissal if workers did not respond to efforts to increase output. Alden explicitly told the Scarman Inquiry that he used to '"press" the workforce in that [the mail order] department' (Dromey and Taylor 2016, 26), and other workers emphasised this too:

> The behaviour of those managers … they were real bullies. They would come in and they looked at you as if you were nothing. If you done a mistake they would shout in your faces 'If you do it again you go through the door'. (A Caribbean woman worker quoted in Thomas 2008)

Grunwick managers operated within a culture of summary
dismissals for any perceived violations by staff that threatened the
level of productivity. The Scarman Report (1977, 17-18) noted that
no code of disciplinary practice appears to have been in operation
to enable staff to appeal against a decision by their managers, nor
were the staff aware of any warning system – such a system was only
first published and posted on departmental notice boards in June
1976, two months before the walk-out. The pressure to maintain
productivity resulted in a labour turnover of some 100 per cent in
a single year. In the mail order department, turnover was particularly high: between 1 and 20 August 1976 thirty-two out of the 102
workers left the plant, with twenty-seven of those departing in the
six weeks leading up to the strike (Rogaly 1977, 37). This would
seem to be a very high rate of turnover at a time when there was
much concern about high and rising levels of unemployment, as
reflected in the slogan 'Labour isn't working', used to such success
in the Conservative Party's election campaign in 1979 (see Beckett
2009, 458).

Flexibility was also demanded through compulsory overtime.
According to Nirmalaben, 'When we filled the form, they had told
us that it was compulsory overtime, and I accepted that', a sentiment reiterated in Dromey and Taylor (2016, 28). Indeed, for some
workers, overtime offered a means of enhancing their otherwise low
pay. The Scarman Report (1977, 16) documents evidence from one
woman who had worked thirty hours overtime in addition to her
thirty-five hours of contracted work in one week. But overtime was
not generously rewarded; it was paid at only 1.25 times the basic rate
for the first six hours, and then at time and a half (Scarman Report
1977, 15). The workforce also resented the way that 'Management
could demand overtime [...] shortly before the normal end of the
working day, without even permitting the workers to telephone
home to arrange for their children to be picked up' (Levidow 1981,
138) – and this was particularly common in the mail order department, which contributed to those employees' grievances. In her
evidence to the Scarman Inquiry, Jayaben Desai – who worked in
that department – stated that although people were willing to stay
until about 7 p.m., after that time 'everybody feels that we should go
home because it was a lonely place and ladies were scared to go alone

even in the evening'.[1] The Scarman Report (1977, 16-17) documents that overtime sometimes extended till 10 p.m.

According to contemporary sources, including the Scarman Report (1977, 15), the pay at Grunwick was 'at the lower end of the rates of pay found in the by no means highly paid industry of photo-processing'. Grunwick workers were paid between £25 and £28 for a thirty-five to forty hour week when they started work. This could rise to £40 per week after two years of employment, though given the high turnover rates, few employees ever achieved these higher rates. This compared to £49.35 per week at Kodak, the highest rates in the sector, and approximately £40 at Ilford. Holiday entitlements, sickness benefits and overtime rates at Grunwick were also inferior to other employees in the sector.[2] However, as the Scarman Report indicates, the strike was motivated by a broader range of issues including compulsory overtime, authoritarian management style and frequent dismissals and threats of dismissals, which created a working culture of fear (Scarman report 1977, 15-18). As Jayaben observed about their action (cited in Rossiter 1977, 18), 'This is not so much a strike about pay, it is a strike about human dignity'.

The ways in which the labour process was managed reveals griev-ances that go beyond the low pay and poor working conditions and entitlements that were common in many small businesses during the 1970s. These broader issues were what ultimately led to resist-ance from some of the workers, who ultimately refused to comply with the system of management by withdrawing their labour from production. They subsequently demanded the right to form and join a trade union that would be recognised within the firm, citing this as the vehicle to resolve labour conflict – what is referred to in the ILO Core Standards as the rights to free association and collec-tive bargaining. However, as the dispute at Grunwick indicates, like the later one at Gate Gourmet, resistance comes not just from the experience on the production line; it is also the result of the inter-section of a range of factors embodied in the workers themselves – their class, ethnic and gendered identities, and also their experi-ence of migration. These all contributed to the workers' perception of injustice and the need for collective action to restore their sense of worth and dignity that had been affronted by unjust treatment in the workplace.

GENDER AND ETHNIC IDENTITY IN LABOUR RELATIONS AT GRUNWICK

The specific identities of the Grunwick workers, including their educational and class positions need to be interrogated in order to understand why, although they appeared to management to be an 'ideal' labour force, speeding up production through managerial control led to resistance and ultimately to the withdrawal of labour.

Because of the ways in which the South Asian diaspora had been integrated into the economies of East Africa, manual and factory labour was new to the Grunwick workers. These women had very seldom been required or encouraged to seek paid work outside the household. All but one of the women we interviewed recalled that they and their female relatives were primarily engaged in domestic work – often the management of domestic labour by servants – while they lived in Africa, though it was increasingly common for such women to do some paid work from home – including dress-making, teaching and tutoring (Herbert 2009). By the 1960s the South Asian communities in the newly independent ex-British colonies in East Africa – Uganda, Kenya and Tanzania – had achieved a relatively privileged social and economic position (Twaddle 1990). However, as we have explained in previous chapters, their very different economic situation in England, caused by their forced expulsion from East Africa in the early 1970s (Mattausch 1998) had propelled them into a manual labour market structured by racial-ised and gendered divisions.[3] They possessed relatively high levels of literacy and education in the English language, as well as the ability to follow instructions and to work accurately at speed, although, in common with women workers elsewhere, their skills were not recognised, rewarded or invested in (Elson and Pearson 1981; Phillips and Taylor 1980). The strikers were mainly from the mail order department, where they were required to perform the complex tasks of processing mail orders, invoices and payments, skills that were treated as typically feminine; these workers were therefore seen as 'unskilled' immigrants, and paid the lowest possible wages.

Management controls played on the gender, race and migrant status of the workers, escalating these demands for higher productivity while seeking to reduce the workforce's control and autonomy over their working days. There are several ways in which the control – and ultimately the resistance of the Grunwick workforce can be understood as both gendered and racialised. Levidow (1981, 144) – with no supporting evidence – claims that 'Asian women are severely burdened with an ethos of female purity', arguing that working together with other women from the same community made it inevitable that norms of conformity were enforced. He also argued that the fact that George Ward, the Director of Grunwick was an Anglo Indian meant he knew how to 'take full advantage of Asian women's vulnerability in the factory' – what Levidow (1981, 145) called 'a culturally sanctioned docility which could be exploited by capital as the women began to work outside their families for the very first time'. There is extensive discussion in the research of the 1980s about how assumptions about South Asian women's traditional docility in relation to their vulnerability in the labour market made it easier for them to be pressurised and exploited at work, which also created the imperative for collective action by South Asian women to resist these exploitative conditions (Parmar 1982; Phizacklea and Miles 1987b).

However, as many have observed (for example, Ramji 2003), the class position of the East African Asians complicated this 'culturally sanctioned docility' and the Grunwick women we interviewed, like most of those who had migrated from East Africa, came from households that employed servants, and were used to the status and respect that accompanied their relatively privileged social status. This fuelled the resentment of what they perceived as degrading treatment from management over issues like permission to go to ante-natal clinics (Wilson 1978, 49), restrictions about using the toilets, and the arbitrary imposition of compulsory overtime. Issues of toilet access were mentioned by women who worked in the mail order department at old Wembley premises, as Jayaben Desai remembered:

When women gathered in the toilet, they used to complain to me. Later they had made 'rules and regulations' that you had to get permission to go to the toilets. This woman said to me that she felt ashamed to ask to go to the toilet, so she held back and was in extreme discomfort and felt a burning sensation. I told her,

'Why do you feel ashamed, when he has no shame making you
ask loudly, why should *you* feel ashamed. Learn how to say it in
English – 'I want to go to the ladies' and then just say so without
any hesitation. (Jayaben)

The issue of compulsory overtime is also one that is imbued with
gendered assumptions and constraints. It is widely agreed that the
proximate reason that sparked Jayaben Desai's walk-out on 20
August 1976 was linked to the arbitrary imposition of forced overtime, but there were a broader set of grievances that informed this
decision, which, as suggested above, included the constant threat of
dismissal, and her desire to retain her dignity in the face of continual
management harassment.

THE GRUNWICK WALK-OUT: THE LIONS WHO CAN BITE
OFF YOUR HEAD

On a hot summer's day, when the air-conditioning at the Grunwick
Chapter Road premises was not in operation and the pressure on
the workforce was heavy, during the company's busiest period of the
year, a series of events led to a walk-out by a handful of workers in
response to arbitrary and oppressive management.

The trouble initially flared in the mail order department, which
was supervised by Malcolm Alden, on Friday 20 August 1976.
Earlier in the day, Devshi Bhudia was given the task of supervising
the sorting of thirteen crates of outgoing mail by that evening,
which he felt was an unreasonable expectation. He responded to this
demand by slowing down the pace of his work, and was summarily
dismissed. As he walked out, he was joined by three male workers,
and they remained standing outside the factory till later that evening.

That same day, when Sunil, Jayaben's son who was a casual
student employee in the summer of 1976, giggled whilst at work
when a student friend tickled him, he was reprimanded by Malcolm
Alden, 'Stop chattering like monkeys, this is not a zoo!' Later that
evening, as Jayaben Desai began preparing to go home at 6 p.m.,
Alden confronted her with a demand for overtime. Although she
was already upset by the rebuke to her son earlier in the day, faced
with an abrupt demand that she extend her working day – and

mindful of the complicated bus journey home – she protested. Upon her refusal, she was invited into the glass cabin by Alden, where an altercation followed. Jayaben recalls her words as she demanded her cards and walked out:

> As I go, I would like to say this. You had said earlier that this is not a zoo. Well, what you run here is not a factory, it is a zoo. There are monkeys here who dance to your tune, but there are also lions here who can bite your head off. And we are the lions, Mr Manager! I want my freedom! (Jayaben)

George Ward records that she then addressed the staff in the open plan office of the mail order department. She asked her fellow workers, 'Can't you understand what these managers are doing to us?' at which point she and Sunil were escorted out by two managers (Ward 1977, 39).

Whilst the immediate pretext for the walk-out was the imposition of a compulsory overtime at short notice, the ways in which the management and control system treated the workers without respect and, in their opinion, robbed them of their dignity and personhood were central to Jayaben's decision to resign, and to walk out before she was publicly humiliated and dismissed:

> I did not think – I just walked out with my self-respect intact. I did not want to work in such a place. I had that power – that I could have found work elsewhere because I knew some English, I could 'present' myself and I was used to working. So I left for my self-respect and because I had confidence in myself. (Jayaben)

Once outside, they were met by Devshi Bhudia and his friends. It was only after a discussion between the five of them that they decided to canvass support among their fellow workers for a union.

Following the spontaneous decision to walk out, Jayaben recalls her husband's reaction when she and her son returned home and recounted the day's events:

> When I came home the first day, my husband scolded me. 'What have you done, do you know what could happen? Our house

could be set on fire, people could kidnap our children. [...] Do you know where this will lead?' I said, 'I have not done this just for myself, I have done it for everyone, don't you worry'. And he never said anything after that. (Jayaben)

According to the Scarman Report (1977, 7), the following Monday, the group stood with placards outside the factory gate at Chapter Road and sought signatures from the workers in a document that outlined their support for a union. Later that day, some fifty workers walked out of the Chapter Road premises. Then, over the next few days, 137 out of a workforce of about 500 joined them. Of these, ninety-one were permanent staff and forty-six were student workers who were there for the summer. Unaware of how to join a trade union and which union to join, the workers sought advice from the Citizen's Advice Bureau, who directed them to the Brent Trades Council and the TUC. By the end of that week, all ninety-one of the permanent staff on strike were members of the Association of Professional, Executive, Clerical and Computer Staff (APEX), a moderate trade union, and received TUC support. Following an unproductive meeting with the co-directors of Grunwick (George Ward was away on holiday), APEX declared the strike official on 1 September 1976, thereby entitling the workers to receive strike pay. The following day, Grunwick responded by sacking the workers for 'participation in strike action' (Scarman Report 1977, 9-10) and the stage was set for what was to become a long and historic battle.

CAUSES OF THE STRIKE: IDENTITY, RESPECT AND RESISTANCE

Central to the workers' decision to walk out was the nature of the managerial control that was exercised at Grunwick. The workers reflected bitterly on the ways in which the management and control system treated them without respect and in what they viewed as undignified ways, according them low status that – given their previous middle-class backgrounds – they were unaccustomed to and unwilling to accept.

The ethnic origin of the workers, and particularly those that went on strike, was also important. This had an impact on the workers' sense of self, on their perceptions of conditions at work and of the way the 'ideal worker' was constructed in gendered and racialised ways that excluded white workers from consideration for the job. In this context, although conditions in the mail order department were the worst in the two premises in being most subject to arbitrary and punitive management pressures, many workers in other departments felt solidarity with those who walked out:

Things were not that bad in some departments. I did not say they were good. Those people were aware of our situation. They knew things could have been better – could get better. That's why they came out. When they saw how we had been treated, they came to support us even before they knew about strike pay. They took a risk and came out to support us out of a tremendous sense of solidarity. These people did not treat us properly and that was why people felt that it was not right. (Jayaben)

Workers who worked at the Cobbold Road premises or those who worked in other departments where the management was less authoritarian and arbitrary therefore decided to join the strikers in an expression of protest at the treatment meted out to their fellow workers. One of the former strikers who had worked in a different section recalls:

It felt bad to see others being treated like that. I had never experienced anything like this before. Many women had never worked outside before. It feels bad for people who have never worked outside the home to have to do so – it's very hard – then hear things like this. I never experienced any of this [difficulties] because I had my mother at home so I did not have to worry about overtime. That's why, I think, I never had any trouble from the managers. But I walked out on the first day with Jayaben mausi [aunty] because I had decided to support her. We were standing outside when Alden came out and said, 'You haven't got any trouble, I haven't [given] you any trouble, so why you want to walk out?' I said, 'I want to have a union in the company'. He said if I came back, they would give me good money and look after me. But I decided to support the union. (Ilaben)

Another worker reiterated this:

> I walked out in solidarity and for union recognition. If the union
> was to come there, it would have been good for everyone. If we
> had any problem, we could have gone to the union. (Nirmalaben)

In his book *Fort Grunwick*, George Ward (1977, 42) attributed the
support for the walk-out to the 'extraordinary importance of family
and personal ties among the Asian community' and Jayaben's position, which he attributed to her age, and which he said brought her
respect and loyalty from the other workers. Ward thereby negates
any role played by the working conditions at Grunwick for trig-
gering the walk-out and depoliticises the actions of the workers,
many of whom – particularly those at the Cobbold Road premises
– did not in fact experience similar levels of day-to-day disrespect
and the forms of managerial control meted out at the Chapter Road
premises. This representation of collective action by South Asian
workers as personal acts of loyalty rather than as political acts of
collective solidarity based on class, race and a sense of injustice is
a common tactic deployed to undermine their struggle. It was also
used by trade union leadership in the Gate Gourmet dispute some
thirty years later (see Chapter Six).

But it is the case that there was not much evidence of solidarity
from the few non-South Asian workers at Grunwick. Although
Grunwick had employed Irish workers in previous times, they were
gradually replaced by more recent non-white migrants. By the time
of the dispute, the few white workers at Grunwick were more likely
to be employed in office and supervisory roles, which explains their
non-participation in the strike. There were some black (African
Caribbean) workers including the male drivers who later came out
in support, but racial segregation within the workplace prevented
any real or lasting cross-racial solidarity. Instead, the labour process
at Grunwick in fact produced divisions on racial lines. These few
so-called 'West Indian women' were employed exclusively in the
film processing department as the 'machine minders' mentioned
above (Levidow 1981, 145); this was a process requiring less supervi-
sion, and which made for less fraught relations with management.
According to Jayaben, West Indian women were deliberately

excluded from the mail order section, as South Asian women, perceived as docile, submissive and bound by community sanctions, were regarded as safe to be entrusted with the task of processing the cheques and postal orders (*ibid.*). Whether or not this really was the rationale, it was clear that there was ethnic segregation at the Grunwick processing plant.

At the time, George Ward actively contested any suggestion that the Grunwick dispute was triggered by racism, and since then, through court action, he consistently challenged any accusation of racism in relation to his management of the Grunwick firm (Limbrick 2007). Ward cited his multi-ethnic workforce as evidence of his racial inclusiveness and to demonstrate that he did not discriminate against any race in matters of employment (Ward 1977, 30). As Ward and others have frequently pointed out, the ethnicity of the owner of Grunwick meant that he could rightly claim common South Asian heritage with the workers – though it should be remembered that it was the white managers he employed who directly interacted with the workforce. More recent writers, including McGowan (2008, 389) also refute any suggestion that the strike had its origins in racist practices at Grunwick.

However, in these accounts, 'racism' is conceptualised in very narrow terms, specifically understood to mean racial discrimination – exclusion on the basis of race – rather than understanding the structural position of the South Asian women that informed their treatment by management, as Smith argues (2017, 173). At stake here was not just the question of whether potential workers were entirely excluded on grounds of their race, but whether the ways in which their racialised identity was constructed informed both the process by which they were differentially and subordinately incorporated into the labour market. As we discussed earlier, such a narrow view of racism does not take into account the structural processes whereby Gujarati women were actively recruited to Grunwick based on stereotypes about 'cheap workers' and in the context of their limited power in the local labour market, consequently producing or reinforcing disadvantage arising from their race and migration history (Parmar 1982). Such a structural account of race – as it intersects with gender – enables us to understand how the constructions of South Asian women by Grunwick as nimble-fingered ideal workers who are cheap, docile and hardworking can be based on positive stereotypes, but they ultimately limit the options of these categories of workers in the labour market.

Over the two years of the dispute, the Grunwick strikers themselves may have interpreted their struggle as that of workers seeking trade union recognition – they were, after all, seeking to appeal to the broad trade union movement for support in what was a very racist political context of the 1970s – but they were also aware of and articulated their struggles in the UK labour market in the context of their gendered and racialised relegation to particular low-status occupations. As Jayaben shouted out to her fellow workers in Gujarati and in English just prior to walking out:

> My friends, listen to this. What is happening to me today will happen to you tomorrow. This man wouldn't speak to white workers like he speaks to us. (Jayaben, cited in Dromey and Taylor 2016, 40)

These accounts of the ways in which the Grunwick workers experienced the intersection of class, ethnicity, migrant and gendered identities in the context of an increasingly pressured labour process offer some insights into the reasons why the dispute at Grunwick blew up when and how it did. This is not a complete account as we were only able to speak to a limited number of those who had participated in the strike and encountered a wall of silence and hostility when we tried to interview people who had remained in employment at Grunwick. Despite our best efforts, we were also unable to speak to any of the black workers who walked out, and whose presence on the picket line is documented in some of the contemporary film footage of the dispute. By the time of our interviews in 2007-2009, it was difficult for Jayaben Desai and other ex-Grunwick workers to remember the details of the day-to-day experiences before the strike. However, the main themes that emerge from our interviews and other contemporary accounts of the labour process and management strategies deployed at Grunwick in some ways echo the later experiences of humiliation and racist practices that were related to us by the South Asian women workforce in the more recent industrial dispute at Gate Gourmet.

THE WIDENING OF THE GRUNWICK DISPUTE

Responding to the sacking of the workers, Roy Grantham, General Secretary of APEX, gave a speech to the annual conference of the TUC on 6 September 1976, seeking to enlist the support of the trade union movement for the Grunwick strikers, who were protesting against 'a reactionary employer taking advantage of race and employing workers on disgraceful terms and conditions' (Scarman Report 1977, 10), indicating the early recognition of the centrality of race to the exploitative conditions at Grunwick. The response of the TUC, which wrote to its affiliated unions enlisting their support in early October, served to bring a local dispute to the national arena over the coming months. But as the dispute was taken up by the wider trade union movement, issues of race and racism receded in the representation of the causes and aims of the dispute, as is visible in the flyers and banners produced by the organisers; the issue of the right to join trade unions and union representation became the one that rallied the rank and file unionists to the cause.

Once they had walked out, the strikers sought to mobilise further support among those who continued to work. The Grunwick strikers pointed out the differing attitudes between workers from different departments at Grunwick. As we have seen, the strikers were mostly the lower paid women workers from the mail order department as well as other women workers in the Cobbold Road factory and the primarily male students who were temporary workers over the summer months. One of the strikers, Nirmalaben recalled trying to persuade a relative to join the strike:

> He was in the accounts department, and I said to him, 'We are standing out here, why don't you join us?' And he said, 'You and I are different. You are in that department, I am in the office, I'm higher up'. That's what he said. What can you say to that? (Nirmalaben)

The South Asian men who were employed on a permanent basis at Grunwick were more likely to be in better-paid roles, while the women and the temporary summer workers were deployed in the work that was labour intensive, highly seasonal and more heavily

supervised. As he was in a 'skilled' job, able to command a better
pay and better treatment from the management, the male worker
referred to by Nirmalaben did not identify with the everyday struggles that had impelled the low-paid women workers to take action.

As Jayaben recounted above with regard to her husband, the
women we spoke to asserted that walking out was a spontaneous
act of solidarity, after which they had to persuade their families
about the validity of their course of action. They were well aware of
the challenge their actions posed to patriarchal assumptions about
their willingness to publicly protest, as well as class-based norms
about appropriate behaviour in public spaces, which protesting and
shouting slogans would violate. For recent migrants who were from
middle-class backgrounds, such protest would also signal to the
whole community their current status as exploited manual workers.
Support from their families was crucial in enabling women to take
part in or continue strike action.[4]

Jayaben recalled that the women workers often faced a range of
different kinds of constraints from their families:

> Some women had a lot of pressure – they used to be pushed –
> 'Don't go, don't go'. Many stopped attending the pickets as well
> because their families said it was not appropriate that our women
> should be standing on the picket line. What will people say? The
> parents used to put pressure. (Jayaben)

Jayaben and other strikers visited the homes of the women workers
to address any concerns they might have had about taking part in
the strike and to persuade their families to allow them to join, but
she recalled that many young women's parents remained worried
about the shame that participating in such a public protest might
bring on the families. Where women were married, Jayaben found
that it was often their husbands who did not want them to take part
– as her own husband had been initially uncertain. Writing about
the women at the frontline of the pickets, Ann Rossiter (1977, 18)
notes that they risked gossip and disgrace for defying the gendered
norms within their community by taking action which put them in
the public eye. Wilson points out that rather than a homogenous
construction of community tradition as curtailing women's agency,

Jayaben was aware of the role of patriarchal ideology in restricting women, when she reflected:

> I don't think it is traditions which are weighing them down [but that] their husbands don't want them to do anything which is not passive and the women end up believing the same [...] Their lives revolve round dressing up, housework, wearing jewellery and things like that. (Cited in Wilson 1978, 63.)

George Ward was aware of these constraints faced by Gujarati women and tried to use them against the strikers. Wilson (1978, 64) cites Jayaben's account of her encounters with George Ward:

> He would come to the picket line and try to mock us and insult us. One day he said, 'Mrs Desai you can't win in a sari, I want to see you in a mini'. I said, 'Mrs Gandhi wears a sari and she is ruling a vast country. I have my husband behind me and I'll wear what he wants me to.' On my second encounter with Ward, he said, 'Mrs Desai, I'll tell the whole Patel community that you are a loose woman'. I said, 'I'm here with a placard! Look! I am showing all England that you are a bad man. You are only going to tell the Patel community, but I am going to tell all of England.' About one girl, he started spreading the story that she had come out only to join her boyfriend. He did this because he knew that if it got to her parents they would force her to go back in. You see he knows about Indian society and he is using it [...] He knows that Indian women are easily shamed.

It seems that Ward was invoking a domestic code of conduct for ensuring a docile workforce by implying that an Indian woman exposing herself on the streets might be considered shameless, a 'loose woman'. Sharpe (1997) notes how Jayaben's response suggests that gendered identities are more complicated than the manager's reliance on the binary opposition of shame and shamelessness might suggest. She argues that Jayaben speaks from within the language of an Indian patriarchy but without subordinating herself to its hierarchy, in that she responds to the taunts from George Ward by deferring to the authority of her husband but only because he already supports her. Through her response, she invokes patriarchal authority – her husband's sanction – for authorising her 'shameless' or 'loose' behaviour of public protest.

There were other constraints that the striking women encountered after the student workers returned to their studies in the autumn. In the months before the wider trade union movement took up their cause, the women cut a lonely figure on the picket line. During these months they regularly encountered racist rebukes from passers-by, the most common of which were loud shouts of 'Paki!' and 'Go back to Paki-land!'[5] Despite this, they picketed consistently throughout the winter months of 1976-1977, as recorded in the documentaries made at that time by Chris Thomas (1977, 1978).[6]

As Grunwick refused to negotiate, APEX referred the issue of the recognition of the union to Acas, the conciliation service to help employees and employers to resolve workplace problems, as it was entitled to do by Section 11 of the Employment Protection Act 1975. Over the first two months of the dispute, the strikers picketed chemists' shops, seeking to dissuade them from sending their films to Grunwick to develop. They also sought to cut off the main route by which films reached Grunwick's mail-order photo processing business, by seeking solidarity action by postal workers. On 1 November 1976, the members of the Cricklewood branch of the Union of Postal Workers (UPW) refused to handle Grunwick mail, on which the firm depended to reach its client base – which George Ward likened to the cutting the company's jugular vein (Scarman Report 1977, 12). Grunwick, which faced imminent liquidation should the boycott of their mail be successful, sought the support of the right-wing National Association For Freedom (NAFF) which threatened to initiate legal action under the Section 58 of the Post Office Act 1953 by seeking an injunction against the UPW.[7]

Apart from the involvement of NAFF, which proved to be crucial to Grunwick's ability to resist the union through the later months of the dispute, there were other factors which explain the subsequent retreat on the part of APEX. On 4 November 1976, an emergency debate on Grunwick was secured with the support of more than a hundred Conservative MPs in the House of Commons. The motion proposed by John Gorst MP was to discuss 'The action of Post Office workers in failing to deliver mail to Grunwick Processing

Laboratories in contravention of the Post Office Act 1953'.[8] APEX succumbed to the pressure exerted by the then Labour government, and the decision to withdraw the postal boycott was announced in the Parliament by the Minister of Employment, Albert Booth. At a point when victory seemed within grasp, instead of relying on solidarity action by the postal workers, APEX agreed to a compromise to abandon the 'blacking' of the mail in return for what proved to be a shallow promise by Grunwick to co-operate with Acas.

On its part, Grunwick sought to hold on to its remaining workforce by increasing the pay of those who had not joined strike action. In November 1976, Grunwick granted a general wage increase of 15 per cent, with a further 10 per cent rise in April 1977. Holiday and sickness benefits were also improved. The Scarman Report (1977, 16) notes that these changes served to make Grunwick pay and benefits comparable with, and in some respects better than, those paid by other comparable firms in the industry.

As part of its mediation process, Acas sought to survey both the sacked workers and those still working for Grunwick about their opinions on trade union representation. Grunwick refused to co-operate and demanded that Acas only ascertain the opinions of those still working for Grunwick, and not those who had been sacked. Over the winter months, a stalemate was orchestrated by the company who refused to allow Acas access to its current employees, or even to provide a list of their names and addresses. In an effort to undermine the Acas process, on 28 February 1977, Grunwick released the findings of a survey which it had itself carried out, of employees still working in Grunwick, which found that 86.4 per cent were in favour of retaining the status quo (i.e. no union membership or recognition). None of the strikers were part of the survey and the Scarman Report recognises the pressure that the workers might have perceived to respond in the way acceptable to the management (Scarman Report 1977, 13-14).

The Acas report recommending union recognition was published on 10 March 1977, but was rejected by Grunwick, and would remain mired in court action over summer of 1977. But in spring 1977, the claim that had been taken by fifty-nine strikers to the Industrial Tribunal asking for their reinstatement or compensation was also thrown out, as the tribunal held that it had no jurisdiction over the situation.[9]

In the face of these setbacks in 1977, with the summer approaching, the strikers responded with a strategy to escalate their picketing during the company's busy period. Brent Trades Council supported the strikers who undertook a tour around union branches in different parts of the country, addressing fellow trade unionists directly and seeking their support for mass pickets of the Grunwick factory. The rank and file of the different trade unions responded and the tactic of mass picketing, which had been developed during the miners' strike in 1972, was vigorously deployed at Grunwick with support coming from a range of traditionally masculine unions such as the National Union of Miners as well as range of anti-racist and feminist groups. Grunwick became the cause célèbre of the trade union movement.

The mass pickets began on 13 June 1977, with a 'women's day of action' when the police arrested eighty-four picketers, and further arrests continued over the following week. The Yorkshire and Scottish miners joined the picket line later that week (Rogaly 1977, 178), where Arthur Scargill (President of Yorkshire Miners) and Audrey Wise MP were among those arrested. At the height of the mass picketing, on 15 June, the postal workers at the Cricklewood sorting office began to boycott Grunwick mail with support from the UPW's London District Council. The mass pickets, combined with the postal boycott created a period of intense mobilisation and suggested the real possibility of a victory. Growing support from rank and file trade unionists, students, workers, anti-racist and feminist groups as well as political parties on the British left swelled the ranks of the pickets week after week to an estimated 18,000 on a 'National Day of Action Against Grunwick' on 11 July 1977 (Rogaly 1977, 182).[10]

As the dispute intensified, women's role on the picket line came under the glare of the national media day after day. But like women workers everywhere, the sacked women found that the 'second shift' of domestic work (Hochschild 1989) had to be managed alongside their responsibilities on the picket line. For women who travelled to address trade union members across the country, this created particular difficulties. Jayaben indicated that the long hours spent in meetings and the travel meant that the distribution of domestic responsibilities had to be negotiated and her husband supported her by taking on more responsibilities. But of her own accord – perhaps in response to community constructions of the strikers as women who neglected their domestic responsibilities – Jayaben also emphasised that she found a way to manage her domestic responsibilities whilst maintaining a very public role:

> Once a BBC woman came to interview me and she asked my husband what he thought about my role in Grunwick, and he said, 'We did not feel she was involved in such a big strike. We did not miss her at home. We used to get our food on time, everything was done as usual. She used to come and go and manage her time such that we did not realise that it was such a big event.' (Jayaben)

Despite the enormity of the struggle she was engaged in and the challenge she posed to patriarchal norms through her actions, Jayaben's words also invoke her simultaneous adherence to these norms. She affirms her conformity to the gendered responsibility for social reproduction in order to justify her public role, on the basis that she was able to manage the two effectively. Other women who had fewer responsibilities on the picket line also described how they balanced their reproductive work with the time spent protesting:

> I used to get up in the morning and make their packed lunch – sandwiches or whatever – and give everyone their breakfast and then head to the picket. When I came back in the evening, I used to cook the dinner. Everything at home was the same as before. (Lataben)

Jayaben described how the demands on her time increased as the mass pickets gained momentum, and she reiterated the crucial role of the support she received from her husband in enabling her to continue leading the strike:

> I used to go for meetings and come home at 9 p.m. One day we had a call at my house. Someone – the Grunwick boss – must have told his secretary or some girl at the office to call. She said I laugh and am overfamiliar with the men […] But my husband said, 'Shut up, I know my wife better then you do. If such a call comes ever again, I will call the police.' And after that, no such call ever came! (Jayaben)

Aware of the role of South Asian men in policing 'their' women's sexuality, this caller's strategy to invoke these norms to curb Jayaben were ineffective in the face of her husband's support for her.

The Grunwick strike made national news headlines every day, which focused on public disorder, rather than on the politics of the strike. On the first day of the mass picket, which was earmarked as women's day, the police kicked the women who gathered, dragging some women by the hair as they were arrested. By the end of the day police had arrested more than eighty women picketers. Subsequent days of mass picketing saw further aggressive policing and many further arrests. In their coverage of the mass pickets, the media minimised or totally ignored the widely prevalent police violence, overwhelmingly representing the picketers as aggressors. One Grunwick striker, Nirmalaben, recounted her surprise as she watched the evening news about the day's events with her family: 'We used to be surprised – is that what happened yesterday we used to wonder. We were 'amazed' by what they showed. Because we did not see any of that happening.'

There were more than 550 arrests during the strike, which was then more than in any industrial dispute since the General Strike of 1926. The notion of 'company police' took hold among the supporters of the Grunwick strikers, as the police action seemed to be designed to curtail the right to picket. These same aggressive police tactics were subsequently deployed during the 1984-5 Miners' Strike, most notably in the form of the violence inflicted on the striking miners at what came to be known as 'The Battle of Orgreave'. But the Grunwick dispute also marked the first time that the Special Patrol Group (SPG), an elite paramilitary-style squad trained to deal with public disorder and acts of terrorism, was deployed in an industrial dispute. Special Branch files released in 2016 (Hughes 2016) and whistleblower accounts showed that there was extensive surveillance of the strikers and their supporters by the Metropolitan Police undercover unit, the Special Demonstration Squad (SDS) (Evans 2016). These documents reveal that Special Branch was receiving information from regional police forces concerning the plans of demonstrators travelling to London to join the Grunwick pickets, as well as from an undercover officer embedded in left-wing groups that supported the strikers (Evans 2016).[11] Documents released to The National Archives reveal that concerns for the policing of public order at Grunwick reached the highest echelons of British government. The Commissioner of the Metropolitan Police came under increasing pressure to take preventative action against the escalating demonstrations. Notes from a meeting at Chequers on 26 June 1977 suggest that the Prime Minister James Callaghan encouraged the Home Secretary to pressure the Commissioner into adopting a more proactive response to the demonstrations and pickets, mindful of the 'danger of bringing the government down'.[12]

Concerned at the scale of the industrial dispute, the Labour government of the day appointed Lord Scarman to lead a Court of Inquiry on 30 June 1977. Jayaben Desai and another woman worker on the Strike Committee, when they spoke to us, recounted their resistance to the unions' withdrawal from the rank and file tactics that had attracted such support for the pickets and gained visibility for the strikers and their cause. They were concerned that pulling back from the mass pickets would result in a loss of momentum that would be hard to regain. However, they were overruled by their union, which was under pressure from the Labour government, as the subsequent release of documents revealed.

On 10 July, the NAFF launched 'Operation Pony Express' to get Grunwick mail out of London and franked and sent by the Royal Mail, thus circumventing the postal boycott. Though secondary picketing was legal at that time,[13] the UPW leadership threatened the Cricklewood postal workers with expulsion from their union. As they therefore risked losing their jobs, the postal workers voted to call off their action against Grunwick by forty-nine to forty-six votes on 29 July (Dromey and Taylor 2016, 177). The same day, Lord Denning sitting in the Appeal Court overturned the High Court decision that had backed the Acas report. In a third blow to the strikers that day – which came to be known in union literature as the 'black Friday' – the Strike Committee were pressurised by APEX leadership to vote to call off a mass picket planned for 8 August 1977.

THE SCARMAN REPORT AND THE END OF THE DISPUTE

The Scarman report was published on 25 August 1977. It found that the strikers had a genuine sense of grievance on account of the low pay at Grunwick, the arbitrary use of compulsory overtime, the everyday indignities and humiliations inflicted on the work-force, the overbearing management style and the constant threat of dismissal which caused anxiety. It recommended that the company should re-employ those strikers who were full-time employees prior to the strike. It argued that the company had acted within the letter but outside the spirit of the law in dismissing the strikers (Scarman Report 1977, 22), but it did not offer the strikers any method for obtaining the recognition that the findings implied. Jayaben, speaking at a conference on 23 August, just before the report was published, said the strikers had 'drowned in sympathy but thirsted for action' (Barrett 2016). The management at Grunwick refused to accept the findings of the Scarman report.

Prime Minister Jim Callaghan's Labour government had a wafer-thin majority and did not want to be associated with a mili-tant strike that threatened the ideals of the Social Contract, an accord between the TUC and the Labour Party in 1970s Britain whereby the unions would take responsibility for moderating wage claims in return for a redistributive welfare state and legal reforms on collective bargaining. Finding themselves under pressure from the government to rein in the dispute, the TUC insisted that the trajectory of the dispute must be determined by the APEX executive rather than the workers or their Strike Committee, who were calling for a resumption of mass pickets (Forbes 1977).

In the absence of support from the trade union leadership, the strikers found it impossible to revive the militancy of June and July. It was not for want of trying though, and a mass picket on 17 October 1977 attracted 5000 supporters. A further mass picket on 7 November was 8000 strong, but the movement was losing ground. In the context of this wrangling between the APEX leader-ship and the Strike Committee, the final episode of the Grunwick strike took place on the steps of the TUC, as it was the umbrella organisation for trade unions in Britain. The strikers' plan was to persuade the TUC to use its influence to interrupt essential services to Grunwick, such as electricity, water and gas. On 21 November, Jayaben Desai, Yasu Patel, Vipin Magdani and Johnny Patel launched a hunger strike outside the TUC headquarters to shame them into action. As Jayaben, by far the most prominent of the members of the Strike Committee, later put it, support from the

TUC 'is like honey on your elbow: you can smell it, you can see it, but you can never taste it!'[14]

But the TUC took no notice. As the four, backed by the chair and secretary of the Strike Committee, Kamlesh Gandhi and Mahmoud Ahmed, had taken this action in defiance of their union, APEX suspended all six of them from union membership. Those strikers who had tried for fifteen months to recruit members to a trade union were now cast out themselves, leaving them feeling abandoned by the trade union movement. In an interview with Women against Racism and Fascism (WARF) at the end of the hunger strike, Jayaben said:

> Oh they talk! They make rules and regulations. We can't make any hunger strike, can't make any demonstration, can't make any mass picket, can't do anything. Now it means they are going to tie the workers' hands and we will have no chance to do anything. (Jayaben, cited in Sivanandan 1977b, 292)

On 14 December 1977, the House of Lords confirmed an earlier decision made by the Appeal Court against the implementation of the Acas report, thus closing the last procedural route that remained for the sacked workers. Not only did the bureaucratic procedures, such as mediation through Acas and the Scarman Court of Inquiry, have no legal teeth, they also served to curtail the momentum built up by the rather more effective secondary action by the postal workers and the mass picketing. The trade union leadership viewed the collective action emerging from the rank and file support as out of control and unmanageable. In the WARF interview, Jayaben argued that the trade union leadership had not served the workers well, even though they had managed to mobilise a range of trade unionist workers in an unprecedented show of solidarity:

> The union views itself like management. There's no democracy there. Its own strikers have no right to do anything. The union says we have to accept everything they say. We are the real fighters – the ones who came out of the company to fight for our rights. But the union just looks on us as if we are employed by them. They have done the same thing to us as Ward did – they have suspended us. And now we have to fight to be reinstated in the

union and then also to be reinstated in the company. (Jayaben, cited in Sivanandan 1977b, 293)

Over the following months, there was little by way of picketing, nor was much progress made towards meeting the strikers' demands. At the final meeting of the Strike Committee, where the strikers conceded defeat, Jayaben told them that they should be proud as 'We have shown that workers like us, new to these shores, will never accept being treated without dignity and respect' (Firmin 2011). In the end, the strike was abandoned on 14 July 1978, without any of the strikers' demands being met.

REMEMBERING GRUNWICK

After the dispute, the sacked Grunwick workers managed to secure jobs with relative ease because of their youth and the nature of the labour market in North London in the late 1970s – quite different to the present day. But by the time of our interviews, the former strikers recounted mixed feelings about the impact of the strike:

> Because of us, the people who stayed in Grunwick got a much better deal. When the factory moved, the van used to come to their home and pick them up because it was difficult for them to get to the new place. Can you imagine that?! And they get pension today! And we get nothing. That was because of us, because of our struggle. (Nirmalaben)

Others talked about the impact taking part in the dispute – which was in the early years of their entry into the UK labour market – had on them as workers. For most women, their subsequent work was in similar low-paid assembly work in factories. However, they recounted the difference that Grunwick made to their sense of self at work and in the community:

> I: I felt great that I can do something. I was no longer scared.

> Q: Scared of what?

> I: Of our community. Of what people will say – 'Look at what

she is doing!' I was initially also scared that I would get 'black-listed' for participating in a strike and that no one would give me a job again. But later I was no longer scared. I had become completely confident – I was able to talk to anyone and say what I needed to say. I got 'guts'. That was it. (Ilaben)

One woman reflected on how their actions had challenged prevailing stereotypes of South Asian women as passive and unversed in trade unionism, beliefs that some women themselves might have come to accept prior to their participation in Grunwick:

It made employers think that these people know how to stand up and fight. It made the women who were involved in it stronger – they could do the things that previously they thought only men could do – you know, like they'd say that women don't know what a strike is! [Laughs.] Now they knew, and they had done it! (Naliniben)

Despite the ultimate failure of the struggle to achieve its initial aims, most of the women from Grunwick also recounted positive feelings about the transformative potential of their agency, feelings of solidarity and of friendships forged on the picket line.

N: It was amazing […] I was completely astonished that so many people turned up to support us. Happiness bubbled up from within – human faces everywhere!

L: We never imagined we would get such support. And look at us now! She [Nirmalaben] has become my 'best friend'! Whenever one of our families go away for a holiday, we call the other to our house and we stay together for a few days. We have fun then!

N: And we stay up chatting! (Nirmalaben amd Lataben)

When they looked back at their experiences at work, the women we spoke to assessed the impact of their actions on their subsequent lives and their identities. As discussed, gendered and culture-specific notions of shame within the community were part of the ways in which women workers at Grunwick were controlled and were deterred from taking part in the pickets. Women, too, often worked with these notions to argue that they had been treated with disrespect and to explain their actions (Dromey and Taylor 2016; Sharpe 1997; Wilson 1978, 57-65). Although other commentators have noted the gendered, racialised dimensions of shame (Parmar 1982; Sharpe 1997; Wilson 1978), what has been less well explored is the role that class position plays in women's perception of it.

While all the Grunwick strikers we spoke to recounted their participation in the dispute with pride, one worker recollected feeling ashamed during particular aspects of picketing – collecting donations.

N: This was the first time I addressed meetings, collected funds [pauses] and to tell you the truth, I felt shame!

Q: Why shame?

N: Because we had to go to the public and ask for money. When we did the picketing people gave in front of us, but who knows what they said behind our backs? We had never done such a thing before – spread our hands in front of strangers for money. (Naliniben)

Naliniben's sense of shame arose because participating in the Grunwick dispute and asking for donations was a public acknowledgement of her class dislocation – she felt that she had moved from being a member of a class that gave donations, to one that had to spread their hands to ask for them.

Another Grunwick striker went on to recall the positive impact that participating in the struggle had on her subsequent working life and explained that it had enabled her to challenge exploitative conditions wherever she encountered them:

I later worked for eleven years for this company which used to make security alarms. There was no union at that place. One evening, they called us to their office and told us that they were making us redundant and that we should not come the next day. I was completely shocked. The company did not give us any notice – they slapped on the redundancy, just like that! I felt very depressed for a while, then I told my friends who were made redundant with me that I wanted to get advice from Citizens Advice Bureau (CAB). My husband used to say that nothing would come out of it, but I insisted, so my family supported me. Most of the other sacked workers were scared that they would get a bad name. So only three of us went to the CAB. They helped me fight a case against the company, which went on for two years and when the decision went against us, we appealed to the High Court and we won! It was because of Grunwick that I knew what to do, I was able to do it. In my last job before I retired too, the wages were very low and I called the union and got the workers to join – the bosses were not happy! Now I hear from my friends that a lot of the women there are in the union and whenever new people start work there, they join the union straightaway. It feels good to know that I have fought and won. (Ilaben)

Jayaben Desai has now become an iconic figure in her community and beyond (Manzoor 2010); her voice has been taken to represent all the striking women, and with some representations suggesting that she had exceptional agency, for a South Asian woman. Jayaben herself was all too aware of this construction of her as an icon and as an unusual South Asian woman, and she frequently sought to dispel it. She recounted a question from a journalist:

She asked me a question that her husband had posed – given that Indian women were 'suppressed', how did I manage to lead the strike? I replied, 'Tell your husband to go and read about Indian history. There is a Margaret Thatcher here now, we had an Indira Gandhi long before. We had strong women like that throughout the ages. During the British rule, we had the Rani of Jhansi, who rode into battle against the British with a sword in her hand and her infant son strapped to her back! You have not heard about them', I said. (Jayaben)

Aware of how Jayaben has been regularly approached by the media to retell the story of Grunwick and her role in it, and how repeated telling of narratives can burnish them into smooth and seamless accounts, this research documented the recollections of four strikers in addition to Jayaben's. These women had not been part of, nor were they aware of, the celebratory accounts of Grunwick that were subsequently constructed by the trade unions (Dromey and Taylor 2016; Rogaly). Our interview was the first time one of them reflected on the historical significance of her actions. She recounted how she had first told her grandchild about this part of her life that very morning:

> My little grandson, he has been very excited all morning – that it's the day of my interview! I told him all about it and he was surprised. [...] He feels very proud of me that I did such thing in my life. 'You!' he says – 'I can't believe you went on strike, grandma!' (Lataben)

Her grandson went on to undertake a school project on Grunwick.

Writing about South Asian Americans, Narayan (2004) argues that the transmission of stories in the diaspora is an important link to a South Asian past and identity formation. Family history is an important theme in these gendered accounts of pioneer (male) migrants overcoming adversity (Herbert 2009; Narayan 2004). This Grunwick striker's 'surprising' narrative about her agency contributed towards writing an alternative story that foregrounds South Asian women workers' struggles for their rights.

But for the Grunwick workers who had regained their middle-class family positions over the last thirty years, the reconstructions of their actions on the picket line were also laden with memories of their class dislocation that the strike invoked. McDowell et al. (2007) argue that the construction of people's identities reflects the time, place and context in which those identities were formed. Class position, as well as other aspects of identity, changes as they move across space as well as through an individual's own life-course, and the changing political landscape that they inhabit. So the ways in which individuals and groups construct a sense of themselves relates both to previous experiences and to their current structural locations. These women's narratives reveal the manner in which their migration histories, and their gendered and classed locations within the labour market have informed their agency at work, as well as their memories and reconstructions of their actions.

CONCLUSION: THE LEGACY OF GRUNWICK

The Grunwick workers resorted to collective action as the result of cumulative experience of injustice. This was based in a large part on the discordance between their perceptions of themselves and their identities as women and as workers – as formed by their experience of migration and their class dislocation – and their experiences of indignities, overt racist or discriminatory practices. It is only by understanding their location at the intersection of gender, race and class, and in the context of their histories of migration and settlement, that we can understand their agency and their perceptions about their actions, as well as their inspiring and sometimes contradictory constructions of these actions.

Though the strike ended without having obtained its goals, leaving the women feeling abandoned and disillusioned with the trade union movement, Grunwick is celebrated as a turning point in the UK's labour history that signals the inclusion of black, minority and women workers within the trade union movement. Based on accounts by women who participated in the dispute, as well as the wider historical accounts, this chapter has sought to reconstruct the events of that summer when trade unionists, ordinary workers, students, feminist and anti-racist campaigners converged on the narrow streets of Willesden to voice their solidarity with a small group of migrant women workers. However, this chapter has demonstrated that while the dominant narrative of the dispute has been written and claimed by the trade union movement, a more complex, critical and somewhat contradictory account emerges when we pay attention to the recollections of the women workers who went on strike at Grunwick.

The Grunwick dispute, which has since assumed an iconic status in British labour history, reflected the circumstances of the 1970s, a particular moment in British Labour history characterised by mass solidarity action during the heyday of industrial militancy. Grunwick marked a departure, in that this solidarity was in support of South Asian women workers who were recent migrants, in a period characterised by a rising tide of racism and anti-immigrant sentiment. Satnam Virdee locates the significance of the dispute in the context of 'the depth of racist sentiment within the British working class' in the 1970s, which he argues socialist opinions at the time had greatly underestimated (Virdee 2014, 128). This racist sentiment is evident in the industrial disputes at Mansfield Hosiery Mills factory and in the Imperial Typewriters strike in the early 1970s, where white trade union members worked with the employers to deny South Asian workers support in their fight for an end to pay, bonus and promotion differentials based on race. In relation to the Mansfield Hosiery strike, the Race Relations Board found that the union 'connived with management to prevent Indian workers' advancement in training' (Smith 2018: 148) and the defeat of the Imperial Typewriters strike demonstrated the unwillingness of trade unions to represent their black members or to acknowledge the discrimination they faced in their everyday working lives because of their race (Dhondy 1974; Race Today 1974).

Virdee argues that the Grunwick dispute was one of the key events and episodes through which the development of the anti-racist standpoint can be charted within one key strand of the trade union movement, resulting in the formation of an anti-fascist, anti-racist, working-class politics (Virdee 2014, 124). For instance, he notes the significance of the presence on the Grunwick picket line of the London Dockers, who carried the Royal Docks Shop Stewards' banner at the head of the mass picket (Virdee 2014, 133), given that about a decade previously, members of the same union had marched to the Houses of Parliament in support of Enoch Powell's 'rivers of blood' speech, demanding an end to black immigration. He attributes the solidarity displayed by rank and file trade unionists during Grunwick to a shift 'from being attached to a narrow understanding of class that nested within dominant conceptions of race and nation […] towards a more inclusive language of class that could now also encompass racialised minority workers' (Virdee 2014, 135). In Virdee's analysis of the significance of both racism and anti-racism in the making of the English working class, Grunwick 'crystallised […] how, in the space of less than a decade, parts of the working class had undergone a dramatic, organic transformation in their political consciousness'. The 'language of class' of socialist activists, which had previously 'nested neatly within dominant conceptions of race and nation', had come to 'encompass racialised minority workers', although the convergence between the white left and ethnic minority workers diverged again soon after (Virdee 2014, 135).

Virdee argues that although Grunwick ended in a defeat, the significant and enduring legacy of this dispute was the public perception of what had happened:

> A generation of black migrant workers saw the British trade union movement support a group of Asian women workers in what would appear to be a small and strategically relatively unimportant industry. A generation of white workers also saw a group of Asian women at the forefront of a ferocious industrial dispute. (Virdee 2000, 555)

Virdee suggests that the solidarity displayed at Grunwick marked a significant change in the consciousness and perceptions of both black and white workers, and was a very 'visible manifestation of rank and file, inter-racial, working-class solidarity' (ibid.).

Against this extraordinary mobilisation of support from the rank and file unionists and the support of trade union leadership in the early stages of the dispute stands the failure of this leadership in truly incorporating the interests and the issues faced by the South Asian workers at Grunwick. Over the course of the dispute the union leadership clashed with the strikers as it sought to control the trajectory of the dispute and the actions of the workers themselves. As the dispute gained national media attention, the bureaucratic structures of the TUC responded to the pressure by prioritising their own relations with the government as well as being mindful of trade unions' role in preserving the Social Contract. The trade union let down the women workers through its reliance on procedure and in failing to forge ahead on the strength of the support that it had helped build for the strikers.

The Grunwick dispute also went a long way towards challenging the dominant representation of South Asian women as passive victims, constrained to the domestic sphere by the patriarchal norms of their community. While South Asian women had taken part in many industrial disputes before and since Grunwick, this dispute received unprecedented media attention as it appeared on the front pages and as the headline news over several weeks – though often framed as a 'law and order' issue because of the numerous arrests during certain phases of picketing. Stereotypical representations of the South Asian woman were most famously dislocated by the images of them arguing furiously with the police, pushing back against police ranks and walking defiantly between surging crowds. These images continue to be important representations of South Asian women in the UK.

The prioritisation of Jayaben Desai as the icon of the Grunwick dispute was central to its representation (McDowell et al. 2012). As the strike leader, she was pictured in the media walking between the serried ranks of police on the packed streets of Willesden. Her achievements are indeed significant. However, constructing Jayaben and Grunwick as exceptional also reinscribes the stereotypes of other South Asian women workers as passive, confined to the domestic sphere and lacking agency, despite the challenge to this narrative that the Grunwick dispute poses. Focussing on an iconic figure and on exceptional lives also serves to individualise collective struggles and to obscure the long and active role played by women of South Asian origin in the UK labour movement as they challenged racism and sexism within their workplaces, demanded the dignity that was seldom accorded to migrant workers in the low-status jobs that were available to them, and challenged trade unions to better represent black and women workers.

The phrase frequently used by the media – 'strikers in saris' – for the Grunwick and other subsequent striking women of South Asian origin suggests a continuing surprise at their militant agency. Strike after strike seems to fail to disrupt this narrative. What was exceptional about Grunwick was not just the agency of South Asian women workers in acting to defend their rights – after all, women of South Asian origin had taken part in many such disputes before and since – but that, for a brief moment, white working class people in the UK saw that they shared a common cause with migrant women workers and they mobilised to support workers facing exploitation and indignities on grounds of their gender, race and class.

However this was a brief moment. Despite the extent and significance of the support for the Grunwick strikers, subsequent events challenge any certainty that the Grunwick dispute marked a permanent internalisation of issues of race and gender among trade union leadership as well as the white rank and file members. As the following chapter demonstrates, the efforts of another group of South Asian women workers in defending their jobs at Gate Gourmet some three decades after Grunwick did not evince widespread support either from white union members or from the leadership of the trade union movement. Rather it can be argued, they endured another betrayal by their union, albeit in a very different political, economic and regulatory context.

NOTES

1. Taken from the Minutes of Proceedings of the Court of Enquiry on 5 July 1977, from the Shorthand Notes of W.B. Gurney & Sons (photocopy from the Warwick University Contemporary Records Centre).
2. APEX report on pay and conditions at Grunwick Processing Laboratories 1976; Warwick Archives.
3. Dromey and Taylor (2016, 34) note that the Political and Economic Planning (PEP) Report of 1974 showed that of all the immigrant groups in Britain the East African Asians had the highest qualifications and education but the lowest average earnings. They were mainly from middle-class backgrounds, but were forced into situations in which their only option was to do unskilled or semi-skilled work.
4. Accounts from the strikers suggest that a few women who walked out that first day lacked such support and had to report back to work. Despite our efforts we were not able to interview these women.
5. This is according to Graham Taylor, addressing the Grunwick 40 conference (Taylor, 2016).
6. See the two documentaries by Chris Thomas, *Stand Together*, UK (for Newsreel Collective) and *Look Back at Grunwick*, (for Newsreel Collective), which were filmed during and immediately following the Grunwick dispute (Thomas 1977, 1978).
7. NAFF threatened to bring legal action on the basis of the Post Office Act 1953, which stated that any officer of the Post Office who 'wilfully fails to handle mail' will be guilty of misdemeanour.
8. The full text of the debate is available at HC (1996).
9. Case numbers 40224/76/C and 40282/76/C, 2 March 1977.
10. A de-classified report from the Special Branch, estimated that some 30,000 participants were gathered at different points around the Grunwick site on that day of action (Special Branch 'Story', n.d.).
11. See Grunwick Dispute – Files overview, Special Branch Files project (Special Branch 'Overview', n.d.).
12. Notes from a meeting between the Prime Minister and ministers, 26 June 1977, 3, Available on: www.documentcloud.org/documents/2746963-PREM-16-1491-46.html#document/p3/a281793 (Accessed 29 November 2016.)

13. In the first of a series of anti-trade union legislation introduced by the Thatcher government, secondary picketing was restricted in The Employment Act of 1980.

14. Quoted in a 1977 *Socialist Worker* pamphlet entitled 'Grunwick', Modern Records Centre, University of Warwick, archive document reference 464/36, p. 16 and in several newspaper articles over the years.

CHAPTER 6

'You have to fight for your rights' [...] No one gives them to you on a plate': The Gate Gourmet dispute

Almost thirty years after the Grunwick strike, another bitterly fought dispute involving South Asian women workers erupted at Heathrow, at airline catering company Gate Gourmet, that for a time grounded British Airways (BA) planes. These striking women were part of a long-established diasporic community, and they had partly been attracted to this part of West London by the growing demand for labour in airport-related services. The women were part of the Punjabi community that had arrived from the 1960s to the 1980s, and many had been young brides or daughters of migrant families, typically from rural backgrounds. Although educated to secondary level, they reported that they were able to speak little English on arrival, and had to settle for unskilled work, with low pay and prospects. Even though they had moved jobs frequently in search of better pay and conditions, and in response to changing labour demand, they had always been restricted to low-skilled and low-paid jobs within a very local area, which explains their (often) long employment history at Heathrow, not only in food processing but also in airline cleaning and other similar occupations. The occupational position of the South Asian women workers involved in the Gate Gourmet dispute had changed little over the previous three decades, in spite of changes in the labour market conditions and in union legislation over the same period. Many of these South Asian employees of Gate Gourmet had participated in the slow incorporation of minority women into unions in the UK, which had been particularly marked within the public sector, and were therefore long-standing members of TGWU at the time of the dispute in 2005.

Gate Gourmet was originally established as a Swissair subsidiary in 1992. It grew into a global concern, taking over other catering firms including BA Catering in 1997, as BA, along with other carriers, outsourced their non-core services. By 2001, Gate Gourmet employed over 32,000 people in 34 countries (Flying Pickets 2007). The rise of the 'budget airlines' in the mid to late 1990s was premised on cutting costs and services, which included reduced or non-existent in-flight catering. Following a decline in the company's fortunes, Gate Gourmet was sold to Texas Pacific Finance Group in 2002, which restructured its debt and disposed of it in 2007.[1] It would appear that Gate Gourmet had been involved in negotiations about restructuring with TGWU for at least two years before this dispute in the Heathrow South premises (Box 2005).[2]

But the events at Gate Gourmet that took place in the wake of these changes followed a different trajectory to the Grunwick strike of thirty years earlier (Anitha et al. 2018). As we have seen, Grunwick is remembered as a turning point in British labour history, a moment that marked the beginning of a process of recognition of black and women workers' needs by trade unions and the beginning of the incorporation of race as well as gender within the conceptualisation of a British working class. However, the Gate Gourmet dispute, ongoing at the time of the thirtieth anniversary celebrations of Grunwick by trade unions, was swiftly forgotten – by the media, the members of the local community and the trade unions. Yet, despite the very different profiles of the two disputes, the very different contexts in which they unfolded, and the different migration histories and ethnicities of the South Asian women involved, there remain many similarities in terms of the nature of the workplace coercion the women experienced, as well as in the ineffectiveness of trade unions in maintaining their support for South Asian women's struggle for their rights. A close examination of the Gate Gourmet dispute enables us to consider the changes and continuities in South Asian women's position in the UK labour market.

NATURE AND FORMS OF WORKPLACE COERCION AT GATE GOURMET

At the time of the dispute, the majority of the Gate Gourmet workers were older women of South Asian origin – primarily direct migrants from Punjab plus a few twice-migrants from Gujarat – who had worked at Gate Gourmet for a considerable length of time. Apart from one Gujarati and one Punjabi woman from East Africa, all the twenty-seven Gate Gourmet workers we interviewed were direct migrants from Punjab. For most of these women, their jobs at Gate Gourmet followed a working life that had involved working in a variety of jobs in both the public and private sector, as they negotiated their way through a changing labour market. Many anticipated that this would be their last job before they retired.

Most of the women had fond memories of their early years at Gate Gourmet, though some offered more ambivalent accounts about working there, particularly in relation to the constraints they faced in particular departments. While work in the washing-up department was generally felt to be demeaning as it entailed handling people's left-over food, those working there also pointed out that the working environment was warmer than in the 'tray-set' section, where the workers assembled food in low temperatures. Though engaged in manual work that was considered unskilled, the women took pride in their work and the skills required to carry it out properly; they felt a sense of responsibility for the tasks allocated to them, recalling how they would work often beyond their shift if a need arose, and were committed to performing their work to the highest standards even though they were obliged to keep up with the fast-pace at the conveyer belt:

> When we assembled dishes, we didn't just throw things in, our work was 'artistic'. It was not just that we chucked it in, we were making a shape. We had high standards. (Kiran)

For a few women who had studied to degree level whilst still in India, talking about their work at Gate Gourmet was also laced with bitterness and they saw it as a reminder of how their aspirations for a better job had come to nothing because manual work was all they could secure in London's labour market. Most women who worked at Gate Gourmet were from low-income families who struggled to make ends meet, even though the families were predominantly homeowners.

A small minority of the women who spoke to us did enjoy a comfortable middle-class existence and perceived their wages as 'an extra' for their families and for themselves. For these women, their working lives were incongruent with their life outside work:

> If I had studied then, I would have had a better job, things would have been different now. I would have been a different person, I would have had more confidence in myself. I would not have been at Gate Gourmet. Instead of raising myself upwards, I lowered myself when I came here. In that catering industry, the people were mostly from villages. The way they speak is different. My language changed and became, like, rural. My brother, he said to me, 'We educated you for twenty-one years, and you have lost all that'. (Leena)

Like most of the women, those who were ambivalent about certain aspects of their working lives at Gate Gourmet still presented positive accounts of their time working for the company when it was still part of BA:

> When the BA managers were there, they understood our problems. Like, if we needed a day off to do something and we could not get that, they would move things around, try their best to switch days with someone. If we were working on the belt, and we needed something, they would reach out and pass it over to you. If you really needed to go to the toilet while the belt was moving, they would let you, sometimes they would even cover for you for four-five minutes till you got back. But all that changed. (Sukhwant)

Following the outsourcing of the company from BA to Gate Gourmet in 1997 and particularly after the subsequent loss of the Virgin Atlantic contract in March 2005, the workers experienced an intensification of the work process imposed by the new management in order to reduce costs. There were continuous initiatives to introduce new working practices aimed at speeding up the throughput of meal packs in the assembly process, which met with sustained resistance from the exclusively female and predominantly South Asian workers in this section (Pearson et al. 2010). The union (TGWU) had, with limited success, attempted to moderate proposed changes in pay and conditions. But behind these bare facts, a similar intersection of issues raised in the analysis of the Grunwick walk-out are apparent in Gate Gourmet as well.

Changes in the labour process, the concomitant changes in the management style, and the response of the company to increasing competition and changes in the market environment demanded a labour force that was required to be increasingly flexible, and ultimately disposable (Wright 2006). Where, in the 1970s, recent South Asian women migrants comprised the most flexible labour force for Grunwick, Gate Gourmet's unionised South Asian women workers, who had substantial work experience, became an increasingly less flexible workforce and thus increasingly undesirable to the employer. The working conditions and management practices perceptibly worsened as time went on, and the company failed to replace workers who left with new ones, intensifying the work for everyone:

> They started trying to cut staff numbers by not replacing people who left. The work would obviously fall behind. We all had things to do. It was not that we were sitting there, hands on our lap, were we? But they were trying to squeeze work out of us, like you squeeze blood out of meat. (Kulvinder)

The Gate Gourmet management tried to speed up the pace of work by introducing a hierarchical structure, but the workers were unaccustomed to this. The changes introduced to increase the workers' productivity and maximise the time they spent on the production line, were implemented by newly appointed managers. In a context where the workers in certain departments were used to tea breaks as well as a lunchbreak in the middle of the day, to help them offset the cold temperatures in which they worked, changes to this system were perceived as particularly oppressive and unreasonable:

> They wanted to change the conditions at work. Like the breaks. It was just a ten minute break, not even enough to drink a cup of tea properly. Just enough time to go to the toilet, relax for a few minutes. This is the break they wanted to take away. That break was needed because it was so cold at work, we needed it to relax our bodies. You had to bend down in the cold, stretch to get

things, obviously it will have an effect on your body. Look at the
women today, so many of them have arthritis and pain in their
joints and back. That's what you needed the break for, to stretch
yourself, ease your aching muscles. (Kulvinder)

Other changes included attempts to re-categorise the time spent
changing into/out of work clothes as outside working hours, thereby
seeking to reduce the time calculated for the workers' hourly wages
by about twenty minutes. These efforts were successfully resisted
by their union. Then the management introduced a zero tolerance
policy concerning clocking in, with penalties attached to it, which
the workers were also particularly aggrieved by:

They started the clock card system – you had to clock in at exactly
the minute you came in. If you came in even a few minutes late,
they used to catch you out. If you were a minute more than three
minutes late, they would dock fifteen minutes wages. But even
then, there was favouritism, and some people got away with it.
And that created tensions with those who did not [get away with
it]. And they used to give us just three minutes to change into
work clothes. (Leena)

The workers also resented the increasing, and in their view unneces-
sary, strictness about finishing shifts:

Even the change-over times. You know how you mill around
when a shift ends. You had five minutes to wash hands, get yourself sorted. You [previously] had a target for the day's work, and
if you met that, it might mean that you had a few extra minutes
at the end of the day. But now, if you exceeded your target, they
always found more work for you till the last minute. (Harjot)

Another issue was the reduction in the training given when there
were changes in the kind of work required or when new employees
were recruited:

Earlier, when we did new work, you got proper training. Like a
week's training for some things. Or let's say there was this work,

and you got training for it, you were given more time to do it the first day, and slowly, in a week, you were expected to work at par with those who had been in that job for a while. But now at Gate Gourmet, you got a little time one day, and the next day you had to work with someone and start doing the full job straight away. (Harjot)

The strategy deployed at Gate Gourmet was remarkably similar to that at Grunwick, where managers pressurised the women workers and played upon their sense of insecurity and fear of losing their job to extract the maximum productivity from them. They used techniques such as displaying a list of 'good workers', and other similar strategies, which were management tools long established in assembly lines employing women worldwide (Grossman 1979).

They used to warn us not to stand still chatting – keep your hands working while you talk, they used to say […] Work more, work more, that's how it was […] They used to put photographs up saying this is a 'good worker'. So some women used to try to outdo the others to become a 'good worker'. (Meeta)

These changes in the labour process were part of a long term strategy to reduce costs, but at the same time they reduced the autonomy of the workers, who resented them not just because of the speed-up of production, but also because of it took no account of their working experience and it degraded their skills on the production line. The workers took exception to the escalation in managerial control that amounted to what they perceived was 'rudeness' or lack of respect for the women as individuals and as competent workers:

There was a lot of pressure to work hard. The managers had no respect for you, they used to talk rudely, and the shop steward never listened to us either. (Rajdeep)

The workers recalled that when BA was their direct employer they had enjoyed holiday entitlements, sick pay, overtime and job security, but in the months before the dispute broke out, the hiring of new workers, or any renewal of existing contracts was invariably on the basis of new and less beneficial terms and conditions. The workers felt that their union had not thrown its full weight behind resisting these changes. Eventually, when the company tried to alter the pay and entitlements of the longstanding workers, they responded with an escalation in their resistance, in spite of efforts by the union to reach an agreement on these changes:

> Then they started telling us that the company was losing money, so our wages should go down. We had heard of wages going up, but never of wages that go down! The price of food, of everything else is going up. So why should we accept a cut in wages? Like sick pay – they wanted to bring a rule that you could only take five days off sick in one year – but you can be sick any time. It is not that you will check out the calendar before becoming sick. The union balloted two-three times, but we rejected the changes. (Rajdeep)

Apart from increasing productivity and reducing costs, other mechanisms of managerial control were also implemented that were particularly resented as they represented attempts to alter the culture of the workplace. Workers reported that the managers started trying to regulate the mode of worker's communication with each other, frowning upon those who spoke to each other in Punjabi and stopping the workers from listening to Punjabi programmes on the radio:

> We used to have the music on while we worked there and when Gate Gourmet took over, we continued with that. It was not like we were just listening to the music, but it provided the background against which our hands moved to do the work. But when the new managers came, what can I say? It was like, they were jealous of us, of us Asians working like that, making the work 'atmosphere' that way. So they stopped the music. (Kulvinder)

The women perceived the banning of South Asian radio programmes as an attack on their collective identity and belonging which was bound up with a sense of shared linguistic and cultural sense of self.

Women used various mechanisms to resist these changes to the conditions and culture at work and to their salary and entitlements, with or without the support of their trade union representatives.

These included 'work to rule', wherein workers strictly limited their work to their required hours and duties.

It [work to rule] happened three times in six months. First time was when they said they did not want to give us fifteen minutes to change and report for work – they said we would have to do all that in our own time. So our women, they carried on working according to the rules, you know what I mean? But those who had put down their names for overtime withdrew saying they could not do it anymore and it went on like this for three days. The floor manager, he had been on his holidays at that time, he flew back straight on a Sunday and landed on the shop floor! […] He backtracked and said, 'If you need the fifteen minutes to change, that's OK by me. Please don't delay the Concorde, if the Concorde gets delayed, I will lose thousands of pounds.' (Jasminder)

Another incident took place shortly before the dispute erupted in August 2005:

They moved this young man from his usual place without any explanation, and they did this again. He got cross and asked the manager why he was being shunted around, and some angry words were exchanged. The manager said, then and there, 'You give me your card, I am sacking you'. Now he was going off on holiday the very next day for a month and was not sure if he would have a job to come back to. So he spoke to the shop steward who assured him that they would sort it out when he came back. How can that be? The matter was hot that day, and in a month's time, things would have cooled down, moved on. That would have been the end of it. He phoned everyone – we all have our mobiles on us. So the word spread everywhere. There was no way they would listen to him when he came back from his holiday. And if the union was not ready to do anything now, what would make them act in a month's time? So we took action ourselves. The word spread like a wildfire, and within ten minutes all the workers were assembled in the canteen. The shop steward was pretty shaken up. Within ten minutes, the entire management

turned up and they apologised for the behaviour of that manager
and they told us they were reinstating the sacked worker right
there. So if there was anything, I'm not saying we left work and
marched off every time, but we used to, whenever needed, handle
things ourselves. We did not bother so much with the shop stewards. (Kulvinder)

Such informal mechanisms of collective bargaining are part of
the general repertoire of action available to trade union members,
and are not new. At Gate Gourmet, the women workers who were
informally accepted as 'leaders' frequently initiated such action and
received the backing of other women workers in their unit, often
without recourse to their official union representatives – the shop
stewards – who were mostly men. The workers had a strong sense
of collective solidarity and an established culture of industrial militancy at work, as Kulvinder recalled, 'Some managers used to say
that it's the workers who run the show here'.

GENDER, GENERATION AND ETHNICITY AT GATE GOURMET

In our interviews, the ways in which the Gate Gourmet workers
related the salience of their ethnic origin and their migration experience to their militant protest – against what they saw as unfair
dismissal in contradiction to their rights as workers – was complex.
According to our interviewees, and as documented in other studies
(for example, Dhindsa 1998), these women came from households
in their countries of origin wherein two or three generations cohab-
ited, and for many, there were servants to share the domestic work;
certainly, they had never experienced outside wage labour under
non-family management. When they migrated to the UK, they
were isolated from their peers, were often in nuclear or vertically
extended families, rather than in multi-generational households
and had to manage housework and childcare on their own. As
we have seen, waged work offered an escape from this isolation
– as well as an opportunity to contribute earnings to the household budget and to gain some control over their own finances (see
Westwood 1984; Whitehead 1981). The camaraderie at work was

fondly remembered by several women who compared working at Gate Gourmet to going to college with friends and attending a family wedding.

R: We used to be happy there. You know how a wedding day goes by with all of you talking and working together? That's how it used to be. As if you had come to a family wedding!

Q: Others have said this as well.

R: The women who work at Heathrow are mostly Punjabi, as you will see. We used to be together as a 'group'. (Rajdeep)

The following comment, typical of many, reflects the positive aspects of working in a place where there were women from similar backgrounds, echoing other research on women workers (Holgate et al. 2006):

There were mostly our women there. Four or five women would work together, chatting, laughing and that's how we did it! It was fun. I have changed so many jobs, but I was happy there. I told myself that this is going to be my last job. I did not want to leave that place. It was like one large family. (Raminder)

It was in terms of the relationship with supervisors and managers, rather than with co-workers, that negative experiences of racialised hierarchies in the UK were expressed:

This manager at Gate Gourmet once invited some of the workers for a meal. But there he began to say some things that were completely out of order. Like, you know, that wages in India are much lower, that we must be used to those kind of wages, that we could have such and such a life if we went back with our pounds, and things like that. (Kulvinder)

One worker identified some workers' compliant responses to the intensification of work as an aspect of their gendered and racialised incorporation into the labour market. She suggested that the fear of losing their jobs led them to accommodate adverse changes to working conditions that other categories of workers would perhaps not have tolerated:

> They increased the speed at which the belt moved, and where there were earlier three women doing the job, they'd say, 'Let's try it with two women instead'. Of course at the beginning, or as a one-off you can adjust it into the old time scales by working faster, but it can't work out like this in the long run. But I don't know what it was with them, some of our women are scared about losing their jobs, I think. They would do whatever it took to adjust any extra work into their current load, and so they kept piling on more work. (Jasminder)

But many of the workers also felt that the practice of setting individual workers in competition with each other stemmed directly from their migrant as well as their ethnic status:

> I think it's with our Asian women, you know, they say, 'divide and rule'. Well, that's what they did, by saying this person is a 'good worker' and putting pressure on everyone like that. Some women did everything they could, went all out to show that they could cope with anything. They then held them up as a 'good worker' and held them up as the standard for everyone to work to. And now, it's even worse. (Jasminder)

The experience of South Asian women at Gate Gourmet reflects a common reality for migrant women workers employed in a highly competitive production process, in which managers from the dominant ethnic group apply practices that would not be tolerated by local workers (Kusakabe and Pearson 2010; McDowell et al. 2007; Waldinger and Lichter 2003; Wright 2006). The issue of control and harassment of women's use of the toilets, discussed in relation to the Grunwick strike, was also a major issue with the women workers at Gate Gourmet. This was especially the case in the two years before the dispute erupted, when the managers began monitoring how often the workers went to the toilet, and how much time they spent there:

If you were not back in a couple of minutes, it was like, come to the office now. 'What were you doing there, inside, for so long?' I had just come back from the toilet one day and was back at my place on the belt when the manager sent for me. So I accompanied him [to the office]. There were four to five [male] managers sitting there. He began questioning me again and again, 'What were you doing there? Why did you go there?' I asked back, 'Why do people go to the bathroom?' He would not stop. The same question, again and again. You feel 'embarrassed'. So I lost all caution, I thought, this shameless man, let me give him such an answer that he feels shame himself. I said, 'I went to change my pad!' He was quiet. What else could he say? I had said it aloud, and he felt shame. I asked him back, 'Why did you ask me these questions? Is this the way to speak?' He just sent me back to the belt. After that he would pick on me for everything. (Kamalpreet)

There is considerable evidence from other research on women workers in a range of production situations – manufacturing, assembly, horticulture (Pearson and Seyfang 2002) – that managerial control over women's access to toilets is a frequently-used, gendered strategy. It is rarely deployed with male workers who generally have more autonomy over their physical mobility in the workplace as well as different biological needs. It is not possible to ascertain from the few contemporary ethnographies of women workers in the UK whether this is a generalised practice across UK industry and/or whether it is a strategy that is more usually found with women of migrant origin, or women of colour. But our research indicates that the women of migrant origin working at both Grunwick and Gate Gourmet workers felt humiliated by this practice.

Although the Gate Gourmet workers acknowledged that the company was in difficulties by early 2005, they claimed that in previous years, flexibility had been achieved by supplementing the core staff with temporary casual staff for peak periods rather than by replacing the existing workforce to manage costs. However by the time the dispute broke out, the management strategy seemed to have been to circumvent any worker resistance by replacing permanent workers with agency staff, who could be employed on new contracts.

It is therefore evident that there was simmering resentment before the events of August 2005, particularly at the discussions of the introduction of agency workers and how these were being linked to issues of changing working conditions and increasing the pressure for higher throughput and productivity. The final straw was the introduction of non-unionised agency workers, reportedly from Eastern Europe (Blanchflower et al. 2007). By 2005, there was a new wave of 'cheap' migrants available to the management in West London, predominantly from Poland or other countries from the recently enlarged EU (McDowell et al. 2007). The South Asian women felt that management had failed to acknowledge how they themselves had increased their productivity, and accepted (albeit reluctantly) deteriorating conditions at work; instead they believed that Gate Gourmet had deliberately provoked them by introducing agency staff whose pay and conditions were even worse than their own, and thereby threatening their own positions. The women also construed racial undertones to the fact that the new workers were white:

> The place where I used to work, that job is still going, and there is a Polish person doing that job now. What's the meaning of this? Why did they throw me out, only to replace me with someone else? This means that they removed me because we were Asian. I heard on the radio that Eric Born [the Managing Director of Gate Gourmet] had said that he could not work with 'these people' – who are 'these people'? We Asians, that's who! (Kulvinder)

The dispute enabled management to renegotiate the working conditions of the existing workforce as well as utilise more recent, and more exploitable migrant labour from the EU Accession countries. Indeed, one of the factors that made the Eastern European migrant workers so attractive was their temporary nature; unlike the settled Punjabi diaspora in West London, the assumption at that time was that Polish workers were not 'here to stay'; nor were they likely to resist to become organised or militant union members. MacKenzie and Forde (2009) document employers' active recruitment strategies to attract immigrant workers already in the national labour markets or recruit directly from abroad – often strategically recruiting one group of migrants after another, as settled migrants organise themselves or expect better conditions and pay. The nature of 'cheap labour' had shifted since the 1970s, and being brown and female was no longer sufficient to guarantee a docile and malleable workforce. Migrant rather than immigrant labour was required, and young and temporary rather than old and permanent were preferred.

By this period, South Asian women had a substantial history of shop floor resistance to management attempts to introduce non-negotiated cost-reducing measures. It was in this context that the events that led to the Gate Gourmet dispute unfolded on 10 August 2005.

THE EVENTS OF THE GATE GOURMET DISPUTE

The dramatic events of 10 August are much disputed, with diversely varying accounts presented by the workers, their trade unions and the management. We have put together this account based on interviews with the sacked Gate Gourmet workers, newspaper reports and the evidence presented at the Employment Tribunal hearings.

On the morning of 10 August 2005, there were some unusual activities at the offices of the Gate Gourmet factory. Several women we interviewed reported noticing this when they reported for their morning shift:

> The management offices had been open when the workers started their shift at 6 a.m. The personnel office was also open – we had never seen their offices open that early in the morning – and there was security outside, at 5 a.m. How did they know they would be needed? (Kulvinder)

According to our interviewees, when the workers returned from their mid-morning tea break, they found around fifty, mostly Polish, agency workers installed in their places.

> We started our work as usual, and then we went for our morning tea break and when we came back, we saw that in the place of those in the wash-up department, not ours, there were the agency workers doing their job. They [the workers at wash-up] told the agency workers to move because it was their job. (Parjot)

Backed by the managers, the agency workers refused to make way. In response to what was seen as clear management provocation, about 200 of the Gate Gourmet employees left their work stations and assembled in the canteen to discuss their response to the presence of the agency workers. Gathering in the canteen in response to various problems was a strategy that had been deployed by workers at Gate Gourmet many times in the past.

> That's what used to happen at Gate Gourmet – that's where the workers used to assemble to discuss their issues and talk. Because they could not all meet at any other place or in each department. So the workers did the same this time as well. (Rajdeep)

Most of the shop stewards were absent from the shop floor on that day because they were attending a union meeting, apart from one male shop steward called Mr Singh. According to several accounts, a few of the workers made phone calls to another shop steward, Mrs Atwal, who joined them.

> We went to the canteen and there the managers gave us a warning to get back to work. Some of us wanted to head back, but Atwal told us to wait for Dhillon [the shop steward convenor], like this [gestures with arms spreads out, as if blocking the way]. She said, 'Is the union dead? We are here to fight for you. You stay put.' So we stayed there. (Parjot)

At the request of the workers and apparently also by the management, they were soon joined by other TGWU shop stewards including the convenor, Mr Dhillon. The position of the shop stewards was that the workers should not return to the line until the management had agreed to talk to their union representatives, a normal procedure in a dispute.

However, in a move that was widely considered by the women we interviewed to have been planned in advance, the management declared they were dealing with an unofficial strike and that anyone who did not go back to work immediately would be dismissed. According to the women we interviewed, the management issued a verbal warning through a loudspeaker, asking the workers to return to work or face dismissal. The shop stewards demanded that the management rescind the warning that they would be dismissed before the workers could return to work. As one worker noted:

> If the workers had gone back to work, the threat of dismissal would have disappeared by itself. At the most, they would have got a warning letter that they had left the shop floor once and if they did it again, they would be dismissed. But Dhillon kept saying, 'You remove the threat first, then I will get the workers to return to work'. (Kulvinder)

The management issued the above mentioned verbal warning over the megaphone three times, but the workers followed the advice from their union representative and remained in the canteen. They were then sacked by megaphone in the presence of the shop stewards. When they refused to return their ID cards they were detained in the canteen by security guards for about seven hours, a form of internal 'kettling'. After they finally left the premises, a lockout was imposed by Gate Gourmet preventing the workers from returning to work. Dismissal notices were handed out stating that those involved in the strike would not be allowed to re-enter the workplace until they had signed a new contract. This information was relayed to those in the canteen by megaphone; many employees from other shifts who did not know what was going on as they had not been present at the time of the initial walk-out were given the information by security guards who had surrounded the canteen, whilst others found out about the events through phone conversations with those who were directly involved. Subsequent dismissals took the number of sacked workers to 813.

The workers recalled the circumstances of their dismissal with anger and bitterness:

> When the third announcement came, I was shocked. I was not well at that time. I had just had my hysterectomy and was taking these tablets. I needed to go to the toilet regularly and could not hold back. I asked three times, but they said no. Then they put this bucket there – right in front of everyone, in front of the men, and were like, 'Here, you go here'. [...] Only we know what we

went through. Then the managers took our IDs and they made us take our gowns off right there. We felt such shame because we did not have the dupatta [long scarves] underneath our gowns – they were in our lockers. The managers were standing there, looking at us, laughing. We felt terrible. We have worked there all these years, worked so hard, and they threw us out like we were some fly in the butter. (Kamalpreet)

The practice of assembling at the canteen as well as the informal mechanisms of collective negotiations with the management, which were valued by these South Asian women workers for their immediacy and perceived effectiveness, had developed at Gate Gourmet through years of experience of union membership and organisation, and the women were acting in accordance with well-established norms. The sacked workers also conformed to the formal mechanisms of representation on the shop floor by heeding the advice of their shop stewards whilst in the canteen. The unionised workers present in the canteen had confidence in the guidance and instructions of their union representatives, as one worker recalled:

They made the announcement, but we stayed on because we wanted to follow our union. We trusted the union and thought they must know best. There were union shop stewards there that day, and they told us to stay there, so we listened to them. (Satinder)

However, as we recount below, the union bureaucracy of the then TGWU progressively distanced itself from these norms, practices and mechanisms that it had arguably shaped over the years.

Subsequent dismissals over the next two days included those on other shifts. Even some who were on holiday or registered sick had received dismissal notices by courier at their houses that afternoon (Flying Pickets 2007). Initially the TGWU supported the Gate Gourmet workers; airport baggage handlers and other workers who were members of the same union undertook solidarity action and refused to work in a move that grounded BA flights for two days, but this was deemed illegal under 1982 legislation outlawing secondary picketing (Milward and Stevens 1987). Over the next few days, the sacked Gate Gourmet workers assembled on a hill nearby to protest at their sacking, and initially received some support from their community.

> The people in the community supported us. They knew that we are hardworking people who have faced injustice. People used to send us food; the gurdwara used to send us food. Sometimes shopkeepers used to send us cartons of juice, packets of crisps and chocolate. They understood how difficult our situation was. But the support dwindled over time as Gate Gourmet took some people back in – the workers got divided, you see. (Amanjot)

In many ways echoing the experiences of Grunwick workers in the first few months on the picket line before their cause was taken up by the wider trade union movement (see p.122), the Gate Gourmet workers too recalled the racist abuse they were subjected to, whilst picketing:

> Some white people used to stop their cars and shout abuse to us, 'Fucking bloody bastards! You go back to your country!' and this and that, but some of us also shouted back at them. I have been in this country for so many years but I have never been at the receiving end of such abuse. The things I had to hear there! (Hansa)

Assembling in the canteen was construed as unballoted action under Section 26 of the Employment Act 1990, so the TGWU repudiated the workers' action in order to protect itself against being fined and against any residual damages claims on their funds. However, this distancing ignored the actions of their own shop stewards in this incident, and, in particular, ignored the stewards' failure to warn the workforce of the very real threat of dismissal.

'WAS THE UNION LEADERSHIP'S ACTION "OFFICIAL"?' ON THE DECISION-MAKING PROCESSES BEHIND THE UNION'S COMPROMISE AGREEMENT

Three weeks into the dispute, on 26 August 2005, TGWU District Officer Oliver Richardson announced to the sacked Gate Gourmet workers who were picketing the company's premises at Heathrow

Airport that a Compromise Agreement had been negotiated with the management at Gate Gourmet.[3] The terms of this agreement included: re-engagement of selected workers from those who had been sacked (on new terms and conditions); some voluntary redundancies; and compulsory redundancy for 144 workers who would be offered compensation in a single payment, to the amount of twice what they earned in a week multiplied by their number of years of service. Subsequently, a meeting of the sacked workers and their union representatives was organised in the Monsoon Club in Southall on 28 September 2005 to discuss the Compromise Agreement.

According to the women workers we interviewed, at that meeting the TGWU officials recommended that all workers accept the agreement negotiated by their union. Without having been given the opportunity to read the full text of the agreement, or even to hear the full agreement being read out to them, those present were asked to indicate their acceptance by a show of hands. Many of our interviewees were critical of the conduct of this meeting. They reported that there were no interpreters present, and the information given by the union representatives was difficult for them to follow. They also reported that they were not fully informed about the terms of the agreement:

> They did not read out the deal to us, they just showed us the papers, just like that [waves an imaginary sheet in the air] and that's how they did it. No one read out the papers to us, no one told us what it was all about. It was only later, when we realised what it said, we were shocked at what happened. (Sukhwant)

Many of these women indicated that they had not understood the details of what had been agreed on their behalf. But the reassurance from the union representatives that they would have the chance to read and endorse the agreement later was crucial to their decision to give the deal an initial go-ahead.

> In the beginning, they said, 'You will get a letter detailing everything, and then when you read it, you can decide' – and that's what should have happened – 'and when you get the details, if even one of you does not sign the agreement, it will not stand'.

Everyone assumed that if they had any objections later, they would not sign and the deal would fall through. So there was nothing to be lost by saying yes then. But then they broke their word. (Gurinder)

The circumstances in which workers' agreement was secured has subsequently been challenged by some of the sacked workers. This position has also received support by some members of the TGWU Executive Council, one of whom attended a fringe meeting to discuss the Gate Gourmet dispute during the TUC conference at Brighton on 8 September 2008. The meeting was also attended by one of the authors of this book. A member of the TGWU Executive Council when the Compromise Agreement was negotiated, who requested anonymity, told us in a detailed interview that he had believed that the Agreement would be put to the vote by the sacked workers before it was endorsed. In his view, the show of hands called for at the Monsoon Club fell far short of being an actual vote. He told us that the TGWU Executive Council:

> were told it [the Compromise Agreement] was going to be taken to the workers, that they would have to agree, that our recommendation was that they accept it. I couldn't believe it when I heard, I thought, 'What, didn't you actually vote on it?'

This lack of compliance with the union's own agreed procedures is especially problematic given legal regulations that require a ballot of the membership before any industrial action can be mobilised by trade unions. According to another union official who we interviewed, 'There are always some losers in any compromise deal'. The sacked workers remained aggrieved at the outcome and particularly at the process, which they felt had not been transparent or democratic.

In the eyes of many of the Gate Gourmet workers, the way in which the union called out the baggage handlers in solidarity, and then negotiated the Compromise Agreement was unacceptable. In making this agreement with the company, the union in fact allowed Gate Gourmet to select for redundancy those workers who had been active members of their union and hence deemed to be 'radical'

(Milner 2005), as well as other 'undesirable' less productive workers. As one worker we spoke to reported:

> They chose the people they just did not want – and they were mostly those from the kitchen. Because the kitchen ladies were strong, they would speak out – they were not the type to keep quiet if something was not right. They used to fight, they were 'troublemakers!' (Puneet)

Indeed, at the height of the dispute, the Gate Gourmet chairman, Dave Siegel, claimed there were up to 200 'radicals' among those sacked by the company (Tran 2005). *Personnel Today* reported that the Gate Gourmet UK & Ireland managing director, Eric Born reiterated his company's stance on 'militant' staff: 'We will not re-engage employees who instigated the wildcat strike in August or their more militant followers' (Thomas 2005). *The Times* (2005) reported on a secret internal briefing presented to bosses at Gate Gourmet, which read: 'Recruit, train and security check drivers. Announce intention to trade union, provoking unofficial industrial action from staff. Dismiss current workforce. Replace with new staff.' The draft document set out a fifteen-week timetable for provoking employees into striking so that they could be replaced with lower-paid Eastern European workers, who had trained in secret in order to reduce the size of the workforce and to alter the pay and conditions of those who remained. These were the aims towards which the company was then negotiating with the union.

Compulsory redundancies also included those workers who were older, who had a history of taking sick leave or who had ongoing health problems, as some workers who spoke to us reported:

> I was on sick leave because I had been injured at work. A loaded trolley fell on my shoulders. This happened in May and I went back to work towards the end of July. When I went back to work, they told me that I had taken too much time off sick. I said, this wasn't sick leave, it was injury at work. They said, we will give you a warning letter. I said, 'Yes, do that. I will fight it'. And that case is still ongoing. I think that's why they got rid of me. (Gunwant)

Over time, however, most workers accepted the new contract or opted for redundancy, but fifty-six workers, of whom fifty were women, continued their dispute with the company and refused to sign the compromise agreement. Rejecting the redundancy payments – which amounted to between £4000-£7000 depending on their number of years of service, a considerable sum for these workers – was not a decision made lightly. The women recounted the reasons why they decided to pursue their claim of unfair dismissal. A feeling that they had been wronged, a strong sense of injustice at what had taken place and the urge to fight for their rights were articulated by many women:

> I felt this had become a matter of my 'self-respect'. The way they had thrown us out was wrong. There have to be three warnings, a verbal warning, then a written warning and only then can you sack an employee. The way they went about it – that was not the way to do it. After working there for so many years, they just threw us out, as if we meant nothing! It was something in my heart that made me feel that I must not condone a wrong thing, that I will not sign it when I knew that it was a wrong thing, that I was right and they were wrong. Why should I accept that I have done something wrong? That was the basis of my fight. (Kamalpreet)

As another woman noted:

> I was aware right at the beginning that I was taking a risk by not signing the agreement – we could have won but we could have lost everything as well. But you have to fight for your rights. (Gunwant)

Drawing information from Gate Gourmet's own website, Hendy and Gall (2006, 2) note that of the '813 workers sacked, 272 were reinstated and 411 given the equivalent of their redundancy entitlement. For 130 there was neither employment nor compensation. In short, Gate Gourmet was able to shed 541 workers' jobs by paying the equivalent of redundancy to 411.' Additionally, the changes to workers' contracts – including reduced annual leave and sick leave and lower rates for overtime work – enabled Gate Gourmet to increase productivity and to reduce the rights of long standing employees to labour protection. Eric Born, managing director of Gate Gourmet UK and Ireland published a report documenting the increased productivity at Gate Gourmet in April 2006, and noted, 'The changes we've been making to working practices are clearly paying off' (CAPA 2006). Compared to the first quarter of 2005, the number of hours lost to sickness reduced by 58 per cent and the number of paid overtime hours was reduced by 76 per cent. Additionally, indicating the intensification of the labour process, these figures also document that the number of economy class bar trolleys packed at the Heathrow South unit increased from thirty-four per employee per day to fifty-three per employee – an increase of 56 per cent (CAPA 2006). After a rush of initial media reports (Box 2005) there has been little continuing interest, and virtually no reporting of the twenty cases taken in 2009 to Employment Tribunals for unfair dismissal.

GENDER, ETHNICITY AND UNION REPRESENTATION: FROM COLLECTIVE ACTION TO INDIVIDUAL CLAIMS THROUGH THE EMPLOYMENT TRIBUNAL

The union's role

Thirty years after the Grunwick strike, the Gate Gourmet dispute threw into sharp relief the continuing inadequacies in the trade unions' representation of minority ethnic women and demonstrated the impact of the Thatcher-era legislation curtailing the capacity of trade unions to organise effectively. The TGWU's initial position was that the women were provoked, which is why the union supported the walk-out in the beginning. However, according to the prevailing legislation this constituted unballoted action, so the union did not use the term 'strike' and the workers were not given 'strike pay' but instead received payments of £50 per week from the union 'hardship fund'. The union were aware that they had to acknowledge this unballoted action under Section 26 of the Trade Union and Labour Relations (Consolidation) Act 1992 (as amended) to protect themselves against any claims for damages.

However, as stated above, this effectively meant that they ignored the alleged role of their own shop stewards in advising the workers who were convening in the canteen against returning to the shop floor when the management warned that failure to return to work would result in their dismissal. The issue of whether action by shop stewards constitutes direct representation of union policy is contested in academic literature (Terry 1995), and this ambivalence about the role of their shop stewards posed a real problem for the TWGU in 2005.

Having initially supported the women, the union's position changed over time, and support for the strikers who refused to sign the compromise agreement was withdrawn. In an address to a conference in London, Tony Woodley (2007), the then General Secretary of the TGWU, stated: 'If they [Gate Gourmet workers] were provoked enough into stopping work then there was nothing that their union could do', through which he sought to imply that the union and the shop stewards were unconnected to the workers' actions. Woodley appeared to be trying to distance these actions from mainstream union practices, again apparently ignoring the alleged role of his union shop stewards in this dispute. The union leadership has consistently refused to engage with any criticism of their role and has continued to put the blame for any negative outcome from the ongoing dispute firmly on the shoulders of the workers.

Many of the women involved consider that their union's progressive abandonment of them was linked to the solidarity actions of other workers at Heathrow, who were also TGWU members. In response to the events of 10 August at Gate Gourmet, BA baggage handlers, bus drivers and ground staff staged solidarity strike action, paralysing BA for 48 hours as they were forced to ground over 100 short and long haul flights, costing them about £40 million (BBC News 2005).

The response of the union leadership was telling. Woodley (2007) asserted the illegality of secondary action, at the same time down playing the walk-out as an expression of community support rather than workers' solidarity: 'We have to say to those workers, "Sorry there is nothing we can do to help you because the law will not allow us to do so" [...] The law did not allow for these women's husbands, sons, neighbours and friends to come to their aid'.

The Gate Gourmet workers resented the ways in which the union had disseminated misleading information, presenting the solidarity action from their co-union members as solely resulting from the close networks and the community strengths of ethnic and family relationships amongst the (Asian) workers at Gate Gourmet and BA. Several workers refuted the suggestion that there were any family connections between them and the baggage handlers, which had brought them out in support:

> There was nothing. Even when we were on the hill, lots of people – reporters – asked us about these connections, but we were not aware of any close connections. Maybe there are some people who may be distant relatives of those at Gate Gourmet – in this area people often know of each other in our community – but we were not aware of any close connections. I think it was just a rumour that was spread by the union because the union wanted to step back from what they had started, and this was a good way of doing that, and everyone believed it. That's why I feel that the union never really supported us, they have always used the workers. When one worker supports the other, when things are like this, if the union leaders were to stand with the workers, then a lot of the struggles would end in victory. (Kulvinder)

Constructing the secondary strike action by the baggage handlers at Heathrow as personalised and a result of family links, was a way of depoliticising the support for those sacked by Gate Gourmet rather than recognising it as an act of class solidarity by workers based on their common interests (also see McDowell et al. 2012). In doing so, Woodley was reaching for all too familiar stereotypes that construct black and minority ethnic workers' industrial action as exotic and somehow different from the norms and practices of the mainstream union (Martinez-Lucio and Perret 2009a). Such representations continue to construct minority ethnic workers, particularly women workers, as on the one hand hard to organise, but, on the other hand, when the women's industrial militancy exceeds the unions' capacity for action under increasingly restrictive legislative frameworks, they are alternatively configured as naïve and impulsive (Bronfrenbrenner 1998, cited in Martinez-Lucio and Perrett 2009a, 239).

Subsequent events revealed the efforts the TGWU made to draw back from the potentially illegal secondary action by other (mainly male) workers at Heathrow. Twelve months later – on 18 September 2006 – *The Guardian* revealed that the TGWU had made payments totalling £600,000 to the two shop stewards who had been involved in bringing the BA baggage handlers out in solidarity for the workers at Gate Gourmet, in order to compensate these union officials for losing their jobs. In turn, the two men agreed not to respond publicly to allegations that they were following union orders by organising the secondary strike (Hencke 2006). When the sacked Gate Gourmet workers heard about *The Guardian*'s disclosure, they felt betrayed by their union's manoeuvres to protect itself while the rank and file members like them were 'hung out to dry'.

> They [the baggage handlers] came out in strike in sympathy, with the support of their union. But when BA wanted to investigate why the baggage handlers went on strike, that's when the union decided to give the shop stewards a lot of 'hush money' to close their months. And the poor workers who stood up for us, they lost a day's wages. (Kulvinder)

The women we spoke to therefore indicated that they felt aggrieved by their treatment, not just by their employer (Gate Gourmet) but also by their own union, who they felt did not act to defend their interests.

Against the backdrop of this dissatisfaction with the behaviour around the baggage handlers' strike and the manner in which the Compromise Agreement had been negotiated and agreed, and uncertain about the extent of the union support for their cause, the workers began filing claims for unfair dismissal with the Employment Tribunal, hoping for a more favourable outcome through the judicial process. However even at this point, it was clear that they were not a priority for their union. It was only on the very last day it was possible to register claims that the union's legal representatives filed claims for unfair dismissal on behalf of all the dismissed workers, leading to a total of approximately 1000 claims on behalf of the 813 sacked workers (Abbas and others v. Gate Gourmet London Ltd, paragraph 9). The union's delay in acting on behalf of its members had led to a duplication of some of the claims already submitted by sacked workers who had utilised their own resources to hire lawyers. The first of these hearings was held in November 2006, and considered the preliminary point of whether the workers in the canteen and those who were dismissed for failing to attend work on the subsequent days were participating in unofficial industrial action. Subsequent cases concerned particular categories of workers, including shop stewards. One of the authors of this book attended these later tribunal hearings at Reading where nineteen cases were heard between September 2007 and June 2008,[4] and was therefore able to observe the tribunal proceedings, talk to the solicitors and to some of the dismissed workers and gather information from those discussions.

Limitations to union powers

Starting under the Conservative government in 1979, and continuing up to and under New Labour from 1997, and in all subsequent governments, collective rights have been increasingly limited and degraded. During this same period, there has been greater legal regulation of workplace relations through employment protection offered by statutory individual rights – such as the rights associated with national minimum wage, working time regulations, parental and maternity benefits and anti-discrimination legislation (Dickens 2002). Since the 1980s, the industrial relations policy and workings of British labour laws have asserted 'the primacy of the individual relationship over the collective' (Deery and Mitchell 1999, 4). The rise of individualised forms of resolving employment disputes has been concurrent with the declining levels of unionisation and the declining number of stoppages due to industrial action. During the 1970s, an average of 21.9 million days each year were lost to strike action, peaking at 29.47 million in the 1979 'winter of discontent'. Since then, strike days have continued to fall – in 1989 there were 4.13 million days lost to strike action, but by 2005, when the Gate Gourmet dispute took place, the number had fallen to less than 158,000 (ONS 2012). This reflects the growing constraints on trade unions' power to mobilise collective action as well as the increasing casualisation of the labour force. This has reduced the numbers of full-time, male (blue collar) employees, who were historically the stalwarts of union membership and activism. Meanwhile, union membership in the UK declined from 13.2 million in 1979, the year after the Grunwick dispute ended, to just under 7.5 million in 2005, when the Gate Gourmet dispute erupted, a drop of over 43 per cent (Achur 2011, 30).

Although the causes for decline in unionisation and stoppages are complex and multifactoral (Colling 2006, 142-2), it has been argued that there is nonetheless a link between two trends. Novitz (2002) argues that the legislative reforms undertaken by New Labour since 1999 seem to provide a pyramid of representation, whereby trade unions *can* establish their relevance. However, this is primarily when they 'accompany' individual employees in grievance and disciplinary proceedings, and when they act as recipients of information and consultation. She suggests that a barrier to the achievement of this objective is the particular conception of 'partnership' adopted by New Labour, which deviates from that conceptualised by the trade unions. This 'partnership' is essentially individualistic in character, procedural in form, and unitary in specification. For example, in a review of the Employment Relations Act 1999, the Department of Trade and Industry (DTI) asserted that 'the definition of union services should focus on those services received by union members as individuals' (DTI 2003, 40, cited in Colling 2006, 143). Bagguley, however, does not consider these changes to represent a decline in class-based collective action. Instead, he argues that 'the repertoire of contention has changed, both in terms of its form and content. People pursue their economistic class interests in an individualised manner, but they are dependent on collective actors such as trade unions in pursuit of these interests' (Bagguley 2002, 1).

In the context of the increasingly individualised nature of workers' rights and the decline of collective bargaining (Brown 1999), the caseload of the Employment Tribunal has steadily increased over the last two decades. Employment Tribunals (originally named Industrial Tribunals) were created by the Industrial Training Act 1964 to enforce workers' statutory individual rights. They received just over 40,000 claims in 1978-9 (Dix et al. 2008, 9), the year when the Grunwick strike ended. Concurrent with the decline in union density, there has been a rise in the number of claims made to

Employment Tribunals, with over 130,000 claims in 2005-6 (Dix et al. 2008, 9), the year the Gate Gourmet dispute began.

Employment Tribunals

Despite this increasing recourse to Employment Tribunals over the last two decades, the limits of utilising individualised tribunal processes rather than the traditional collective tactics of withdrawing labour and disrupting the production have been widely noted (Bagguley 2002; Brown et al. 2000; Oxenbridge et al. 2001). Colling (2006) argues that, in contrast to negotiation, which is the common tool of collective bargaining, recourse to a legal process merely provides a blunt instrument which creates a winning and losing side. In doing so, it often fails to achieve an outcome which is acceptable to both sides. He also observes that it remains notoriously difficult to obtain any long term advantages that might be the result of settling a dispute, or indeed to ensure final enforcement of the judgement.

The legal process did not unfold smoothly for the Gate Gourmet workers either. In spite of the fact that the union initially backed the workers' actions, they had changed their position by the time the cases for unfair dismissal came to be heard in the Employment Tribunal in 2007. Although the role of the union shop stewards had been one of the most debated aspects of this dispute, accounts from the Gate Gourmet workers and from the tribunal judgements indicate that the union's solicitors focused on the company's role in allegedly encouraging the workers to assemble in the canteen, presumably with the aim of demonstrating constructive dismissal. Several women mentioned that they were advised by the union solicitor to keep the union out of their accounts of what happened on the day:

> Some people were saying that the managers sent them there, and others were saying they went there themselves. The union did not let them tell it as it was. The union was like, 'The union should not be named, the union should not be named'. That's what happened at the tribunal. (Puneet)

The workers' narratives of the events recalled a far messier and nuanced reality than was presented at the adversarial tribunal system which pitted the management against the union. Where the workers' narratives of the events did not accord with the union's public narrative, the workers felt that their voices had been muffled by their own representatives, who were seeking to furnish the requisite evidence to prove their unfair dismissal claim. In the event, the claims for unfair dismissal were not upheld, although the tribunal chair did question the role of the shop stewards in not acting decisively in defence of their members' interests.

The written tribunal judgement corroborates the women's accounts about the action of their shop stewards in preventing them from returning to their work once the warnings had been given. The judgement, in fact, states that Mr Dhillon [the shop steward] 'followed the advice given to him by Mr [Brendan] Gold, the National Secretary [of the TGWU], which was to seek a withdrawal of the threat of dismissal before the staff returned to work' (Abbas and Others v. Gate Gourmet London Ltd, paragraph 54). However, since their union had not officially authorised the walkout, the court decided that it was the workers' 'own choice' not to return to work. In fact the judgement criticised the actions of Mr Dhillon:

> What none of the tribunal could understand is why, having heard how the respondent [Gate Gourmet] viewed this congregation of employees, Mr Dhillon [the convenor] did not address the entire group to advise them that whatever their concerns might be this was a matter which the union had been due to consider [...] including what if any industrial action was appropriate [...] and that they should return to work. Had he done so none of these problems would be before this tribunal. (Abbas and Others v. Gate Gourmet London Ltd, paragraph 75)

As discussed, Woodley's (2007) construction of the primary group of sacked workers as easily provoked and therefore to blame for the situation sought to erase the role of the union shop stewards in failing to advise the workers of the very real threat of dismissal they faced. The women who spoke to us were very critical of the role of the trade union in facilitating the events at the canteen on that day.

Q: Who do you think is to blame for the way things turned out?

G: I would say it is the union. They should have followed the proper procedure. After they [Gate Gourmet] gave us the warning, the final warning, they [the union] should have known that we have to ballot before a strike. We were there just for a meeting, but they should have known the danger when the company started giving us the warnings. We were just following their advice. The union made a mistake that day. They should have known what the law is, what their duties were. But then the company gave us a written warning in different languages. That also makes me think that the company knew what was going to happen – they must have set this up. How could they have arranged to print and translate it in so many languages in such a short time? That makes me also suspect the company. They were looking to get rid of us in any case. So it was both of them – the union and the company. (Gunwant)

The sacked workers were left disappointed not just by the outcome of the tribunal decision but also by the procedure that they felt had not served them well. The importance of language in legal processes has been noted in light of the ways in which lawyers use language in courtrooms to constrain, control, or coerce the evidence of witnesses (Cotterill 2003), and this is an issue that can impede minority workers' access to the judicial process. During one of the Employment Tribunal hearings, there was considerable wrangling over the role of the interpreter. One of the workers was able to understand the question, 'What is your name?' and answer it before the interpreter translated it for her. The tribunal judge then decided that there was no need for an interpreter and proceeded to hear her evidence directly, till the distress of the claimant and her inability to understand complex questions made it evident that translation was indeed necessary. The level of competence needed to understand simple questions is vastly different from that needed to tackle questioning in a court, especially when much depends on witness accounts.[5]

The complexity of making one's voice heard in the tribunal process was evident in another subsequent case (Mr B. L. Mayo and twenty-two others v. Gate Gourmet London Ltd). Some workers claimed that they had been prevented from entering Gate Gourmet and assumed they had been dismissed and *then* proceeded to join the picket line. As one of the sacked workers recounted:

> Once they locked me out, obviously I had to go and join the others on the hill and shout slogans. I am not going to sit at home with my hands folded in my lap, am I? (Kulwant)

The company argued that the workers had joined the picket line instead of reporting for work and were subsequently dismissed. The interpreter provided by the court translated the questions posed to the claimant to establish the sequence of events: 'Did the person at Gate Gourmet [security guard/staff] stop you from entering the premises when you reported for work that day?' When the sacked worker answered in affirmative, the next question was, 'Did they say that you were not allowed to come in because you had been dismissed?' The claimant explained that the security guard had not explicitly uttered those words. It was the claimant's solicitor who sought further clarification – 'Did you understand their actions to mean that you had been dismissed?' The interpreter, however, translated this into exactly the same words as the last question – 'Did they say that you were not allowed to come in because you had been dismissed?' The claimant, who had in earlier accounts asserted that she joined the picket line *after* she understood herself dismissed because she was denied entry to Gate Gourmet, replied with a 'no' to this mistranslated question because this had not been explicitly said by the security staff, and she had never claimed that it was indeed the case.

The nuances of evidence gathering had therefore been completely missed in the translation process, it seemed, to the detriment of the claimant. Colling's (2006, 152-4) reservations about the tribunal process and the nature of evidence gathering are very pertinent here, highlighting that much depends on what evidence you give in court – say the wrong thing and it could go the wrong way.

In all, out of more than 700 cases, the tribunal found that only eighteen workers had been unfairly dismissed, most of whom were those workers who been off work sick, on holiday or on compassionate leave when they were sacked. The convenor of shop stewards,

Mr Dhillon, who was deemed to have been present in the canteen at the request of the management and workers when he was sacked, rather than participating in the unofficial strike action, won his case for unfair dismissal.[6] But the remaining workers whose claims were thrown out by the tribunal remained unsatisfied by the judicial process, which they felt did not accommodate their voices.

In both the Grunwick and the Gate Gourmet dispute, the adversarial process evidently did not serve the South Asian women workers well. When fifty-nine of the Grunwick strikers took their cases to the then Industrial Tribunal (case 40224/76/c and 40282/76/c) in 1977, it was thrown out because of a lack of jurisdiction.

The Grunwick strikers had also been ill-served when they presented evidence to the Scarman Committee. Workers feared that an overreliance on the Scarman Committee's report would result in a loss of the momentum that had been built up by the mass pickets, a fear which turned out to be well-founded. In many respects, the inquiry process was intended to find a legal basis for determining which side in the dispute was right according to the law; in practice, its conclusions were not legally binding, but they had a negative effect on the ongoing dynamics of the strike by slowing the momentum that had been built up after several months of picketing.

The model that has developed since the 1970s, of trade unions as the providers of services and legal support to their members in the tribunal process, did little to meet the expectations of the Gate Gourmet women. They anticipated that the unions would support and facilitate their collective action against management actions and policies, rather than just supply individual, and potentially divisive advice on submissions to the Employment Tribunal. These women's experiences also indicate that the individualised mechanisms of redress now available to workers are not easily accessible to minority women workers who may be disadvantaged by their lack of linguistic precision, and in this case, they had to rely on the union solicitors to act in their interest. This was problematic, given that, as we detailed above, the women workers' own accounts of the origins of the dispute did not accord with their union's version of events, to the detriment of their cases. This was not because of the commonly held view that, as migrants, they were unfamiliar with the procedures of British trade union activism. On the contrary, they were longstanding and disciplined unionised workers, but they fell victim to the lack of transparency and flexibility of the legal system to which they turned for redress, as well as by the inconsistency of the union's processes and priorities.

Martinez-Lucio and Perrett (2009a, 329-330) argue that the changing context of industrial relations presents unique challenges for trade unions in representing workers, because employment is regulated in a variety of ways. Well-traversed routines thus have come to be circumscribed by this increasingly restricted labour legislation in the UK since the 1980s (Colling 2006; Smith and Morton 2006). In a discussion about labour action by minority ethnic workers and the role of community organisations and support groups, as in the case of the strikes at Imperial Typewriters and Burnsall,[7] Wrench and Virdee (1996) argued that in the process of incorporating changes to their practices to conform to regulation, the trade unions have lost their radical edge. The Gate Gourmet case would seem to confirm this view.

MEMORIES AND REFLECTIONS ON THEIR STRUGGLES

By the time we interviewed the Gate Gourmet workers in 2008-2009, they had exhausted almost all the avenues for legal action against the company. Some of the women held out the hope of holding their trade union to account for dereliction of duty. They felt that this was an accurate description of the shop stewards' failure to advise the workers to return to the shop floor. They had, at this point, been abandoned by the mainstream left movement and were primarily being supported by the Workers' Revolutionary Party, which facilitated periodic meetings of the sacked women. Most women who attended these meetings welcomed the opportunities to get together, and continued to attend the annual May Day rallies in the years following the adverse tribunal ruling. They organised community events to keep their cause alive, even when there was widespread perception among the local community in Southall that the dispute had been resolved following the Compromise Agreement.

Most of the sacked workers remained in touch with friends who had been re-employed at Gate Gourmet under new contracts. We managed to speak to three of these re-employed women. Although

they were particularly wary of anyone finding out that they had talked
to us, as they feared losing their jobs, they also wanted to speak out
about the changes imposed on the workers after the Compromise
Agreement and the reinstatement of the selected workers on new
contracts. They reported that the managers organised a meeting to
explain these changes soon after the workers' reinstatement:

> They had a meeting where they told us that they would reduce
> the number of breaks from three to two, and the length of the
> breaks and that of the lunch break was cut short. The pay was
> also not the same as before, and now you get five sick days a
> year, that's all. But the biggest difference is that they have started
> giving us a 'hard time' at work now. Earlier, if there was some-
> thing wrong, the workers could go to the union, the workers
> would get together. But now it is not like that at all. The union
> is nothing, it's there in name only. If we have a problem, there is
> no one to talk to, and if you complain, you get into trouble. They
> send people home, they sack people for little things. There is no
> one to listen to us. It has changed, totally changed. (Satinder)

Those who went back to work for Gate Gourmet reported that
given the significant deterioration in their working conditions and
benefits, the women who chose to remain did so for want of other
options. These women spoke for themselves and for others still at
Gate Gourmet, when they described their futile search for other
jobs, in the hope that they could hand in their notice and move
on to more secure employment. In a context where the local labour
market was becoming increasingly competitive at the bottom end,
management strategies played upon workers' fear of losing their jobs
to extract the maximum productivity from the workforce:

> The number of women doing the work has reduced on each
> belt, so you have to hold it together yourself. If something goes
> wrong, which it does, because there are very few people doing
> the work that used to be done by a lot more workers earlier, it's
> our problem. That's how it is now, we are held responsible and
> fear for our jobs, so that creates a lot of pressure. But we are still
> working there. You see, a lot of the women there do not know

much English, or they live close by, that's why they are putting up with all this. In any case, it is a lot harder to find jobs now, particularly for people who have worked there for a long time, those who are older. So they carry on, and the more they get scared, the more the company scares them. That's the story of that place now. (Satinder)

For those who had been made redundant, the loss of their wages created many difficulties for their families. A few women spoke of the ongoing repercussions of their initial decision to join their co-workers in the canteen and their subsequent refusal to sign the Compromise Agreement and decision to turn down the redundancy payments:

My husband was very angry. Things were really difficult at home. He told me not to ask him for any money, he told me he had no money to spare. I had to borrow on my credit card to buy food for the children, pay the bills as he would not help out. So I stopped using my car, as I had no money for petrol. It was hard, so hard. We had arguments, fights every day, every day. I will never forget those ten months. I went through hell and back. (Parjot)

Parjot managed to get through those months because of the support of her adult daughter, who worked extra shifts to contribute to the household budget when her father refused to do so. In an interview conducted at Parjot's home, in between her mother-in-law's repeated visits to the room where the interview was taking place, Parjot managed to convey a whispered account of how, in an ongoing abusive marriage, the physical violence escalated over the months that the dispute lasted. Loss of her wages exacerbated the power imbalance in her household, and she felt that she had paid a heavy price for her stance.

While a majority of the women talked about the support they had received from their families, some, like Parjot, reflected on the ways in which the gender relations within the household shaped their capacity to challenge their treatment at work. Kulvinder, who was widely regarded as one of the leaders of the dispute and who, in the early weeks and months, regularly attended public meetings to garner support for their cause, recalled the difficulties of managing the competing demands of her new post-Gate Gourmet job, campaigning on behalf of the sacked workers, and her role as the primary carer of a young child:

> It was very difficult for me, doing all the housework, looking after my daughter, and meeting people and attending events all over the place. I took her with me everywhere – that was not easy, not for her and not for me. It is not just me, all women face this pressure. Men never want women to put themselves forward. They just want women to sit at home or work. It's not that previous battles have been fought only by men, women have fought too. I have to play my role in this, and to do that I have to fight outside the home, and sometimes I have to fight within the house too. If they [men] have some spare time, they can go and visit friends, or go to the pub or wherever, but if we go to meetings in our spare time, they will never like that. They will say, 'Why don't you stay at home, there are so many things to do around the house'. (Kulvinder)

Given that they were often older, and given the changing nature of the local labour market where there existed a pool of 'disposable workers' in the form of new migrants from the European Accession countries, many of the sacked workers struggled to find another job. They felt that the public profile of their dispute and the perception that those selected for redundancy were undesirable workers rendered them particularly unemployable. It was in this context that some of the women talked about their feelings of worthlessness and loneliness from being house-bound after decades of paid work:

> After being out of work for some time, I began to get depressed. I began to see myself as a 'loser'. Wherever I went, to one or two places, agencies where I gave my name – nothing came out of it. People used to hear 'Gate Gourmet' and lose interest in me. (Leena)

For women who were the only wage-earners in their family, the difficulties were compounded:

It's been hard for us. After I lost my job, we had to sell the house. The mortgage on the house was still ongoing. I used to do double shift – I would say about sixty-five to seventy hours a week at Gate Gourmet. The whole house was running on my wages. Then, when I lost my job, it felt like everything is over for us. It was so hard to sell the house, we had to sell it for less than we wanted to. (Kamalpreet)

The difficulties created by this resistance to hiring sacked workers from Gate Gourmet, and the pressures placed on existing social networks by the number of newly sacked women who were seeking work in the local labour market, led some women to seek work outside the ethnic enclave where they had spent their working lives. Up until that point, they had moved from one job to another, each secured through their social networks. Several women secured new jobs in the growing number of firms delivering home-based social care, where they earned a fraction of their earlier wages, for body-work that was arduous and considered demeaning. Others secured retail work in small shops and a few women found what they deemed better work, at supermarkets and high street stores. Those who did the latter were younger women, who had more options in the changing labour market in West London. These women compared their current jobs with their previous employment at Gate Gourmet, and felt that they now had better opportunities working outside ethnic enclaves:

You know, there were a lot of white people who work here – so I had thought, you know, that there will be some issues – you know what I mean – but there was nothing like that. It was easy-going here. Where there are more Asian people working in a place, you have to work harder. The management puts pressure on you, and our people also work harder, so they expect more out of you. Where white people work, where one goes to smoke, others go off too. In places where our people work, if you go to the loo twice within a short time, they will point out, 'She just went a while back, and there she goes again!' Here, if the manager has to say something to me and other people are present, she will ask to see me in private – meaning you get 'respect'. And at Gate

Gourmet, the manager would come and even if there were ten
people around you, they would, you know, say whatever they had
to say to you, in front of everyone. (Harjot)

In expressing her experiences, Harjot here associates the improved
conditions at her new workplace – a supermarket – with the diverse
workforce there, and contrasts it with her experiences at workplaces
where a majority of the workforce was of South Asian origin. She
astutely attributes the labour practices of firms at the bottom end of
the labour market to perceptions about the capabilities of minority
ethnic workers for hard work, and their perceived tolerance of high
levels of managerial control. Leena, speaking for a group of three
friends who had taken voluntary redundancies said:

We have no regrets at having lost that job because we have got
better jobs [at a post office, at Marks and Spencer, and at the till
of a petrol station]. What was my job at Gate Gourmet – just
chopping vegetables. And that place, it was full of 'common' attitude and jokes. I have changed, my job is different today. I meet
people from different walks of life, I have had to learn to deal
with them, I have felt a change in my personality. I feel, there
must be something good in me, something worthwhile that I
have been given this office job now. (Leena)

Unlike most workers at Gate Gourmet, these three friends were
from middle class families, and, because of the gendered deskilling
that operates upon migration, their working lives were in sharp
contrast to those of their male relatives who were professionals in
salaried, secure jobs. Though they spoke fondly of the fun they had
whilst working at Gate Gourmet, they also disassociated themselves from the other workers on account of their class, education
and urban backgrounds, and looked down upon the 'rural peasant'
culture that they felt had prevailed there. Due to these memories
of their status dislocation associated with working there, they were
ambivalent about their participation in the struggle for their rights
– particularly the public protests following the sackings. Although
they had assembled in the canteen and, at earlier points in their
interviews they had spoken about how they stood up to managerial

control whilst at Gate Gourmet, they pointed out that throughout their time on the picket line they 'never asked for donations, never. I could never do anything like that!'; 'We did not like doing all that. We used to consider all that very "low"'. And 'I was there, but I did not shout slogans'.

The key point of interest, here, is not whether they took part in these aspects of picketing or not, but that they felt the need to distance themselves from what might be seen as working-class, rural and unfeminine behaviour, such as shouting slogans and asking for donations. Their account is similar to that of Naliniben, one of the Grunwick strikers we quoted (see p.132), who looked upon her participation in that dispute as a reminder of her class dislocation upon migration.

These women, however, were in the minority of those we interviewed. Most of the sacked workers – perhaps surprisingly given their current difficulties and the loss of any compensation because of their decision to fight – recalled their pride at the stance they had taken in defence of their rights:

> Maybe I will not gain anything in this fight, maybe I will fail, but my children will at least be able to say, 'My mother fought for her rights'. The tree that I plant today may not give me any fruits, but others will surely eat its fruits. As for me, I would say that there is still a deep anger inside me, that what happened with us was not fair. That anger is what drives me to carry on, to keep speaking up for my rights. You have to fight for your rights, it is only by fighting that you get your rights. No one gives them to you on a plate – 'here, you take this', do they? (Kulvinder)

Despite their difficulties, they saw their fight as part of a wider and longer term struggle for workers' rights, and this gave them a sense of solidarity with other workers and of their place in history:

> Financially it's been hard. But we are fighting for our rights. If you stand up for your rights then you know what your rights truly are. If you don't fight, tomorrow workers will have no rights. That's what I have understood in this process. If you are sick, you are sick. What can you do about it? Are workers not allowed to

be sick? Anyone can be sick. Others will learn that if you are sick you can get sacked, so they will somehow bear their illness and come to work. Why should that be? Today it has happened to me, tomorrow it can happen to others. (Devinder)

CONCLUSION

At both Grunwick and Gate Gourmet, changes in the labour process combined with different elements of the women workers' experiences and identities, which propelled them into collective action against their employers. The issues of dignity and fairness were central to both the Grunwick and the Gate Gourmet disputes. Grunwick was a spontaneous act of resistance to managerial control, while the underlying grievances behind Gate Gourmet were downward pressures on pay and conditions and the growing use of agency and contract labour. The workers involved in both resorted to collective action as the result of a cumulative experience of injustice. This was based in large part on the discordance between their perceptions of themselves in terms of their identities as women and as workers and their actual experiences in the workplaces. Their responses were thus formed as much by their experience of migration and their class dislocation, as by any overt racist or discriminatory practices.

Our framework for understanding these disputes draws upon feminist analysis of intersectionality, which stresses the significance of interlinking different aspects of identities. As both the disputes indicate, resistance comes not just from the experience on the production line; it is also the result of the intersection of a range of factors embodied in the workers themselves – their class, ethnic and gendered identities, and also their experiences of migration. These all contributed to their perceptions of injustice and their belief in the need for collective action to restore their senses of worth and dignity, which had been affronted by unjust treatment in the workplace. Both of these disputes were about recognition as well as rights.

What happened at Gate Gourmet in the summer of 2005 indicates that, in spite of longstanding union membership and a history of industrial activism, South Asian women workers were once again subject to arbitrary management, treated as a 'disposable' labour force (Wright 2006) and left unprotected by the wider labour movement. These migrant women workers did not receive the full and unconditional support from their union that was their due, and they felt that their lives and their jobs were treated as unimportant. In spite of the fact that their trade union had initially recognised their grievances, the union was unable, or unwilling, to prioritise the workers' situation and instead left them to depend on a legal procedure – through which they were also given only minimal support – and which ultimately gave them no resolution and no satisfaction.

After the Grunwick dispute, it was claimed that the union movement had changed the ways in which women and minority workers were to be incorporated into mainstream policy and practice. However, the experience of the women workers at Gate Gourmet indicates that it was their very ethnicity and 'difference' that was invoked by their union to justify the way it distanced itself and ultimately abandoned their struggles for dignity and justice at work.

NOTES

1. Texas Pacific Finance Group sold Gate Gourmet to Investment Bank Merrill Lynch in March 2007 (www.reuters.com/article/idUSL0214903620070302).
2. At the time of the dispute, according to information available on the Gate Gourmet website, there were 3000 staff employed by the firm, of whom around 2000 worked at Heathrow: 983 in Heathrow South producing 36,000 on-board meals for 70 flights, 810 in Heathrow West producing 29,500 meals for 195 flights, and 139 at Hatton Cross producing 22,000 meals for 70 flights. The number of flights handled by Heathrow South was smaller than Heathrow West because they only dealt with BA long-haul flights. Up until the end of Concorde flights, in October 2003, Gate Gourmet had also fulfilled this contract, and their role there was to provide the more exclusive meals with higher quality standards, similar to those given to first class passengers today. Unlike the shorter flights that had meals delivered from Heathrow West and Hatton Cross, long-haul passengers would not be satisfied with a few sandwiches and a bottle of mineral water. This made Heathrow South of strategic and financial importance to the Gate Gourmet firm and therefore particularly vulnerable if there was action by workers.
3. Details of the Compromise Agreement can be found on www.leeds.ac.uk/strikingwomen.
4. These cases were Mrs L. K. Saran and Thirty-Two Others v. Gate

Gourmet London Ltd (case no: 2702017/05 & others) on 17 and 18 September 2007; Mr B. L. Mayo and Twenty-Two Others v. Gate Gourmet London Ltd (case no: 2701778/05 & twenty-two others) between 25 February 2008 and 3 April 2008; Unite the Union v. Gate Gourmet London Ltd (case no: 2701992/05) between 25 February and 5 March 2008; Mr S. Bhatti v. Gate Gourmet London Ltd (case no: 2701292/07) between 1 April and 3 April 2008; Mr H. S. Cheema v. Gate Gourmet London Ltd (case no: 2702004/05) and seven other cases heard on 24 and 25 April 2008; and Mr K. Sehmi v. Gate Gourmet London Ltd (case no: 2702507/200) on 18 June 2008.

5. A similar situation can be observed in the evidence given at the Scarman Inquiry, where Lord Scarman compliments Jayaben Desai on her English and she denies her language ability as observed in the minutes of the proceedings of the Court of Enquiry on 5 July 1977, from the Shorthand Notes of W.B. Gurney & Sons, Warwick University Contemporary Records Centre.

6. Among the few cases for unfair dismissal that were upheld by the tribunal, four were brought on behalf of former TGWU shop stewards.

7. Burnsall was a metal finishing company in Smethwick, Birmingham. Twenty-six mostly Punjabi women walked out demanding union recognition, equal pay and basic health and safety and were subsequently sacked for going on strike. There were several disagreements between the union (GMB) and the strikers about the form and nature of the strike action, with the strikers increasingly resisting the union's attempts to limit the strike within the constraints imposed by the changes to employment law over the past decade. Though the women had had strong community support, the strike was eventually called off after a year by the GMB, who decided it was unwinnable (Wrench and Virdee, 1996, 259-263).

CHAPTER 7

Minority women and unionisation in a changing economy – where are we now?

T his book has sought to throw new light on the work and lives of
women of South Asian origin who have, at different times, been
celebrated as industrial activists, but also cast aside as inconveniences
to the trade union movement in the UK. In this chapter, we examine
the ongoing challenges faced by trade unions in seeking to offer
effective representation for migrant women workers, some forty
years after the 'turning point' represented by the Grunwick dispute.
We reflect on the continuities and changes in how South Asian
women have related to their trade unions, as illustrated by the very
different experience of those involved in the dispute at Gate Gourmet
in comparison with the earlier strike at Grunwick. This leads us to
analyse the complexities involved for trade unions in representing
minority ethnic women workers given the changing gender and
ethnic composition of the labour force, the changing nature of the
labour market, and following the significant shifts in industrial relations legislation outlined previously. We recognise the impact of
recent anti-discrimination legislation which requires individualised
mechanisms, such as recourse to Employment Tribunals by vulnerable groups of workers, instead of the solidaristic notions of
recompense for grievances that lay behind earlier collective actions.

This book has also given a voice to the women involved in the
actions at Grunwick and Gate Gourmet, which is especially important given that those voices have hitherto been ignored. We have
sought to listen to them and to understand how their experiences
of these events are mediated by their identities and grounded in

their historical and material realities. Both groups of women were migrants, and both faced the disruption that was concordant with arriving in the UK from the late 1960s onwards, entering a country in which the society and culture were becoming increasingly unwelcoming to immigrants.

For the Grunwick workers, who had sought refuge from the escalating persecution they experienced in the newly independent countries of East Africa, the UK was seen as a haven where they would be free to pursue their families' and communities' goals of improving their lives, educating their children and integrating into the wider society. Instead, as we have seen, they had little option but to seek manual work, which they had never undertaken before. Not only did this work represent a serious class dislocation for these women, given their relatively privileged pre-immigration lives, but they also came face-to-face with a management regime which exploited gendered and racialised hierarchies in its pursuit of profitability and productivity in what was a newly emerging industrial process. This was not what they had expected.

The women involved in the Gate Gourmet dispute had a different background. But by the beginning of the twenty-first century, they had accumulated significant employment experience in this country, all in relatively low-paid and so-called low-skilled occupations both in the public and the private sector. The visions they had before they migrated from their native Punjab, of what life would be like in Britain, were also shattered by the reality of the lives they found when they got here. Many of them were young when they arrived in West London in the 1970s and 1980s. Although, like the majority of migrants from poorer parts of the world, they belonged to relatively comfortably off communities of peasant farmers, they had not been educated in English in post-independence India and their primary expectations of life in Britain centred on family, marriage and children – and for many, the opportunity to work. They had not anticipated that they would have to go out to work in manual jobs, which they often had to do very soon after they arrived in the UK, and they had not anticipated that they would have to take jobs which involved anti-social shift hours and to face direct racism at work from both supervisors and co-workers. For many, the fact that they had to combine paid work with often primary responsibilities for housework, cooking and childcare was a difficult challenge which they remembered with pain. The 'better life' of their pre-immigration dreams turned out to be elusive, replaced by the reality of their gendered roles in the family and their gendered and racialised identities in the labour market. They experienced these realities as lifelong challenges, as they sought to make themselves comfortable and secure in a Britain which was rapidly changing in many ways.

Basing our analysis on the accounts of the disputes provided by women who were directly involved in them is an attempt to acknowledge the complexities of their lives, to understand their motivations for action, and the ways in which they experienced their dealings with their trade unions and others. This account therefore differs both in emphasis and in detail from some of the previous representations of these events. We are not suggesting that the women's version is the only valid account. However, it is *as* valid as other accounts, even though it does at times de-centre the widely disseminated trade union stories in favour of a narrative that is grounded in the women's own lives. By the time we interviewed the five ex-Grunwick strikers more than thirty years after the event, they were relatively elderly, and, with the possible exception of Jayaben Desai, the significance of the strike had diminished as their lives progressed over the years. They remembered it as important, however, often rather wistfully, though they considered that the beneficial consequences of it were enjoyed by those that came after them, rather than directly by themselves.

For the trade union movement, the Grunwick strike remains hugely significant, primarily because of its implications for the labour movement in incorporating the interests of women and migrant workers of colour. The women we spoke to were less concerned about the impact of their actions on trade unions, and more interested in how it had affected them as individuals and as workers, impacted on their roles in their families and their communities, as well as the influence their actions had on popular perceptions about South Asian women. Because we were able to conduct the interviews in Hindi, allowing them to reflect on their past in a language they were comfortable with, we were able to produce an account which is not based on the frequently repeated assertions in other research, but that instead represents a more direct account of the women's own experiences. Because this dispute was so significant for the labour movement in this country, it is important to formulate a record of it in the principle protagonists' own words.

Our interviews with the women at Gate Gourmet who rejected the settlement agreed by their union also fills a significant gap in the accounts available of South Asian women's involvement in industrial activism. This dispute broke out in a different place and at a different time from the Grunwick dispute, and, as we discuss below, the world had changed in many different ways in the intervening thirty years. As we have made clear, unlike the events at Grunwick, the Gate Gourmet dispute is not celebrated as an indication of the agency and political determination of the women involved. Rather, it has been ignored not least because the actions of those women were in opposition to the decisions of their trade union, and deemed by some to be weakening, rather than strengthening the unions' cause. Recording these women's direct experiences is also important. Because of their long years of employment history in the UK, their interviews give a unique account of the complexity of the lives of migrant women workers as they lived the intersectional reality of work and family, production and reproduction, and faced the often conflicting norms and expectations of community and society. As with the Grunwick interviews, these interviews were also conducted in Hindi, which reinforced our ambition of allowing the women to relate their own personal analysis of how their lives had unfolded, both before and after the dispute, and the reasons they opposed the settlement agreed between the company and the trade union. If we want to understand the ways in which the relations between the trade union movement and migrant women workers has changed, we need to listen to the voices of those directly involved.

FROM GRUNWICK TO GATE GOURMET: A CHANGING WORLD

The different responses by the unions to the disputes at Grunwick and Gate Gourmet have to be understood in terms of the changes in the regulatory and political environment in which trade unions operate. Compared to the context of mass solidarity in which

Grunwick dispute unfolded, the strategies and practices of trade unions in the early-twenty-first century had changed very significantly. Through the Thatcher years and beyond, restrictions had been placed on trade unions' capacity to organise, and increasingly the options for collective action had been narrowed, to be replaced by systems of individual and legal complaints. Plus, an increasingly globalised economy resulted in changes to the labour market, and all of these played important roles in the outcome of this dispute.

Changing context of industrial relations legislation in the UK between Grunwick and Gate Gourmet

By 2005, when the Gate Gourmet workers began their dispute at Heathrow, the days of mass production were becoming a distant memory and an increasing proportion of workers in both manufacturing and service occupations were working for employers who were themselves operating as subcontractors, or supplying outsourced services. This inevitably was partly responsible for the declining levels of unionisation in the UK as well as the diminishing level of employment protection enjoyed by those in the organised sectors.

Workers' legal rights had also evolved considerably during this time. Successive legislation had been enacted which strengthened workers' legal rights, including anti-discrimination and equal pay laws. However, these changes had been accompanied by the weakening of other rights that had facilitated collective bargaining, such as the right to take industrial action in support of other workers (secondary picketing). The Conservative government elected in 1979 with Margaret Thatcher at its helm, was from the outset ideologically committed to reducing union power and effectiveness. The bitter struggles over the miners' strike in 1984 merely strengthened their resolve to reduce unions' power, and a series of measures were introduced which profoundly changed the regulatory framework in which unions operated, and would continue to do so in the following decades.

There were five major pieces of trade union legislation between 1979 and 1990: the 1980 Employment Act, the 1982 Employment Act, the 1984 Trade Union Act, the 1988 Employment Act, and the 1990 Employment Act. These together served to remove the legal space for collective action that had been used by trade unions, imposing severe restrictions on the ability of unions to organise lawful industrial action whilst also making them liable to claims for damages in the event of unlawful action. The Acts also introduced strict controls over unions' internal governance and voting arrangements, imposed restrictions on the compensation for union shop stewards' work, and removed all immunity in the case of secondary (solidarity) action (Crouch 1996; Miller and Steele 1993) all of which had a significant impact on the Gate Gourmet dispute.

The Labour government elected in 1997 largely continued with the trend towards reducing workers' collective rights, whilst at the same time introducing legislation which sought to improve workers' individual rights such as parental leave entitlements and equality rights. These changes were in line with EU directives based on the Social Charter, although according to many commentators, the application of these directives in the UK was 'minimalist' (Smith and Morton 2006, 405).

The shift from collective to individual rights is evident in the number of claims made to Employment Tribunals, which increased from an estimated 40,000 in 1978-9 (Dix et al. 2008, 9), the year when the Grunwick strike ended, to 191,451 claims in 2012-13 (Ministry of Justice 2010, 2). These numbers have declined dramatically following the introduction of the fee regime in July 2013 to 61,308 claims in 2014-15 (Ministry of Justice 2015). Inevitably these shifts in the regulatory context within which trade unions operate have had a profound impact not only on the nature of industrial activism, but also on the role of trade unions in supporting their members. The Grunwick dispute is primarily remembered for the mass solidarity picketing as well as the secondary action by the postal workers and others in support of the strike. In contrast, the Gate Gourmet dispute unfolded in 2005 in a very different regulatory context for the trade unions. The sorts of mass action on the streets of London that characterised the Grunwick dispute and indeed the limited solidarity action by airline baggage at Heathrow airport was no longer permitted in UK law.

These changes in the legal framework in which trade unions can operate are a mirror image of the increasing deregulation of employment relations in the UK. Workers from minority communities increasingly found work in small workplaces in privately owned service sectors as new sorts of products and services were produced for individual or corporate consumption. Just as the Grunwick operation had developed in response to the new and growing market for processing holiday and family photographs in the 1970s, the Gate Gourmet workers were employed in an outsourced operation, which prepared passenger meals for a privatised airline that had previously been a publicly owned national carrier. And while the rush by public and private corporations alike to reduce their direct operations to their core functions and to contract out a range of peripheral services such as IT, payroll, management, cleaning, maintenance and catering was put forward on the grounds of efficiency, it was widely recognised that a major incentive for this was also to avoid unionised workplaces and the necessity of negotiating and being bound by collective bargaining.

This was not a solely British phenomenon. Guy Standing (2011) has named the expanding numbers of low-paid unprotected workers in industrial economies the 'precariat' and observed the ways in which the working conditions and security of those in unorganised and insecure employment placed a downward pressure on the conditions for all workers in such economies. It is clear that certain sections of the workforce, mainly in well-established generally male-employing occupations, such as transport workers, as well as in professional occupations in the education and health services, have remained (at least until recently) a 'labour aristocracy'. However, the majority of low-paid jobs in a range of previously organised sectors such as building, retail, hotel and catering, agriculture, care work and cleaning are not protected by collective agreements between employers and employees. This change has been accelerated by the increasing proportion of public services which have been contracted out to private suppliers – not just in health and social care – and the unrelenting privatisation of different parts of previously publicly owned enterprises such as postal services and railways, ideologically driven by a belief in the efficiency of the private sector. This has inevitably resulted in a weakening of union membership, representation and potency. In this context it is quite clear that regulation of individual workers' legal rights has been enacted in direct contrast to the restrictions on union activities and resources.

One result of this outsourcing was the growth in the employment of agency workers. This had been common during the preceding decades, and by 2011, there were an estimated 1.4 million agency workers in the UK. The employment rights of such workers have been partially enhanced, in line with EU directives, so that after twelve weeks in the same role with the same employer, agency workers would be entitled to the same employment and working conditions as permanent employees, including pay rates, shift allowances, holiday pay, bonuses, and maternity rights. However such entitlements did not include occupational sick pay, redundancy pay and health insurance (BBC News 2011). These exceptions reinforced the trend towards precarious employment which had continued since the Conservative government took office in 1979. New entrants to the labour force, including minority women of migrant origin were often likely to be in situations where they lacked employment protection, and were seen as flexible – and thus disposable – workers by their employers.

In every aspect, the Gate Gourmet story reflects the result of these changes. Secondary picketing was outlawed by 2005, which put pressure on the union to sign a far-reaching Compromise Agreement and allowed the company to dispense with workers that they deemed to be insufficiently productive. In spite of initial support from the workers' own trade union, including from other categories of workers at Heathrow, fear of litigation and reputational damage led the union to withdraw support from those who refused to accept the compromise agreement. In the view of many of the sacked workers, this rode roughshod over individuals' rights and principles.

Changes in the world of work and the decline of unionisation

The thirty year period between Grunwick and Gate Gourmet was characterised by a shift from Fordist to post-Fordist modes of production, with concomitant changes to the labour market and to the nature of the preferred workforce and to workers' employment relations. The old modes of economic production, which had featured large firms, mass production and standardised work where workers could expect long term employment (though such secure employment was never available to most women or migrant workers) were supplanted in large part by an economy which demanded flexible, knowledge-based labour, working in a largely service context. It has been argued that this marked a shift from technical, financial or bureaucratic controls to cultural coordination, internalised commitment and self-discipline among employees (Thompson 2003).

However, these were not the features of a post-Fordist labour market that were experienced by those at the bottom end of the employment market, where features of the old economy persisted, albeit without the relative security enabled by mass production systems and extensive collective representation. Gorz (1999, 45) argued that large companies and organisations have now largely eliminated the capital-labour antagonism 'for the stable core of its elite workers' and shifted those antagonisms outside its field of vision, to the peripheral, insecure and unprotected labour force – what Standing (2011) terms the new and growing 'precariat'. Successive governments in the UK have been slow to counter the tendency for capital to compete to reduce labour costs, so the 'race to the bottom' on the basis of lower labour costs through deregulation has continued apace.

One of the consequences of these changes in the UK was the decline in unionisation and the rise of new forms of atomised employment. The Grunwick strike took place in a period marked by high levels of trade union membership, which has, with brief exceptions in 2014-15, been in decline since then (ONS 2016, 4). But these general trends hide important variations within the workforce; although unionisation amongst white workers was high in the 1970s, the rates of union membership amongst women, and amongst black and South Asian workers was much lower, a trend which lasted well into the 1990s (Bradley 1999; EOC 2004; Kirton and Healy 1999; Sinclair 1995). Since 2002, women's union density levels have increased consistently; in the current decade, union membership rates amongst women has been higher than among men, a trend which has primarily been attributed to the greater proportion of women workers in the public sector (Achur 2011, 3-4). This greater propensity of women to unionise is particularly marked for some categories of women, including such as those of South Asian origin; in 2013, 26 per cent of South Asian workers were members of trade unions, compared to 15 per cent of South Asian men (TUC

2014, 1). On the whole, unionisation levels have been highest for white workers, followed closely by black or black British workers, with lower levels documented for other categories including workers of South Asian origin (ONS 2016). In the majority of unions, BME groups continued to be under-represented as shop stewards, health and safety representatives, conference delegates and on union executives in relation to overall membership (TUC 2014, 2).

The growth in women's labour force participation in the UK: How did minority women fare?

Women's participation rate in the labour market (as a percentage of women of working age) in the UK increased steadily, from 60 per cent in 1981 to 76 per cent in 2001 (Jaumotte 2003). However, much of this employment is restricted to part-time and low-paid jobs, mainly in the service sector (EOC 2002). This trend has been exacerbated in recent years, due to a combination of aggressive 'austerity' policies which have further reduced in-work benefits and coerced even mothers of young children, particularly lone parents, into the labour force where they often have no choice but to accept minimum wage in insecure and part-time work. Working women in the UK confront a series of structural inequalities in the labour market as the result of their structural gendered realities. They have uniquely gendered relationships to a number of life course events and circumstances, including marriage, child-bearing, childcare, care for older or disabled relatives, life-stage and level of qualifications, all of which have had a negative effect on the quality of women's occupational and earnings opportunities (Anyadike-Danes and McVicar 2010; Dex et al. 1998; Elliot et al. 2001).

Recent research also indicates that women's ethnicity has a strong bearing on their labour market activity. The presence of a partner is identified as having the greatest impact on Pakistani and Bangladeshi women's employment, while the presence of a pre-school child is most significant for white women's economic participation. White women continue to have a higher rate of part-time working than all other ethnic groups, and the high rates of full-time work which black women have undertaken most likely reflect the lower earnings of BME men (Bruegel 1979). Interestingly, whilst minority ethnic women in non-manual occupations have occupational profiles similar to those of white women, those in manual occupations fare worse than their white counterparts, despite the fact that a larger proportion of minority ethnic women are in full-time employment overall (Dale and Holdsworth 1997).

The employment patterns of women from diverse ethnic backgrounds have historically varied significantly across different sectors, reflecting the diversity of women's experiences from different minority backgrounds (Botcherby 2006; Buckner et al. 2007; Dale et al. 2006; Lindley et al. 2004). For example, the Labour Force Survey data for 1979, just after the end of the Grunwick dispute, indicates that BME women were more heavily concentrated in the manufacturing sector. Compared to the 25 per cent of the employed British-born white women who worked in manufacturing in 1979, the corresponding figures were 58 per cent for Indian, 45 per cent for African-Asian, 54 per cent for Pakistani and 50 per cent for Bangladeshi women (Dustmann and Fabbri 2005, 445). However, this employment was not in the unionised factories employing male workers such as car manufacture or iron and steel production, but in the traditionally feminised workplaces and sweatshops of the garment and footwear industries.

The pattern of relegation to low-paid, low-status occupations, described as the 'ethnic penalty' in employment, has continued over the years and for black African, black Caribbean, Pakistani and Bangladeshi workers (Heath and Cheung 2006). Recent research indicates that BME workers' disadvantage in the labour market has continued, though patterns vary between different ethnic groups. Analysis of the 2011 census revealed that Pakistani women's unemployment rate was more than three times that of white British women, and for black Caribbean women, unemployment was more than double that of white British women (Nazroo and Kapadia 2013).

Black and minority ethnic women's struggles against their experiences of gender-based and racial discrimination and disadvantage in the labour market has also been extensively documented (Bryan et al. 1985; Mirza 1997; Parmar 1982; Wilson 1978), though, as in the case of the Grunwick and Gate Gourmet workers discussed in this volume, this has not always been with the full support of their trade unions (Wrench and Virdee 1996).

Given the history of minority women's labour market activity, their substantial participation in industrial activism and their high rates of union membership over recent decades, it is all the more problematic that the myth of South Asian women's assumed orientation towards domesticity has persisted (Anitha et al. 2012) alongside the inaccurate view that minority women workers are difficult to unionise, in spite of research to the contrary (Wrench 1987; Holgate 2005).

STRIKING CONTRASTS: GRUNWICK VERSUS GATE GOURMET

The facts of the two disputes, their causes, their protagonists, the outcome and the legacy are matters of historical record. But what these events tell us about the experience of migrant women workers with respect to British trade unions is very different.

The beginning of the Grunwick dispute in 1976 occurred just under a century after Disraeli's government passed the Conspiracy and Protection of Property Act in 1875, which effectively legalised union industrial actions such as withdrawal of labour and picketing. Grunwick was a cause that was embraced by a trade union movement confident of its power and its place in the British political context. The trade union movement in the 1970s was ambitious; its more progressive elements recognised that the world of work, or at least the world of the workforce was changing. They could no longer restrict themselves to the traditional white male working class which had sustained their growth for the previous hundred years.

However, since the 2000s, trade unions have encountered new problems in reaching out to BME workers, particularly recent migrants who are more likely to work in low-paid and precarious jobs where unions have little influence. This 'ethnic division of labour' (Wills et al. 2009) poses new challenges to trade unions' capacity to represent the most vulnerable sections of the workforce, and research documents recent efforts by unions to organise beyond traditional structures and alliances (Wills and Simms 2004), in what has been termed as 'community unionism' (Martinez-Lucio and Perrett 2009b).

Since the events of 2005 which precipitated the dispute at Gate

Gourmet, industrial relations have also been further complicated by the imposition of new rules about employment protection and the introduction of fees for industrial tribunals, as well as by the austerity policies by the (2011-15) coalition government and the subsequent (2015 -) Conservative government. These changes have taken place in the wake of the so-called financial crisis of 2008 in western economies dominated by unregulated financial services, as the structures of unsustainable debt supported by creative financial instruments crumbled before the horrified eyes of the world. But in the decade since the crisis, the finance sector has remained unregulated, whilst the power and reach of trade unions has been further diminished.

GLOBALISATION AND UBERISATION: KEY CHALLENGES FOR THE FUTURE

The changes in the world of work reflect changes in global realities, and these represent ongoing challenges for the trade union movement. The trends towards diminishing employment protection continue apace, not least because of the nature of globalisation, in which deregulation of the operations and mobility of capital has become entrenched, in contrast to increasing controls on migration and limitations on the international mobility of labour. The story of the relocation of Cadbury chocolate manufacturing plant from Somerdale in Somerset to Skarbimierz in Poland is representative of the ways in which the global mobility of capital is able to take advantage of cheap labour in different parts of the world to reduce costs, destroying unionised, protected jobs but also laying the foundations for the replacement of even low-paid unprotected jobs with technological innovations in the future (Meek 2017). In the Cadbury case, the union that represented a well-established and organised workforce in the UK was unable to prevent the company relocating to a take advantage of cheap labour. So it is not surprising that unions have found it increasingly difficult to protect an atomised workforce that is divided along ethnic and gendered lines.

The Grunwick film processing plant closed down in 2011 following a marked decline its business caused by the digital camera and smart phone revolutions. In 2009, British Airways started to withdraw the provision of in-flight meals on short-haul flights, and this policy is now being considered for long-haul flights as well (Farmer 2017). Whilst the offer of supermarket pre-packed food is the substitute service, the jobs which were lost in airline catering close to the Heathrow hub are now dispersed and carried out by a very different – though also largely migrant – workforce in different parts of the UK.

The nature of work is also being transformed by the so called gig economy – defined by the US Labour Bureau as 'single project[s] or task[s] for which a worker is hired, often through a digital marketplace, to work on demand' (Prettys 2017). Examples of this include taxi-hailing app Uber and food delivery service Deliveroo; in both of these, customers request services via apps or online, and employees are selected from an available pool. This form of technologically enabled piecework enables employers to access workers' services in response to flexible levels of demand. It is a form of employment relations which ensures that the worker bears all the risks without access to employment protection or entitlements while the employer incurs no employment related costs or taxation (Tomlinson and Corlett 2017). Recent estimates indicate that 2.5 per cent of workers in the UK already get more than half their income from such online platforms, a figure which is likely to increase in the future (Huws 2016).

These developments, together with the growth of self-employment, particularly amongst women, are indications of the rapid changes in the UK labour market, which challenge old models of labour organisation based on the large scale geographically static workplaces of previous eras. Some workers have indeed successfully challenged the way those employment practices falsely classified employees as self-employed despite their working on a regular basis for the same organisation, thus absolving the employer of all costs entailed in employing their flexible workforce and putting all the risk on to the workers. Reactions against this include the recent and ongoing legal challenges against Uber and Deliveroo. On 28 October 2016, two drivers, James Farrar and Yaseen Aslam, brought a case to the Employment Tribunal on behalf of a group of nineteen Uber workers who argued that they were employed by the San Francisco-based firm Uber, rather than working for themselves. The

Employment Tribunal ruled that Uber drivers are not self-employed and should be paid the national minimum wage. In their judgement, the tribunal found that Uber had resorted 'in its documentation to fictions, twisted language and even brand new terminology' to create the fiction of self-employment.[1] Delivery drivers have similarly challenged their categorisation as self-employed freelancers rather than employed by Deliveroo, through a series of strikes demanding changes including a minimum wage and that the company negotiate with the workers as a collective, rather than with individual workers (Day 2016).

The challenge for the trade union movement is to develop appropriate forms of organisation, which will, by necessity, be based on new technology and social media, in order to respond effectively to these new forms of employment relations and work in the twenty-first century.

CONCLUSION

It is in this context that the long term implications for the politics of race and class and gender in UK labour markets and the trade union movement must be analysed. The response of post-2008 governments was to impose fiscal and financial austerity on their populations in order to pursue a monetarist objective of debt reduction and deficit elimination. These policies have had negative effects on the working population in the UK and elsewhere, in several ways. Firstly they have squeezed expenditure and services in the public sector, reducing both employment and access to social security benefits and entitlements. For the UK workforce, not least for working women from migrant backgrounds, this has had direct impacts on the kinds of jobs they have been able to get, since, as we have shown, many of these women had previously managed to obtain relatively secure jobs in the public sector, in the decades before Gate Gourmet. Secondly, the quality and access to services such as health, education and social care was significantly squeezed, whilst the cost of further and higher education, housing and transport escalated exponentially (Pearson and Elson 2015).

Recent research has indicated that women have borne the brunt of these cuts, and particularly women from BME communities. The

Women's Budget Group has calculated that by 2020, the cumulative effect of tax and benefit changes since 2010 on UK-based South Asian women living in the poorest 33 per cent of households, will mean that their average individual income will be 19 per cent lower than it would have been under the tax and benefit system before the 2010 general election. Not only is it clear that the poorest households, and women in particular, have shouldered the greatest burden of austerity measures, it is also the case that the compounding effect of income, gender and ethnicity means that BME households are the hardest hit. Women lose more than men, and black and Asian households lose more than white households. Taken together, this sees the poorest black and South Asian women disadvantaged in multiple ways, by their location at the intersection of gender, race and class (Women's Budget Group 2016).

Although as we have reported above, minority women who have managed to secure non-manual jobs have reduced the wage gaps between themselves and their white counterparts, more recent research by TUC in 2015 indicates that black workers with degrees are paid on average nearly a quarter less than their white peers. Unfortunately, the TUC does not disaggregate these figures by gender, but women like those who were employed in low-paid jobs in Grunwick and Gate Gourmet have remained extremely disadvantaged in the UK labour market.[2]

These trends are only exacerbated by the racialised politics and political discourse which have characterised the post-EU referendum landscape in this country, in which much of the working class has been mobilised on the basis of an exclusionary construction of migrant workers as a threat to 'indigenous workers' – particularly working class – wages and jobs. This reality complicates the claims of the trade union movement to have successfully championed the rights and prospects of black and minority ethnic women.

The recent commemorations of the fortieth anniversary of the Grunwick strike continued to claim that Grunwick changed the trade union movement forever. These claims would appear to conflate the discrete events of Grunwick, in which South Asian women were the leaders and the principal actors, with the cause of minority women workers in general. Although there has been acknowledgement about the role of minority women workers in the decades since the Grunwick dispute, the silence about the fate of other less celebrated South Asian women in trade unions continues. The Communication Workers Union (CWU), for example, marked the fortieth anniversary of the Grunwick dispute at its Black Workers Conference by discussing the significant role the union played in showing solidarity with the mainly South Asian female workforce. It claimed (CWU 2016):

> The outcome of the dispute is of little consequence compared to what the heroic stand itself represented. Some suggest that it marked a momentous shift in the way that BAME people were considered in the world of work going forward and it is the responsibility of the union to continue this legacy.

While this was undoubtedly true, there is a danger that a narrow focus on the Grunwick dispute strengthens the dominant view that Grunwick was a unique event, which requires no further analysis or qualification.

Additionally, internal factors constrained the unions' capacity to defend the rights of the minority women workers at Gate Gourmet. In spite of the way in which the British trade union movement has constructed the now historic Grunwick strike as an emblematic turning point in its representation of black and minority ethnic and women workers, trade union structures, procedures and legal frameworks, it can be argued that they have not been wholly successful in serving minority women effectively. Since Grunwick, trade unions in the UK have adopted a variety of strategies and frameworks to address issues of diversity (Wrench 1996; 2004). However, the union strategies for mobilising and representing black and minority ethnic workers have focused on recruitment and campaigning issues (Martinez-Lucio and Perrett 2009a). The underlying assumption has long been that minority ethnic and women workers lack a propensity to unionise, which has precluded any radical re-examination of those trade union structures and practices that might serve to exclude these women's particular interests. On the whole, trade union approaches to gender have been more effective than those concerning issues of race/racism. Issues raised by the multiple forms of inequalities experienced by the intersectional location of black and minority ethnic women workers remain largely unrecognised as race and gender have tended to be examined as discretely separate, and initiatives to understand their intersection have remained piecemeal and fragmented. As Fine and Holgate (2013, 141) have argued:

> The challenge is then to think how workers' issues can be reframed to reflect their lived experiences as workers and as citizens, recognising how these two parts of people's lives are so very much interlinked, and particularly so for immigrant workers.

We would add to that the importance of recognising that migrant workers are also gendered, and it is essential also to reflect their lived experience as women and men.

This dimension of industrial relations echoes Nancy Fraser's argument that 'only by integrating recognition and redistribution can we arrive at a framework that is adequate to the demands of our age' (Fraser 1997, 12). It would seem timely to apply this analysis to the structures and processes of trade unions in Britain, to forge new strategies which support the legitimate aspirations and expectations of minority women workers, such as the South Asian women who protested their treatment by both the company and their union at Gate Gourmet. In the context of South Asian women's experiences of employment in the UK it is important not only to focus on traditional labour issues of pay, working conditions, rights to free collective bargaining. For these workers, their identities and experiences as migrants and as women are as central as their resistance to low pay and unfair working conditions, and this informed and underlaid the determination and tenacity they displayed in their protest and resistance. But fully integrating this recognition into ongoing strategies remains a formidable challenge in a period when trade unions remain constrained by both the nature of the labour market in an era of globalisation and restructuring, and by the increasing restrictions on trade unions imposed by a neoliberal state in the UK.

NOTES

1. Mr Y. Aslam, Mr J. Farrar and Others v. Uber, Case nos 2202550/2015 & Others, p.27. Available at: www.judiciary.gov.uk/wp-content/

uploads/2016/10/aslam-and-farrar-v-uber-reasons-20161028.pdf. (Accessed 2 May 2017.)

2. These figures are based on the TUC's analysis of the ONS Labour Force Survey figures from Q4 2014-Q3 2015 (TUC 2016). See 'Black workers with degrees earn a quarter less than white counterparts, finds TUC', TUC London 2016. Available at: www.tuc.org.uk/equality-issues/ black-workers/labour-market/black-workers-degrees-earn-quarter-less-white. (Accessed 2 May 2017.)

Bibliography

Achur, J., *Trade Union Membership 2010: A National Statistics Publication*, Department of Business, Innovation and Skills, London 2011.

Ahmad, F., 'Still in Progress? Methodological Dilemmas, Tensions and Contradictions in Theorising South Asian Muslim Women', in N. Puwar and P. Raghuram (eds), *South Asian Women and the Diaspora*, Berg Publishers, Oxford 2003, pp. 43-65.

Alberti, G., 'Mobility Strategies, "Mobility Differentials" and "Transnational Exit": The Experiences of Precarious Migrants in London's Hospitality Jobs', *Work, Employment and Society*, 28, 6 (2014), 865-881.

Allen, S. and Wolkowitz, C., *Homeworking: Myths and Realities,* Macmillan, London 1987.

Alleyne, B., 'An Idea of Community and Its Discontents: Towards a More Reflexive Sense of Belonging in Multicultural Britain', *Ethnic and Racial Studies*, 25, 4 (2002), 607-27.

Andall, J., 'The Space Between: Gender Politics and Immigration Politics in Contemporary Europe', in J. Andall (ed.), *Gender and Ethnicity in Contemporary Europe*, Berg, Oxford 2003, pp. 1-20.

Andall, J., *Gender, Migration and Domestic Service*, Ashgate, London 2000.

Anderson, B., *Doing the Dirty Work? The Global Politics of Domestic Labour*, Zed Books, London and New York 2000.

Anitha, S., Pearson, R. and McDowell, L., 'From Grunwick to Gate Gourmet: South Asian Women's Industrial Activism and the Role of Trade Unions', *Revue Française de Civilisation Britannique* (2018, forthcoming).

Anitha, S., Pearson, R. and McDowell, L., 'Striking Lives: Multiple Narratives of South Asian Women's Employment, Identity and Protest in the UK', *Ethnicities*, 12, 6 (2012), 654-775. Ansari, H., 'Mapping the Colonial: South Asians in Britain, 1857-1947', in N. Ali, V.S. Kalra, and S. Sayyid (eds), *A Postcolonial People:*

South Asians in Britain, Hurst and Company, London 2006, pp. 143-156.

Anthias, F. and Yuval-Davis, N., *Racialised Boundaries: Race, Gender, Nation, Colour and Class and the Anti-Racist Struggle*, Routledge, London 1993.

Anthias, F., 'Evaluating Diaspora: Beyond Ethnicity?', *Sociology* 32, 3 (1998), 557-580.

Anwar, M., *Between Cultures: Continuity and Change in the Lives of Young Asians*, Routledge, London 1998.

Anwar, M., *The Myth of Return: Pakistanis in Britain*, Heinemann, London 1979.

Anyadike-Danes, D. and McVicar, D., 'My Brilliant Career: Characterizing the Early Labor Market Trajectories of British Women From Generation X', *Sociological Methods Research*, 38, 3 (2010), 482-512.

Aston, J., Hooker, H., Page, R. and Willison, R., *Pakistani and Bangladeshi Women's Attitudes to Work and Family*, Department for Work and Pensions Research Report No. 458, HMSO, Leeds 2007.

Atkinson, C. and Lucas, R., 'Worker Response to HR Practice in Adult Social Care in England', *Human Resources Management Journal*, 23, 3 (2013), 296-312.

Aurora, S., 'Grunwick 40 Years On: Lessons from the Asian Women Strikers', *OpenDemocracy*, 22 November 2016. Available at: www.opendemocracy.net/5050/sujata-aurora/grunwick-40-years-on-lessons-from-asian-women-strikers. (Accessed 11 September 2017.)

Bagguley, P., *The Individualisation of Class Struggle*, University of Leeds, Leeds 2002. Available at: www.sociology.leeds.ac.uk/about/staff/bagguley.php. (Accessed 14 July 2016.)

Ballard, R., (ed.), *Desh Pardesh: The South Asian Presence in Britain*, Hurst and Co., London 1994.

Ballard, R., *Riste and Ristedari: The Significance of Marriage in the Dynamics of Transnational Kinship Networks*, The Centre for Applied South Asian Studies, University of Manchester, Manchester 2004. Available at: www.casas.org.uk/papers/pdfpapers/ristedari.pdf. (Accessed 4 April 2017.)

Barrett, E., 'The True Heroes of Grunwick', *The Spiked*, 14 December 2016. Available at: www.spiked-online.com/newsite/article/the-true-heroes-of-grunwick/http/independent.co.uk/news/obituaries/jayaben-desai-trade-unionist-who-shot-to-national-prominence-during-the-bitter-grunwick-dispute-of-2220589.html#.WdTCQV tSzcs. (Accessed 1 October 2016.)

Baumann, G., *Contesting Culture: Discourses of Identity in Multi-Ethnic London*, Cambridge University Press, Cambridge 1996.

BBC News, 'Record Industrial Dispute Settled', *BBC News*, 23 April 2000. Available at: news.bbc.co.uk/1/hi/business/723718.stm. (Accessed 27 September 2017.)

BBC News, 'BA strike chaos starting to ease', *BBC News*, 13 August 2005. Available at: news.bbc.co.uk/1/hi/england/london/4147780. stm. (Accessed 25 October 2017.)

BBC News, 'Agency Workers Get Greater Rights From 1 October', *BBC News*, 30 September 2011. Available at: www.bbc.co.uk/news/business-15115461 (Accessed 26 April 2017)

Beckett, A., *When the Lights Went Out: Britain in the Seventies*, Faber and Faber, London 2009.

Bernsten, L., 'Reworking Labour Practices: On the Agency of Unorganized Mobile Migrant Construction Workers', *Work, Employment and Society*, 30, 3 (2016), 472-488.

Bhachu, P., 'Twice Versus Direct Migrants: East African Sikh Settlers in Britain Volume V. 1989-90', *California Immigrants in World Perspective*, The Conference Papers, 1990. Available at: escholarship. org/uc/item/840862km. (Accessed 24 April 2017.)

Bhachu, P., *Twice-Migrants: East-African Sikh Settlers in Britain*, Tavistock Publications, London and New York 1985.

Bittman, M., Rice,J. and Wajcman, J., 'Appliances and Their Impact: The Ownership of Domestic Technology and Time Spent on Household Work', *British Journal of Sociology*, 55, 3 (2004), 401-423.

Blanchflower, D., Salaheen, J. and Shadworth, C., *The Impact of the Recent Migration from Eastern Europe on the UK Economy*, IZA Discussion Paper No 2615, IZA, Bonn 2007.

Bonizzoni, P., 'Immigrant Working Mothers Reconciling Work and Childcare: The Experience of Latin American and Eastern European Women in Milan', *Social Politics*, 21, 2 (2014), 194-217.

Borchers, A., Lee, R.C., Martsolf, D.S. and Maler, J., 'Employment Maintenance and Intimate Partner Violence', *Workplace Health and Safety*, 64, 10 (2016), 469-478.

Botcherby, S., *Pakistani, Bangladeshi and Black Caribbean Women and Employment Survey: Aspirations, Experiences and Choices*, EOC, Manchester 2006.

Box, G., 'Flyer Liars', *Daily Mirror*, 16 August 2005.

Bradley, H. and Fenton, S., 'Reconciling Culture and Economy: Ways Forward in the Analysis of Gender and Ethnicity' in L. Ray and A. Sayer (eds), *Culture and Economy After the Cultural Turn*, Sage, London 1999, pp. 112-34.

Bradley, H., *Gender and Power in the Workplace*, Macmillan, London 1999.

Brah, A. and Shaw, S., *Working Choices: South Asian Women and the Labour Market,* Department of Employment Research Paper, no.91, Department of Employment, London 1992.

Brah, A., *Cartographies of Diaspora: Contesting Identities*, Routledge, London 1996.

Brettell, C.B., 'Theorizing Migration in Anthropology: The Social Construction of Networks, Identities, Communities and Globalscapes,' in C.B. Brettell and J.F. Hollifield (eds), *Migration Theory*, Routledge, New York 2000, pp. 97-135.

Brown, J. M., *Global South Asians: Introducing the Modern Diaspora*, Cambridge University Press, New Delhi 2007.

Brown, M. S., 'Religion and Economic Activity in the South Asian Population', *Ethnic and Racial Studies*, 23, 6 (2000), 1035-1061.

Brown, W., 'Individualisation and Union Recognition in Britain in the 1990s', in S. Deery and R. Mitchell (eds), *Employment Relations: Individualisation and Union Exclusion*, Federation Press, Sydney 1999, pp. 153-170.

Brown, W., Deakin, S., Nash, D. and Oxenbridge, S., 'The Employment Contract: From Collective Procedures to Individual Rights', *British Journal of Industrial Relations*, 38, 4 (2000), 611-629.

Bryan, B., Dadzie, S. and Scafe, S., *The Heart of the Race: Black Women's Lives in Britain*, Virago, London 1985.

Buckner, L., Yeandle, S. and Botcherby, S., *Ethnic Minority Women and Local Labour Markets*, Equal Opportunities Commission, Manchester 2007.

Bunsee, B., 'Women in Struggle: The Strike at Mansfield Hosiery', *Spare Rib*, 19, 21 (1974).

Butler, D., 'How the Grunwick Strike woke up trade unionists to minority workers' rights', *New Statesman*, 22 November 2016. Available at: www.newstatesman.com/politics/staggers/2016/11/how-grunwick-strike-woke-trade-unionists-minority-workers-rights. (Accessed 11 September 2017.)

Cantle, T., *Community Cohesion: A Report of the Independent Review Team*, Home Office, London 2001.

CAPA, 'Gate Gourmet Figures Show Productivity Rising and Sickness Falling at LHR', 21 April 2006, *CAPA Centre for Aviation*. Available at: centreforaviation.com/insights/analysis/gate-gourmet-figures-show-productivity-rising-and-sickness-falling-at-lhr-974. (Accessed 25 October 2017.)

Carby, H.V., 'White Woman Listen! Black Feminism and the Boundaries of Sisterhood', in The University of Birmingham Centre for Contemporary Cultural Studies (ed.), *The Empire Strikes Back: Race and Racism in 70s Britain*, Hutchinson and Co., London 1982, pp. 212-235.

Carter, B. and Fenton, S., 'Not Thinking Ethnicity: A Critique of the Ethnicity Paradigm in an Over-Ethnicised Sociology', *Journal for the Theory of Social Behaviour*, 40, 1 (2010), 1-18.

Carter, B., Green, M. and Halpern, R., 'Immigration Policy and the Racialisation of Migrant Labour: The Construction of National Identities in the USA and Britain', *Ethnic and Racial Studies*, 19, 1 (1996), 135-157.

Castree, N., 'Labour Geography: A Work in Progress', *International Journal of Urban and Regional Research*, 31, 4 (2007), 853-62.

Chaudhuri, S, Morash, M. and Yingling, J., 'Marriage Migration, Patriarchal Bargains and Wife Abuse: A Study of South Asian women', *Violence Against Women*, 20, 1 (2014), 121-161.

Cockburn, C., *Strategies for Gender Democracy*, European Commission, Brussels 1995.

Colgan, F. and Ledwith, S., 'Diversity, Identities and Strategies of Women Trade Union Activists,' *Gender, Work and Organization*, 7, 4 (2000), 242-257.

Colling, T., 'What Space for Unions on the Floor of Rights? Trade Unions and the Enforcement of Statutory Individual Employment Rights', *Industrial Law Journal*, 35, 2 (2006), 140-160.

Constable, N., 'Introduction: Cross-Border Marriages, Gendered Mobility and Global Hypergamy', in N. Constable (ed.), *Cross-Border Marriages: Gender and Mobility in Transnational Asia*, University of Pennsylvania Press, Philadelphia 2005, pp. 1-16.

Cooper, M., 'The Remaking of the British Working Class: Trade Unions and Black and Asian Worker in Britain 1949-1984', *Historical Materialism Conference*, London, 7 November 2013. Available at:

britishcontemporaryhistory.com/in-the-news/the-trade-unions-and-black-and-asian-workers/. (Accessed 24 April2017.)

Cotterill, J., *Language and Power in Court: A Linguistic Analysis of the O. J. Simpson Trial,* Palgrave Macmillan, Basingstoke 2003.

Cox, A., Sung, S., Oliver, G. and Hebson, G., 'Using Union Mobilisation Theory To Explain the Expression of Gendered Industrial Relations Interests: Two UK Case Studies', *Journal of Industrial Relations,* 49, 5 (2007), 717-739.

Crompton, R. (ed.) *Restructuring Gender Relations and Employment,* Oxford University Press, Oxford 1999.

Crouch, C., 'Atavism and Innovation: Labour Legislation and Public Policy Since 1979 in Historical Perspective', *Historical Studies in Industrial Relations,* 2 (1996), 111-124.

Curran, S.R., Shafer, S., Donato K.M. and Garip F., 'Mapping Gender and Migration in Sociological Scholarship: Is It Segregation or Integration?', *International Migration Review,* 40, 1 (2006), 199-223.

CWU, 'Report of the 2016 Black Workers' conference of the CWU', 2017. Available at: www.cwu.org/media/news/2016/october/12/black-workers-conference-2016. (Accessed 2 May 2017.)

Dahya, B., 'The nature of Pakistani Ethnicity in Industrial Cities in Britain', in A. Cohen (ed.) *Urban Ethnicity,* Tavistock, London 1974, pp. 77-118.

Dale, A., and Holdsworth, C., 'Issues in the Analysis of Ethnicity in the 1991 British Census: Evidence From Microdata', *Ethnic and Racial Studies,* 20, 1 (1997), 160-181.

Dale, A., 'Social Exclusion of Pakistani and Bangladeshi Women', *Sociological Research Online,* 7, 3 (2002). Available at: www.socresonline.org.uk/7/3/dale.html. (Accessed 1 November 2017.)

Dale, A., Lindley, J. and Dex, S., 'A Life-Course Perspective on Ethnic Differences in Women's Economic Activity in Britain', *European Sociological Review,* 22, 4 (2006), 459-476.

Datta, K., McIlwaine, C., Evans, Y., Herbert, J., May, J., and Wills., J., 'From Coping Strategies to Tactics: London's Low-Pay Economy and Migrant Labour', *British Journal of Industrial Relations,* 45, 2 (2007), 404-32.

Davis, M., (ed.), *Class and Gender in British Labour History: Renewing the Debate (or Starting it?),* Merlin Press, London 2010.

Davis, M., McKenzie, R. and Sullivan, R., *Working Against Racism: The Role of Trade Unions in* Britain, TUC, London 2006.

Day, J., 'The Deliveroo Strike', *London Review of Books Blog*, 12 August 2016. Available at www.lrb.co.uk/blog/2016/08/12/jon-day/the-deliveroo-strike. (Accessed 28 April 2017.)

de Certeau, M., *The Practice of Everyday Life*, trans. Steven Rendall, University of California Press, Berkeley 1984.

Deery, S. and Mitchell, R., (eds), *Employment Relations: Individualisation and Union Exclusion*, Federation Press, Sydney 1999.

Dex, S., Macran, S., Joshi, H. and McCulloch, A., 'Women's Employment Transitions Around Childbearing', *Oxford Bulletin of Economics and Statistics*, 60 (1998), 97-115.

Dhindsa, K. S., *Indian Immigrants in the UK: A Socio-Economic Analysis*, Concept Publishing Company, New Delhi 1998.

Dhondy, M., 'The Strike at Imperial Typewriters', *Race Today*, July 1974, pp. 201-5.

Dickens, L., 'Gender, Race and Employment Equality in Britain: Inadequate Strategies and the Role of Industrial Relations Actors', *Industrial Relations Journal*, 28, 4 (1997), 282-291.

Dickens, L., 'Individual Statutory Employment Rights Since 1997: Constrained Expansion', *Employee Relations*, 24, 6 (2002), 619-637.

Dickey S., 'Permeable Homes: Domestic Service, Household Space and the Vulnerability of Class Boundaries in Urban India', *American Ethnologist*, 27, 2 (2000), 462-489.

Dix, G., Forth, J. and Sisson, K., *Conflict at Work: The Pattern of Disputes in Britain Since 1980*, ACAS, London 2008. Available at: www.acas.org.uk/media/pdf/f/j/Acas_Research_Conflict_at_work_03_08-accessible-version-July-2011.pdf. (Accessed 24 April 2017.)

Doyle, M., and Timonen, V., 'Obligations, Ambitions, Calculations: Migrant Care Workers' Negotiation of Work, Career, and Family Responsibilities', *Social Politics: International Studies in Gender, State and Society*, 17, 1 (2010), 29-52.

Dromey, J. and Taylor, G., *Grunwick: The Workers' Story*, Lawrence and Wishart, London 2016. First published 1978.

Duffield, M., *Black Radicalism and the Politics of De-industrialisation: The Hidden History of Indian Foundry Workers*, Avebury, Aldershot 1988.

Dustmann, C. and Fabbri, F., 'Immigrants in the British Labour Market', *Fiscal Studies*, 26, 4 (2005), 423-470.

Dyer, S., McDowell, L., and Batnitzky, A., 'Migrant Work, Precarious Work-Life Balance: What the Experiences of Migrant Workers in the Service Sector in Greater London Tell Us About the Adult Worker Model', *Gender, Place and Culture*, 18, 5 (2011), 685-700.

Eade, J., *The Politics of a Community: The Bangladeshi Community in East London*, Avesbury, Aldershot 1989.

Ehrenreich, B., and Hochschild, A. R., *Global Woman: Nannies, Maids, and Sex Workers in the New Economy*, Metropolitan Books, New York 2003.

Elliott, J., Dale, A. and Egerton, M., 'The Influence of Qualifications on Women's Work Histories, Employment Status and Earnings at Age 33', *European Sociological Review*, 17 (2001), 145-168.

Elson, D. and Pearson, R., '"Nimble Fingers Make Cheap Workers": An Analysis of Women's Employment in Third World Export Manufacturing', *Feminist Review*, 7 (1981), 87-107.

EOC, *Facts about Men and Women in Great Britain*, Equal Opportunities Commission, Manchester 2004.

EOC, *Women and Men in Britain: Management*, Equal Opportunities Commission, Manchester 2002.

Evans, L. and Bowlby, S., 'Crossing Boundaries – Racialised Gendering and the Labour Market Experiences of Pakistani Migrant Women in Britain', *Women's Studies International Forum*, 23, 4 (2000), 461-474.

Evans, R., 'Covert Police Spied on Strikers and Their Supporters in Iconic Dispute', *The Guardian*, 13 April 2016. Available at: www.theguardian.com/uk-news/undercover-with-paul-lewis-and-rob-evans/2016/apr/13/covert-police-spied-on-strikers-and-their-supporters-in-iconic-dispute. (Accessed 24 April 2017.)

Farmer, B., 'British Airways Could Charge for Food on Long Haul Flights', *The Telegraph*, 10 April 2017. Available at: www.telegraph.co.uk/news/2017/04/09/british-airways-could-charge-food-long-haul-flights. (Accessed 28 April 2017.)

Fine, J. and Holgate, J., 'The Countermovement Needs a Movement (and a Counter Strategy)', in L. Adler, M. Tapia and L. Turner (eds), *Mobilizing Against Inequality: Unions, Immigrant Workers, and the Crisis of Capitalism,* ILR Press, Ithaca 2014, pp. 127-145.

Firmin, P., 'A Truly Working Class Hero(ine)', *Red Pepper*, 19 January 2011. Available: www.redpepper.org.uk/a-truly-working-class-heroine. (Accessed 16 November 2016.)

Flying Pickets (ed.) *Sechs monate streik bei Gate Gourmet,* Assoziation A, Berlin 2007.

Forbes, A., 'In the Wake of Grunwick', *Marxism Today,* December 1977, pp. 386-391.

Forde, C. and Mackenzie, R., 'Migrant Workers in Low-Skilled Employment: Assessing the Implications for Human Resources Management', *International Journal of Manpower,* 30, 5 (2009), 437-452.

Fraser, N., *Justice Interruptus,* Routledge, London 1997.

Froystad, K., 'Master-Servant Relations and the Domestic Reproduction of Caste in Northern India', *Ethnos,* 68, 1 (2003), 73-94.

Froystad, K., *Blended Boundaries: Caste, Class and Shifting Faces of 'Hinduness' in a North Indian City,* OUP, New Delhi 2005.

Fryer, P., *Staying Power: The History of Black People in Britain,* Pluto, London 1984.

Gardner, K. and Shakur, A., 'I'm Bengali, I'm Asian, and I'm Living Here', in R. Ballard (ed.) *Desh Pardesh: The South Asian Presence in Britain, UK,* C. Hurst and Co, London 1994, pp. 142-164.

Gedalof, I., 'Unhomely Homes: Women, Family and Belonging in UK Discourses of Migration and Asylum', *Journal of Ethnic and Migration Studies,* 33, 1 (2007), 77-94.

Ghassem-Fachandi, P., 'On the Political Uses of Disgust in Gujarat', *South Asian History and Culture* 1, 4 (2010), 557-576.

Gilroy, P., 'The End of Antiracism', in J. Donald and A. Rattansi (eds), *'Race', Culture and Difference,* Sage, London 1992, pp. 49-61.

Goldfarb, J., 'Gate Gourmet Now Owned by Multiple Investors', *Reuters,* 2 March 2007. Available www.reuters.com/article/idUSL0214903620070302. (Accessed 28 March 2017.)

Gorz, A., *Reclaiming Work: Beyond the Wage-Based Society,* Polity, Oxford 1999.

Grossman, R., 'Women's Place in the Integrated Circuit,' *Southeast Asia Chronicle,* 66 (1979), 2-17.

Hagan, J., Lowe, N., and Quingla, C., Skills on the Move: Rethinking the Relationship Between Human Capital and Immigrant Economic Mobility', *Work and Occupations,* 38, 2 (2011), 149-178.

Hall, S., 'The Question of Cultural Identity', in S. Hall, D. Held and A. McGrew (eds), *Modernity and its Futures,* Polity Press, Cambridge 1992, pp. 274-316.

HC, 'Hillingdon Hospital (Cleaners' Dispute)', House of Commons

Debate, vol. 285 cc320-913, 13 November 1996. Available at: hansard.millbanksystems.com/commons/1996/nov/13/hillingdon-hospital-cleaners-dispute. (Accessed 4 April 2017.)

HC, 'Post Office Act 1953 (Industrial Dispute)', House of Commons Debate, vol. 918 cc1637-98, 4 November 1976. Available at: hansard.millbanksystems.com/commons/1976/nov/04/post-office-act-1953-industrial-dispute#S5CV0918P0_19761104_HOC_293 (Accessed 29 Nov 2016)

Healy, G., Bradley, H. and Mukherjee, N., 'Inspiring Activists: The Experience of Minority Ethnic Women in Trade Unions', in G. Healy, E. Heery, P. Taylor and W. Brown (eds), *The Future of Worker Representation,* Macmillan, Basingstoke 2004, pp. 103-126.

Hebson, G., Rubery, J. and Grimshaw, D., 'Rethinking the Job Satisfaction in Care Work: Looking Beyond the Care Debates', *Work, Employment and Society,* 29, 2 (2015), 314-330.

Hencke, D., '£600,000 for Shop Stewards Fired Over Gate Gourmet Strike', *The Guardian,* 18 September 2006.

Hendy, J. and Gall, G., 'British Trade Union Rights Today and the Trade Union Freedom Bill' in K.D. Ewing (ed.), *The Right to Strike: From the Trade Disputes Act 1906 to a Trade Union Freedom Bill 2006,* Institute of Employment Rights, Liverpool 2006, pp. 247-277.

Herbert, J. 'Oral Histories of the Ugandan Asians in Britain: Gendered Identities in the Diaspora', *Contemporary South Asia,* 17, 1 (2009), 21-32.

Herbert, J., 'The British Ugandan Asian Diaspora: Multiple and Contested Belongings', *Global Networks,* 12, 3 (2012), 296-313.

Hillman, N., 'A 'Chorus of Execration'? Enoch Powell's "Rivers of Blood" Forty Years On', *Patterns of Prejudice,* 42, 1 (2008), 83-104.

Hochschild, A. R., *The Second Shift: The Working Parents and the Revolution at Home',* Avon Books, New York 1989.

Hochschild, A.R. 'Emotion Work, Feeling Rules and Social Structure', *American Journal of Sociology,* 85, 3 (1979), 551-575.

Hodgson, R., *Dignity at Work,* Cambridge University Press, Cambridge 2001.

Holgate, J., 'Organizing Migrant Workers: A Case Study of Working Conditions and Unionization in a London Sandwich Factory', *Work Employment and Society,* 19, 4 (2005), 63-80.

Holgate, J., Hebson, G. and McBride, A., 'Why Gender and

"Difference" Matters: A Critical Appraisal of Industrial Relations Research', *Industrial Relations Journal*, 37, 4 (2006), 310-328.

hooks, b., *Yearning: Race, Gender and Cultural Politics*, Turnaround, London 1991.

Hughes, S., 'Special Branch "Political Police" Spied On Grunwick Strikers', *Morning Star*, 4 March 2016. Available at: morningstaronline. co.uk/a-9eee-Special-Branch-political-police-spied-on-Grunwick-strikers#.WD3No1WLTcu. (Accessed 29 November 2016.)

Huws, U., 'Logged Labour: A New Paradigm of Work Organisation?', *Work Organisation, Labour and Globalisation*, 10, 1 (Spring 2016), 7-26.

IMR, 'Gender and Migration Revisited', *International Migration Review* (Special Issue), 40, 1 (2006).

IPPR, *Irregular Migration in the UK: An IPPR Factfile*, Institute for Public Policy Research, London 2006.

Jarvis, H., 'The Tangled Webs We Weave: Household Strategies to Co-Ordinate Home and Work', *Work, Employment and Society*, 13, 2 (1999), 225-247.

Jaumotte, F., *Female Labour Force Participation: Past Trends and Main Determinants in OECD Countries*, OECD Economics Department Working Papers, No. 376, OECD iPublishing, 2003. Available at: dx.doi.org/10.1787/082872464507. (Accessed 28 April 2017.)

Jayaram, N., (ed.) *The Indian Diaspora: Dynamics of Migration*, Sage, London 2004.

Jha, D.N., *Holy Cow: Beef in Indian Dietary Traditions*, Verso, London 2002.

Jones, E., 'The Bristol Bus Boycott of 1963', *Black History Month*, 365, 2015. Available at: www.blackhistorymonth.org.uk/article/section/bhm-heroes/the-bristol-bus-boycott-of-1963. (Accessed 13 February 2017.)

Kalra, V., *From Textile Mills to Taxi Ranks: Experiences of Migration, Labour and Social Change*, Ashgate Publishing, Aldershot 2000.

Katz, C., *Growing Up Global: Economic Restructuring and Children's Everyday Lives*, University of Minnesota Press, Minneapolis, MN, 2004.

Kirton, G. and Greene, A.M., 'The Dynamics of Positive Action in UK Trade Unions: The Case of Women and Black Members', *Industrial Relations Journal* 33, 2 (2002), 157-72.

Kirton, G. and Healy, G., 'Transforming Union Women: The Role of Women Trade Union Officials in Union Renewal', *Industrial Relations Journal*, 30, 1 (1999), 31-45.

Kofman, E. and Raghuram, P., 'Women and Global Labour Migrations: Incorporating Skilled Workers', *Antipode*, 38, 2, (2006), 282-303.

Kofman, E., Phizacklea, A., Raghuram, P. and Sales, R., *Gender and International Migration in Europe: Employment, Welfare and Politics*, Routledge, London 2000.

Kusakabe, K. and Pearson, R., 'Transborder Migration; Social Reproduction and Economic Development: A Case Study of Burmese Women Workers in Thailand', *International Migration: Special Issue on Women and Migration in Globalising Asia: Gendered Experiences, Agency and Activism*, 48, 6 (2010), 13-43.

Levidow, L., 'Grunwick: The Social Contract Meets the 20th Century Sweatshop', in L. Levidow and B. Young (eds), *Science Technology and the Labour Process*, Vol. 1, CSE Books, London, 1981, pp. 123-171.

Limbrick, S., 'Businessman Sues Guardian Over Web Reference to 1976 Strike', *Press Gazette*, 11 October 2007. Available at: www.pressgazette.co.uk/businessman-sues-guardian-over-web-reference-to-1976-strike. (Accessed 23 November 2016.)

Lindley, J., Dale, A. and Dex, S., 'Ethnic Differences in Women's Demographic and Family Characteristics and Economic Activity Profiles 1992-2002', *Labour Market Trends*, (April 2004), 153-65.

Lucas, K., 'Bluecollar Discourses of Workplace Dignity Using Outgroup Comparisons to Construct Positive Identities', *Management Communication Quarterly*, 25, 2 (2011), 353-374.

MacKenzie, R. and Forde, C., 'The Rhetoric of the 'Good Worker' Versus the Realities of Employers' Use and Experiences of Migrant Workers', *Work Employment and Society*, 23, 1 (2009), 142-159.

Mand, K., 'Gender, Ethnicity and Social Relations in the Narratives of Elderly Sikh Men and Women', *Ethnic and Racial Studies*, 29, 6 (2006), 1057-1071.

Mand, K., 'Gender, the Life Course and Homemaking Across Tanzania, Britain and Indian Punjab', in S.I. Rajan, V.J. Varghese and A.K. Nanda (eds), *Migration, Mobility and Multiple Affiliations: Punjabis in a Transnational World*, Cambridge University Press, Cambridge 2016, pp. 338-359.

Mansour, C., 'The Cross-National Diffusion of the American Civil Rights Movement: The Example of the Bristol Bus Boycott of

1963', Miranda [Online], 10, 2014. Available at: citeseerx.ist.psu.edu/viewdoc/download?doi=10.1.1.679.9863&rep=rep1&type=pdf. (Accessed 13 February 2017.)

Manzoor, S., 'How Asian Women Made Trade Union History and Shattered Stereotypes', *The Guardian*, 20 January 2010.

Marciniak, K., 'Foreign Women and Toilets', *Feminist Media Studies*, 8, 4 (2008), 337-356.

Martinez-Lucio, M and Perrett, R., 'Meanings and Dilemmas in Community Unionism: Trade Union Community Initiatives and Black and Minority Ethnic Groups in the United Kingdom', *Work, Employment and Society*, 23, 4 (2009b), 693-710.

Martinez-Lucio, M. and Perrett, R., 'The Diversity and Politics of Trade Unions' Responses to Minority Ethnic and Migrant Workers: The Context of the UK', *Economic and Industrial Democracy*, 30, 3 (2009a), 324-347.

Mason, R. and Sherwood, H., 'Cameron "Stigmatising Muslim Women" with English Language Policy', *The Guardian*, 18 January 2016. Available at: www.theguardian.com/politics/2016/jan/18/david-cameron-stigmatising-muslim-women-learn-english-language-policy. (Accessed 18 May 2016.)

Mattausch, J., 'After 'Ethnicity': Migration Identity and Political Economy', *Immigrants and Minorities,* 20, 3 (2001), 59-75.

Mattausch, J., 'From Subjects to Citizens: British 'East African Asians', *Journal of Ethnic and Migration Studies,* 24, 1 (1998), 121-141.

Mattaush, J., 'A Case of Mistaken Identity: Why British African Asians are not an 'Ethnic' Community', *South Asia Research*, 20, 2 (2000), 171-181.

McDowell, L., *Migrant Women's Voices: Talking About Life and Work in the UK Since 1945*, Wiley-Blackwell, Oxford 2016.

McDowell, L., *Working Lives: Gender, Migration and Employment in Britain, 1945-2007*, Wiley-Blackwell, Oxford 2013.

McDowell, L., Batnisky, A. and Dyer, S., 'Division, Segmentation and Interpellation: The Embodied Labour of Migrant Workers in A Greater London Hotel', *Economic Geography*, 83, 1 (2007), 1-25.

McDowell, L., *Working Bodies: Interactive Service Employment and Workplace Identities*, Wiley-Blackwell, Oxford 2009.

McDowell, L., Anitha, S. and Pearson, R., 'Striking Similarities: Representing South Asian Women's Industrial Action in Britain', *Gender, Place and Culture,* 19, 2 (2012), 133-152.

McGowan, J., '"Dispute", "Battle", "Siege", "Farce"?— Grunwick 30 Years On', *Contemporary British History*, 22, 3 (2008), 383-406.

McIlwaine, C., Datta, K., Evans, Y., Herbert, J., May, J. and Wills, J., *Gender and Ethnic Identities Among Low-Paid Migrant Workers in London*, Working Paper 3, Queen Mary, University of London, London 2006.

Meek, J., 'Somerdale to Skarbimierz', *London Review of Books*, 39, 8 (2017), 3-15.

Miller, K. and Steele, M., 'Employment Legislation: Thatcher and After', *Industrial Relations Journal*, 24, 3 (1993), 224-235.

Milner, M., 'Gate Gourmet Chief Refuses to Take Back 'Militants', *The Guardian*, 1 September 2005. Available at: www.guardian. co.uk/politics/2005/sep/01/uk.britishairwaysbusiness. (Accessed 26 January 2012.)

Milner, M., *Status and Sacredness: A General Theory of Status Relations and an Analysis of Indian Culture*, Oxford University Press, Oxford 1994.

Milward, N. and Stevens, M., 'British Workplace Industrial Relations 1980-1984', *Policy Studies*, 7, 3 (1987), 50-65.

Ministry of Justice, *Tribunal statistics collection*, Tribunal Service, Ministry of Justice, London 2015. Available: www.gov.uk/ government/collections/tribunals-statistics. (Accessed 2 March 2017.)

Ministry of Justice, *Employment Tribunal and EAT statistics 2009-10 (GB)*, Tribunal Service, Ministry of Justice, London 2010. Available: www.gov.uk/government/uploads/system/uploads/attachment_ data/file/218501/tribs-et-eat-annual-stats-april09-march10.pdf. (Accessed 1 November 2017.)

Minority Rights Group (ed.), 'Asians of East and Central Africa', In *World Directory of Minorities*, St. James Press, Chicago 1990, pp. 222-225.

Mirchandani, K., Mukherhjee, S. and Tambe, S., 'Old Jobs in New Forms: Women's Experiences in the Housekeeping Sector in Pune', in S. Raju and S. Jatrana (eds), *Women Workers in Metro Cities of India*, Cambridge University Press, Cambridge 2016, pp. 121-138.

Mirza, H. S., '"All the Women are White, All the Blacks are Men – But Some of us are Brave": Mapping the Consequences of Invisibility for Black and Minority Ethnic Women in Britain', in D. Mason (ed.), *Explaining Ethnic Differences: Changing Patterns of Disadvantage in Britain*, Policy Press, Bristol 2003, pp. 121-138.

Mirza, H. S., *Race, Gender and Educational Desire: Why Black Women Succeed and Fail*, Routledge, Abingdon 2009.

Mizen, S. (2016) 'The Great British Civil Rights Scandal: The Bristol Bus Boycott', *BBC History Magazine*, August 2013. www.historyextra. com/article/premium/great-british-civil-rights-scandal-bristol-bus-boycott. (Accessed 14 September 2017.)

Modood, T., Berthoud, R., Lakey, J., Nazroo, J., Smith, P., Virdee, S. and Beishon, S., *Ethnic Minorities in Britain: Diversity and Disadvantage*, Policy Studies Institute, London 1997.

Mohanty, C.T., 'Under Western Eyes: Feminist Scholarship and Colonial Discourses', *Feminist Review*, 30 (1988), 61-88.

Mohanty, C.T., '"Under Western Eyes" Revisited: Feminist Solidarity Through Anticapitalist Struggles', *Signs*, 28, 2 (2003), 499-535.

Mooney, N., 'Aspiration, Reunification and Gender Transformation in Jat Sikh Marriages from India to Canada', *Global Networks*, 6, 4 (2006), 389-403.

Murji, K., 'Mis-taken Identity: Being and Not Being Asian, African and British', *Migrations and Identities*, 1, 2 (2008), 17-32.

Narayan, K., 'Haunting Stories: Narrative Transmissions of South Asian Identities in Diaspora', in K. A. Jacobsen and P. Kumar (eds), *South Asians in the Diaspora: Histories and Religious Traditions*, Brill, Leiden and Boston 2004, pp. 415-434.

Nazroo, J. and Kapadia, D., *Dynamics of Diversity: Evidence From the 2011 Census, ESRC Centre on Dynamics of Ethnicity*, The University of Manchester, Manchester 2013. Available at: www. ethnicity.ac.uk/medialibrary/briefingsupdated/Ethnic%20 inequalities%20in%20labour%20market%20participation.pdf. (Accessed 26 April 2017.)

Novara Media, 'Defeat was Snatched from the Jaws of Victory – Remembering the Grunwick Strike', *Novara Media*, 25 August 2016. Available at: www.youtube.com/watch?v=oIrr5e2mHzI. (Accessed 19 September 2017.)

Novitz, T., 'A Role for Trade Unions as Designed by New Labour: The Representation Pyramid and 'Partnership', *Journal of Law and Society*, 29 (2002), 487-509.

ONS, *Annual Population Survey, January 2004 to December 2004*, Office for National Statistics, London 2004.

ONS, *Days Lost to Industrial Action: Labour Disputes*, Office for National Statistics, London 2012. Available at: www.ons.gov.uk/

ons/taxonomy/index.html?nscl=Days+Lost+Due+to+Industrial+A
ction. (Accessed 20 March 2012.)

ONS, *Employment Patterns*. Office for National Statistics, London 2006. Available at: www.statistics.gov.uk/CCI/nugget.asp?ID=96 4&Pos=&ColRank=2&Rank=896. (Accessed 12 June 2010.)

ONS, *Trade Union Membership 2015: Statistical Bulletin*, Department for Business, Innovation and Skills, London 2016. Available at: www.gov.uk/government/uploads/system/uploads/ attachment_data/file/525938/Trade_Union_Membership_2015_-_ Statistical_Bulletin.pdf. (Accessed 15 April 2017.)

Oxenbridge, S., Brown, W., Deakin, S. and Pratten, C., *Collective Employee Representation and the Impact of Law: Initial Responses to the Employment Relations Act 1999*, ESRC Centre for Business Research Working Paper No. 206, University of Cambridge, Cambridge 2001.

Pahl, R.E., *Divisions of Labour*, Basil Blackwell, Oxford 1984.

Palmer, P. and Eveline, J., 'Sustaining Low Pay in Aged Care Work' *Gender, Work and Organisation,* 19, 3 (2012), 254-75.

Parekh, B., 'South Asians in Britain', *History Today*, 47, 9 (1997). Available at: www.historytoday.com/bhikhu-parekh/south-asians-britain. (Accessed 11 May 2016.)

Parker, J., 'Women's Groups in British Trade Unions', *British Journal of Industrial Relations*, 40, 1 (2002), 23-48.

Parmar, P., 'Gender, Race and Class: Asian Women in Resistance', in The University of Birmingham Centre for Contemporary Cultural Studies (ed.), *The Empire Strikes Back: Race and Racism in 70s Britain*, Hutchinson and Co., London 1982, pp. 236-76.

Parrenas, R., *Servants of Globalization: Women, Migration and Domestic Work*, Stanford University Press, Stanford, 2001.

Parry, J., *Caste and Kinship in Kangra,* Routledge, London 1979.

Passerini, L., 'Women's Personal Narratives: Myths, Experiences, and Emotions', in Personal Narrative Group and J. W. Barbre (eds), *Interpreting Women's Lives: Feminist Theory and Personal Narratives,* Indiana University Press, Bloomington 1989, pp. 189-197.

Pearson, R. and Elson, D., 'Transcending the Impact of the Financial Crisis in the United Kingdom: Towards Plan F – a Feminist Economic Strategy', *Feminist Review*, 109 (2015), 8-30.

Pearson, R. and Kusakabe, K. 'Who Cares? Gender, Reproduction, and Care Chains of Burmese Migrant Workers in Thailand', *Feminist Economics*, 18, 2 (2012), 149-175.

Pearson, R. and Seyfang G. "'I'll Tell You What I Want … ": Women Workers and Codes of Conduct', in R. Jenkins, R. Pearson and G. Seyfang (eds), *Corporate Responsibility and Labour Rights: Codes of Conduct in the Global Economy*, Earthscan, London 2002, pp. 43-60.

Pearson, R. and Anitha, S. and McDowell, L., 'Striking Issues: From Labour Process to Industrial Dispute at Grunwick and Gate Gourmet', *Industrial Relations Journal*, 41, 5 (2010), 408-428.

Phillips, A. and Taylor, B. 'Sex and Skill: Notes Towards a Feminist Economics', *Feminist Review*, 6 (1980), 79-88.

Phizacklea, A. and Miles, R., 'The British Trade Union Movement and Racism', in G. Lee and R. Loveride (eds), *The Manufacture of Disadvantage,* Open University Press, Milton Keynes 1987a, pp. 21-30.

Phizacklea, A. and Miles, R. 'The Strike at Grunwick', *Journal of Ethnic and Migration Studies*, 6, 3 (1987b), 268-278.

Phizacklea, A. and Wolkowitz, C., *Homeworking Women: Gender, Racism and Class at Work*. Sage, London 1993.

Piore, M.J., *Birds of Passage: Migrant Labor and Industrial Societies,* Cambridge University Press, New York 1979.

Portes, A. 'Social Capital: Its Origins and Applications in Modern Sociology', *Annual Review of Sociology*, 24 (1998), 1-24.

Prettys, 'Inquiry Into the Rights of Workers in the "Gig Economy"', *Prettys*, November 2016. Available at: www.prettys.co.uk/inquiry-into-the-rights-of-workers-in-the----gig-economy---. (Accessed 1 November 2017.)

Puwar, N. and Raghuram, P., 'Dislocating South Asian Women in the Academy', in N. Puwar and P. Raghuram (eds), *South Asian Women in the Diaspora*, Berg, Oxford 2003, pp. 1-20.

Qureshi, K., 'Shehri (City) Brides Between Indian Punjab and the UK: Transnational Hypergamy, Sikh Women's Agency and Gendered Geographies of Power', *Journal of Ethnic and Migration Studies*, 42, 7 (2016), 1216-1228.

Race Today, 'The Imperial Typewriters: The Continuing Story', *Race Today,* August 1974, 223-225.

Raghuram, P., 'Caste and Gender in the Organisation of Paid Domestic Work in India', *Work, Employment and Society*, 15, 3 (2001), 607-617.

Rahemtullah, O. S. 'Interrogating "Indianness": Identity and Diasporic Consciousness Among Twice Migrants', *Anthurium: A Caribbean Studies Journal*, 7, 1 (2010), 1-20.

Ramdin, R., *The Making of the Black Working Class in Britain*, Wildwood House, Aldershot 1987.

Ramji, H. 'Engendering Diasporic Identities', in N. Puwar and P. Raghuram (eds), *South Asian Women in the Diaspora*, Berg, Oxford 2003, pp. 227-242.

Ramji, H., 'Journeys of Difference: The Use of Migratory Narratives Among British Hindu Gujaratis', *Ethnic and Racial Studies*, 29, 4 (2006), 702-724.

Rand, G., 'Martial Races and Imperial Subjects: Violence and Governance in Colonial India 1857-1914', *European Review of History*, 13, 1 (2006), 1-20.

Ray, R., 'Masculinity, Femininity and Servitude: Domestic Workers in Calcutta in the Late Twentieth Century', *Feminist Studies*, 26, 3 (2000), 691-718.

Riessman, C., *Narrative Methods for the Human Sciences*, Sage, California 2008.

Robbins, P., 'Meat Matters: Cultural Politics Along the Commodity Chain in India', *Cultural Geographies*, 6, 4 (1999), 399-423.

Rogaly, B., 'Intensification of Workplace Regimes in British Horticulture: The Role of Migrant Workers', *Population, Space and Place*, 14, 6 (2008), 497-510.

Rogaly, J., *Grunwick*, Penguin Books, Harmondsworth 1977.

Rossiter, A., 'Risking Gossip and Disgrace', *Spare Rib*, 54 (1977), 18-19.

Sachdeva, S., *The Primary Purpose Rule in British Immigration Law*, Trentham Books, Stoke- on-Trent 1993.

Sanders, C., 'Economic Abuse in the Lives of Women Abused by an Intimate Partner: A Qualitative Study', *Violence Against Women*, 21, 1 (2014), 3-29.

Sangster, J., 'Telling Our Stories: Feminist Debates and the Use of Oral History', in R. Perks and A. Thomson (eds), *Oral History Reader*, Routledge, London 1998, pp.87-100.

Sayyid, S., 'BrAsians: Postcolonial People, Ironic Citizens', in N. Ali, V.S. Kalra and S. Sayyid (eds) *Postcolonial People: South Asians in Britain*, Hurst and Co., London 2006, pp.1-10.

Scarman Report, *Report of a Court of Inquiry Under Lord Justice Scarman, OBE, into a Dispute Between Grunwick Processing Laboratories Limited and Members of the Association of Professional, Executive, Clerical and Computer Staff*, Her Majesty's Stationery Office, London 1977.

Sehgal, D., *Time Shift: The Grunwick Strike*, BBC Bristol for BBC 4, 2003.

Sharpe J., 'The Limits of What is Possible: Reimagining Sharam in Salman Rushdie's Shame', *Jouvert: A Journal of Postcolonial Studies*, 1, 1 (1997). Available at: english.chass.ncsu. edu/jouvert/v1i1/sharpe.htm. (Accessed 22 November 2016.)

Shaw, A., *Kinship and Continuity: Pakistani Families in Britain*, Harwood Academic Publishers, Amsterdam 2000.

Sinclair, D., 'The Importance of Sex for the Propensity to Unionize', *British Journal of Industrial Relations*, 33, 2 (1995), 173-190.

Singh, A. T., and Uberoi. P., 'Learning to "Adjust": Conjugal Relations in Indian Popular Fiction', *Indian Journal of Gender Studies*, 1, 1 (1994), pp. 93-120.

Singh, G., 'Introduction' in B. Parekh, G. Singh and S. Vertovec (eds), *Culture and Economy in the Indian Diaspora*, Routledge, London 2003, pp. 1-12.

Sivanandan, A., *Race, Class and the State: The Black Experience in Britain*, Institute of Race Relations, London 1976.

Sivanandan, A., 'The Liberation of the Black Intellectual', *Race and Class,* 18, 4 (1977a), 329-343.

Sivanandan, A., 'Race, Class and the State: Grunwick', *Race and Class,* 19, 1 (1977b), 69-73.

Smith, C., 'The Double Indeterminacy of Labour Power: Labour Effort and Labour Mobility', *Work, Employment and Society,* 20, 2 (2006), 389-402.

Smith, E., *British Communism and the Politics of Race,* Brill, Leiden 2018 (forthcoming).

Smith, P. and Morton, G., 'Nine Years of New Labour: Neoliberalism and Workers' Rights', *British Journal of Industrial Relations*, 44, 3 (2006), 401- 420.

Socialist Worker,' Here to Stay, Here to Fight – How the Grunwick Strike Changed Everything', *Socialist Worker*, 251, 16 August 2016. Available at: socialistworker.co.uk/art/43226/Here+to+stay,+here+to+fight+++how+the+Grunwick+strike+changed+everything. (Accessed 19 September 2017.)

Special Branch 'Overview', 'Grunwick Dispute Files Overview', Special Branch Files Project, n.d. Available at: www.specialbranchfiles.uk/grunwick-dispute-story/. (Accessed 29 March 2017.)

Special Branch 'Story', 'Grunwick Dispute – Story', Special Branch

Files Project, n.d.. Available at: specialbranchfiles.uk/grunwick-dispute-story. (Accessed 29 March 2017.)

Spivak, G., 'Can the Subaltern Speak?,' in C. Nelson and L. Grossberg (eds), *Marxism and the Interpretation of Culture,* Macmillan, London 1988, pp. 271-313.

Sprung, S. *The Year of the Beaver*, Channel 4, 1985.

Standing, G., *Precariat: The New Dangerous Class*, Bloomsbury, London 2011.

Streets, H., *Martial Races: The Military, Race and Masculinity in British Imperial Culture, 1857-1914,* Manchester University Press, Manchester 2004.

Stylianou, A. M., Postmus, J. L. and McMahon, S., 'Measuring Abusive Behaviours: Is Economic Abuse a Unique Form of Abuse?', *Journal of Interpersonal Violence,* 28, 16 (2013), 3186-3204.

Sullivan, W., 'Black Workers and Trade Unions 1945-2000', *Britain at Work*, London Metropolitan University, London 2012. Available at: www.unionhistory.info/britainatwork/narrativedisplay.php?type=raceandtradeunions. (Accessed 28 March 2017.)

Takhar, S., *Gender, Ethnicity and Political Agency: South Asian Women Organizing*, Routledge, New York 2013.

Tatla, D. S. and Singh, G., *Sikhs in Britain: The Making of a Community*, Zed Books, London 2006.

Taylor, G., 'From Grunwick to Deliveroo', Grunwick40 Conference, Willesden Library Centre, London, 26 November 2016.

Taylor, S., 'Transnational Emotion Work: Punjabi Migration, Caste and Identity', *International Journal of Work and Emotion*, 5, 3 (2013), 281-295.

Terry, M., 'Employee Representation: Shop Stewards and the New Legal Framework', in P. Edwards (ed.), *Industrial Relations: Theory and Practice*, Blackwell, Oxford 1995, pp. 257-284.

The Times, 'Food Firm Considered Provoking a Dispute', *The Times*, 15 August 2005. Available at: www.thetimes.co.uk/article/food-firm-considered-provoking-a-dispute-2j7zdvnh0sx. (Accessed 22 October 2017.)

Thomas C., *Stand Together*, Newsreel Collective, 1977.

Thomas C., *Look Back at Grunwick*, Newsreel Collective, 1978.

Thomas C., *The Great Grunwick Strike 1976-1978: A History*, Brent Trades Union Council, 2008.

Thomas, D., 'Gate Gourmet to Select Redundancy Candidates

From List of Volunteers', *Personnel Today*, 2005. Available: www.personneltoday.com/hr/gate-gourmet-to-select-redundancy-candidates-from-list-of-volunteers. (Accessed 1 March 2017.)

Thompson, P., 'Disconnected Capitalism: Or Why Employers Can't Keep Their Side of the Bargain', *Work. Employment and Society*, 17, 2 (2003), 359-78.

Tomalin, E., 'Writing British Asian Women: From Purdah and the Problematic Private Sphere to New Forms of Public Engagement and Cultural Production', in S. Mcloughlin, W.Gould, A.Kabir and E. Tomalin (eds), *Writing the City in British-Asian Diasporas*, Routledge, London 2014, pp. 179-198.

Tomlinson, D and Corlett, A., *A Tough Gig: The Nature of Self-Employment in Twenty-First-Century Britain and Policy Implications,* Resolution Foundation, London 2017.

Tran, M., 'Gate Gourmet dispute escalates', *The Guardian*, 1 September 2005. Available: www.theguardian.com/business/2005/sep/01/politics.britishairways. (Accessed 2 March 2017.)

TUC, 'Black Workers with Degrees Earn a Quarter Less than White Counterparts, Finds TUC', TUC London 2016. Available at: www.tuc.org.uk/equality-issues/black-workers/labour-market/black-workers-degrees-earn-quarter-less-white. (Accessed 2 May 2017.)

TUC, *Black Workers and Unions*, TUC Equality Audit, London 2014. Available at: www.tuc.org.uk/sites/default/files/Black%20workers%20and%20unions%20-%20TUC%20Equality%20Audit%202014.pdf. (Accessed 15 April 2017.)

Twaddle, M. (ed.), *Expulsion of a Minority: Essays on Ugandan Asians*, Athlone Press, London 1975.

Twaddle, M., 'East African Asians Through a Hundred Years', C. Clarke, C. Peach and S. Vertovec (eds), *South Asians Overseas: Migration And Ethnicity*, Cambridge University Press, Cambridge 1990, pp. 149-66.

Virdee, S. 'Racism and Resistance in British Trade Unions, 1948-79', in P. Alexander and R. Halpern (eds) *Racializing Class, Classifying Race: Labour and Difference in Britain, the USA, and Africa*, Macmillan, Basingstoke 1999, pp. 122-149.

Virdee, S., 'A Marxist Critique of Black Radical Theories of Trade Union Racism', *Sociology*, 34, 3 (2000), 545-565.

Virdee, S., 'Anti-Racism and the Socialist Left, 1968-79', in E. Smith and M. Worley (eds), *Against the Grain: The British Far Left from 1956,* Manchester University Press, Manchester 2014.

Visram, R., *Asians in Britain: 400 years of History,* Pluto Press, London 2002.

Waldinger, R. and Lichter, M., *How the Other Half Works: Immigration and the Social Organisation of Labour,* University of California Press, Berkeley, CA 2003.

Wall, K., and José, J. S., 'Managing Work and Care: A Difficult Challenge for Immigrant Families', *Social Policy and Administration,* 38, 6 (2004), 591-621.

Ward, G., *Fort Grunwick,* Maurice Temple Smith Ltd, London 1977.

Warrier, S., 'Gujarati Prajapatis in London: Family Roles and Sociability Networks', in R. Ballard (ed.), *Desh Pardesh: South Asian Experience in Britain,* University of British Columbia Press, Vancouver 1994, pp. 191-212.

Werbner, P., *The Migration Process: Capital, Goods and Offerings Among British Pakistanis,* Berg, Oxford 1990.

Westwood, S. and Bhachu, P., *Enterprising Women: Ethnicity, Economy and Gender Relations,* Routledge, London 1988.

Westwood, S., *All Day Everyday: Factory and Family in the Making of Women's Lives,* Pluto, London 1984.

Whitehead, A., '"I'm Hungry Mum": The Politics of Domestic Budgeting', in K. Young, C. Wolkowitz and R. McCullagh (eds), *Of Marriage and the Market: Women's Subordination in International Perspective,* CSE Books, London 1981, pp. 88-111.

Wills, J. and Simms, M., 'Building Reciprocal Community Unionism in the UK', *Capital and Class,* 82 (2004), 59-84.

Wills, J., Datta, K., Evans, Y., Herbert, J., May, J., and McIlwaine, C., *Global Cities at Work: New Migrant Divisions of Labour,* Pluto, London 2010.

Wills, J., May, J., Datta, K., Evans, Y., Herbert, J. and McIlwaine, C., 'London's Migrant Division of Labour', *European Journal of Urban and Regional Studies,* 16, 3 (2009), 257-271.

Wilson, A., '"We are the lions, Mr. Manager": Revisiting the Great Grunwick Strike, *Ceasefire,* 15 June 2016. Available at: ceasefiremagazine.co.uk/we-lions-mr-manager-revisiting-great-grunwick-strike. (Accessed 11 September 2017.)

Wilson, A., *Finding a Voice – Asian Women in Britain,* Virago, London 1978.

Wilton, S., 'Promoting Equality? Gendered Messages in State Materials for New Immigrants', *Social and Legal Studies,* 18, 4 (2009), 437-454.

WING (Women Immigration and Nationality Group), *Worlds Apart: Women Under Immigration and Nationality Law,* Pluto Press, London 1985.

Women's Budget Group, *New Research Shows That Poverty, Ethnicity and Gender Magnify the Impact of Austerity on BME Women,* Women's Budget Group, London, 28 November 2016. Available at: wbg.org.uk/news/new-research-shows-poverty-ethnicity-gender-magnify-impact-austerity-bme-women. (Accessed 2 May 2017.)

Woodley, T., 'Gate Gourmet and Beyond', Address to the Institute of Employment Rights Conference, London, 31 January 2007.

Wray, H., '"A Thing Apart": Controlling Male Family Migration to the UK', *Men and Masculinities,* 18, 4 (2015), 424-447.

Wray, H., *Regulating Marriage Migration into the UK: A Stranger in the Home,* Ashgate, Farnham 2011.

Wrench, J. and Virdee, S. 'Organising the Unorganised: "Race", Poor Work and Trade Unions', in P. Ackers, C. Smith and P. Smith (eds), *The New Workplace and Trade Unionism: Critical Perspectives on Work and Organisation,* Routledge, London 1996, pp. 240-78.

Wrench, J., 'Trade Union Responses to Immigrants and Inequality in Denmark and the UK: The Context of Consensus and Conflict', *European Journal of Industrial Relations,* 10, 1 (2004), 7-31.

Wrench, J., 'Unequal Comrades: Trade Unions, Equal Opportunity and Racism', in R. Jenkins and J. Solomos (eds), *Racism and Equal Opportunity Policies in the 1980s,* Cambridge University Press, Cambridge 1987, pp. 160-186.

Wright, M., *Disposable Women and Other Myths of Global Capitalism,* Routledge, New York and London 2006.

Yeates, N., 'A Global Political Economy of Care', *Social Policy and Society,* 4, 2 (2005), 227-34.

Yeates, N., *Globalizing Care Economies and Migrant Workers. Explorations in Global Care Chains,* Palgrave, Basingstoke 2009.

Yuval-Davis, N., Anthias, F. and Kofman, E., 'Secure Borders and Safe Haven and the Gendered Politics of Belonging: Beyond Social Cohesion', *Ethnic and Racial Studies,* 28, 3 (2005), 513-535.

Yuval-Davis, N., *The Politics of Belonging: Intersectional Contestations,* Sage, London 2012.

Index

Acas 122, 123, 127, 129
agency
    alternative accounts 24-6
    impact of Grunwick dispute
        130-4, 138
    industrial militancy 37, 93-6
    migration and marriage 51
    paid work and education 59-61
    productive and reproductive
        labour 91-3
    reworking strategies 93
agency workers 154-6, 192
Ahmad, F. 18, 24
Alden, Malcolm (Grunwick
    manager) 105-6, 107, 112-13
Anitha, S. et al. 142, 196
Anwar, M. 19, 41, 45
Association of Professional,
    Executive, Clerical and
    Computing Staff (APEX) 2,
    114, 119, 122-3, 127, 128,
    129

Bagguley, P. 169, 170
Baumann, G. 23-4
BBC News 96, 165, 192
Bhachu, P. 20, 42, 45
Bhudia, Devshi (Grunwick) 112,
    113
Born, Eric (Gate Gourmet
    managing director) 162, 164
Brah, A. 25, 41, 55, 57

Brent Trades Council 114, 124
British Airways (BA) 5, 141, 142,
    144, 147-8
    changes to airline catering 197-8
    solidarity strike action (baggage
        handlers) 165, 166, 167
British Nationalities Act (1948)
    39
Butler, D. 4-5

Callaghan, James (PM) 127, 128
Cameron, David (PM) 22
care work 75
career expectations and reality
    90-1
cheap labour 1-2, 9-10, 67, 103,
    155
childcare arrangements 80-7
    see also reproductive and
        productive labour
Citizens Advice Bureau (CAB)
    114, 133
class/caste dislocation 65-6, 68-9,
    70-2, 73, 75
    career expectations and reality
        90-1
    domestic responsibilities 77-8
    Gate Gourmet dispute 180-1
    Grunwick dispute 102, 111-12,
        120, 132, 134
cleaning work 70-1
Colling, T. 169, 170, 173, 175

Commonwealth Immigrants Act (1962) 41, 43-4

Communication Workers Union (CWU) 201

community/culture
essentialist notion of collectivity 33
and kinship networks 20
notions of shame 120-2, 131-2
reproduction of 21-4, 52

Compromise Agreement: Gate Gourmet dispute 159-64, 176, 177, 192

Conservative government: legislation 189-90, 192

Cromey, Jack (TGWU) 3-4

Datta, K. et al. 79, 84-5, 87, 91

Desai, Jayaben (Grunwick strike leader) 2, 3, 4, 6, 7, 11, 35, 102
family experience of migration 47-8, 54-5
labour market entry 57
and media 133-4, 138
role and strategies 104-6, 107, 111-14, 115, 116-17, 118, 120-2, 124-6, 128-30

Dhillon (shop steward convenor, Gate Gourmet) 156, 157, 171, 173-4

dignity of work 74-5, 96-9

'dirty' work 70-1, 75

domestic responsibilities 76-87, 124-5

domestic violence 85-6, 98-9, 177

domestic work, paid 70-1

Dromey, J. 3
and Taylor, G. 4, 7, 101, 102, 107, 108, 118, 127, 132, 134

Duffield, M. 27, 28, 40

Dyer, S. et al. 77, 79, 87

East African Asians 42-6, 110
Ugandan 44-5, 48, 56, 104
see also Grunwick dispute; Gujarati/East African twice-migrant women

East European migrant workers 154-6

Elson, D.
and Pearson, R. 10, 103, 110
Pearson, R. and 199

Employment Acts 159, 189-90

Employment Protection Act (1975) 122

Employment Relations Act (1999) 169

Employment Tribunals/Industrial Tribunals 169-70, 190
Gate Gourmet dispute 170-5
Grunwick dispute 74, 123
Uber workers 198-9

English language 56, 58, 62, 69, 90, 102, 110, 112
Employment Tribunal interpreter 172, 173
lack of proficiency 35, 41, 61
twice-migrants 45-6
UK policy discourses 22

ethnicity see race/ethnicity and gender issues

family reunion 12, 14, 20-1, 45, 50-1

family roles see reproductive and productive labour

farm work 88, 89

financial austerity policy 199-200

Firmin, P. 130
food processing work 71-2
Forde, C.
  and MacKenzie, R. 91
  MacKenzie, R. and 67, 104,
    154-5
Fraser, N. 202

Gate Gourmet dispute 141-2
  events of 155-9
  gender, generation and ethnicity
    150-5
  and Grunwick dispute 5-17, 32-
    7, 185-94, 196-7
  memories and reflections 175-82
  nature and forms of workplace
    coercion 142-50
  TGWU
    Compromise Agreement 159-
      64, 176, 177, 192
    limitations to powers 168-70
    role 164-8
    unfair dismissal claims:
      Employment Tribunals 167-8,
      170-5
  see also Punjabi/Sikh migrant
    women
gender and race issues see race/
  ethnicity and gender issues
gig economy 198
globalisation and uberisation 197-9
'good worker' list 147
Gorst, John (MP) 122-3
Grantham, Roy (APEX) 119
Grunwick dispute 1-5, 18, 101-3
  causes of 114-18
  end of 127-30
  and Gate Gourmet dispute 5-17,
    32-7, 185-94, 196-7

gender and ethnic identity in
  labour relations 110-12, 114-
  18
Industrial Tribunal (1977) 74,
  123
labour force, labour process and
  working conditions 103-9
legacy of 135-9
memories of 130-4
Scarman Report/Inquiry 103,
  104-5, 107, 108-9, 114, 119,
  122, 123, 127-30, 174
walk-out 112-14
widening of 119-27
see also Gujarati/East African
  twice-migrant women
Grunwick Strike Committee 2, 4,
  127, 128-9, 130
Grunwick40 celebrations (2016)
  3, 4, 5, 7, 200-1
Gujarati/East African twice-
  migrant women 47-9, 54-5,
  62-3
labour market entry 56-8, 59-
  60, 65-7, 69
see also Grunwick dispute

'hard worker' discourse 66-7, 74-5
Herbert, J. 36, 45-6, 49, 51, 56,
  59-60, 110, 134
Hillingdon Hospital dispute
  (1995) 95-6
Hindi language 12, 35, 36-7,
  187-8
Hochschild, A.R. 54, 76, 84, 124
housing 54-6
hunger strike: Grunwick dispute
  2-3, 128-9

immigration policy 20-3, 40-2,
    43-4, 49-50
Immigration Act (1971) 21, 44
Imperial Typewriters strike (1974)
    28-31, 136, 175
Industrial Tribunals *see*
    Employment Tribunals/
    Industrial Tribunals

Jarvis, H. 76, 80

Labour government 127, 128,
    168, 169, 190
labour market
  Fordist and post-Fordist
    production 192-4
  race/ethnicity and gender issues
    64-75, 194-6
  South Asian women's entry into
    56-62
Levidow, L. 103, 106-7, 108, 111,
    116
life histories research 33-7
Lufthansa Skychef strike 96

McDowell, L. 34
  et al. 37, 134, 138, 154
MacKenzie, R.
  and Forde, C. 67, 104, 154-5
  Ford, C. and 91
management practices, strategies
    and styles 28-31, 72-5, 103-9,
    144-50
Mansfield Hosiery strike (1972)
    28-31, 136
marriage and migration 51, 52-4,
    60-1
Martinez-Lucio, M. and Perrett,
    R. 33, 166, 175, 196, 201

Mattaush, J. 42, 46, 57, 110
meat/food processing work 71-2
'mobility power' 91, 93
Modood, T. et al. 23, 46
Mohanty, C.T. 24, 25
Murray, Len (TUC) 2

National Association For Freedom
    (NAFF) 122, 127
Novitz, T. 169

outsourcing 95, 142, 144-5, 189,
    191-2
overtime: Grunwick dispute 108-
    9, 112

patriarchy 20, 120-2
Pearson, R.
  and Elson, D. 199
  Elson, D. and 10, 103, 110
  et al. 144
  and Seyfang, G. 153
piecework 85, 89, 90, 92-3, 198
policing: Grunwick dispute 126-7
postal boycott: Grunwick dispute
    122-3, 124, 127
'precariat'/precarious employment
    191, 192, 193
Punjabi/Sikh migrant women 41-
    2, 49-56, 62-3
  labour market entry 66, 68-9
  paid work and education 58-9, 60
  trade union membership/
    industrial militancy 93-6
  see also Gate Gourmet dispute
Punjabi/Sikh migrants 39-40, 42,
    46-7
  and Punjabi East African twice-
    migrants 45

Qureshi, K. 53-4

Race Relations Act (1968) 43
Race Relations Board 29, 136
race/ethnicity and gender issues
  Gate Gourmet dispute 150-5
  Grunwick dispute 110-12, 114-18
  labour market 64-75, 194-6
  representations and erasures 18-26
  trade union movement 7-10, 26-33, 136, 199-202
racial hierarchies 32-3, 65, 151-2, 154
  and segregation 116-17
racism
  and class 135-6
  Gate Gourmet 159
  Grunwick 117-18, 122
  and job-seeking 61
reproductive and productive labour 76-87
  Gate Gourmet dispute 177-8
  Grunwick dispute 124-5
resistance 87-96, 114-18
reworking strategies 93
Rogaly, J. 7, 89, 101, 108, 124

Scargill, Arthur (NUM) 3, 124
Scarman Report/Inquiry 103, 104-5, 107, 108-9, 114, 119, 122, 123, 127-30, 174
self, sense of 97-8, 130-1
self-employment 198-9
shame 120-2, 131-2
shop stewards 28-9, 30
  Gate Gourmet 94-5, 149-50, 156-7, 158, 159, 165, 167, 171, 173-4, 175

Siegel, Dave (Gate Gourmet) 162
Sikh migrants see Gate Gourmet dispute; Punjabi/Sikh migrant women; Punjabi/Sikh migrants
Sivanandan, A. 27, 39, 129-30
Smith, E. 29, 30-1, 117, 136
social isolation 51-2, 178
social and kinship networks 20, 61-2, 80-3, 179
social support of co-workers/co-strikers 97, 99, 131, 150-1
solidarity 115, 136, 137, 181-2
  secondary strike action (BA baggage handlers) 165, 166, 167
South Asian migration and settlement 38-47
South Asian women 10-17
  dominant representations and erasures 18-26
  labour market entry 56-62
  migration and settlement 47-56
  work and life histories research 33-7
Special Branch 126-7
Standing, G. 191, 193

Tatla, D.S. and Singh, G. 39, 46, 47, 50, 55
Taylor, S. 54
Thatcher, Margaret (PM) 189
toilet access 111-12, 152-3, 157-8
Tomalin, E. 18, 19-20
Trade Union and Labour Relations (Consolidation) Act (1992) 164-5
trade unions
  decline of 192-4

globalisation and uberisation 197-9

Grunwick and Gate Gourmet disputes 2-10, 187-9, 196-7

legislation 189-92

limitation of powers 168-70

membership/recognition 93-6, 104, 114, 115-16, 118, 119, 122-4, 127

race/ethnicity and gender issues 7-10, 26-33, 136, 199-202

see also specific unions and disputes

Trades Union Congress (TUC)

Gate Gourmet dispute 161

Grunwick dispute 2-3, 101, 114, 119, 128-9

and Labour Government: Social Contract 128, 137

race and gender issues discriminatory practices 27, 29, 31-2

research 200

Transport and General Workers Union (TGWU) 3-4, 29, 30, 34, 96

see also under Gate Gourmet dispute

Twaddle, M. 42, 110

Uber workers 198-9

Ugandan Asians 44-5, 48, 56, 104

see also Grunwick dispute; Gujarati/East African twice-migrant women

unfair dismissal claims: Gate

Gourmet dispute 167-8, 170-5

Union of Postal Workers (UPW) 122-3, 124, 127

UNISON 95

violence

domestic 85-6, 98-9, 177

police 126

Virdee, S. 26, 27, 29, 32, 135-7

Wrench, J. and 32, 175

walk-out: Grunwick dispute 112-14

Wall, K. and José, J.S. 77, 79-80, 84-5, 86

Ward, George (Grunwick owner/director) 1, 103, 104, 107, 111, 116, 117, 121-2

Wills, J. et al. 67, 196

Wilson, A. 24-5, 30, 105, 120-2

Women Against Racism and Fascism (WARF) 129

Women's Budget Group 200

Woodley, Tony (TGWU) 165, 166, 171

work

dignity and struggles 74-5, 96-9

experiences and strategies 87-96

and family roles *see* reproductive and productive labour

and life histories research 33-7

working conditions 103-9, 142-50

Wray, H. 21, 49

Wrench, J. 28, 31, 32, 196, 201

and Virdee, S. 32, 175